WARRIORS
AND THE
BATTLE WITHIN

TERRY THOMPSON

© Copyright 2004 Terry Thompson. All rights reserved.

No part of this publication may be reproduced, stored in a retrieval system, or transmitted, in any form or by any means, electronic, mechanical, photocopying, recording, or otherwise, without the written prior permission of the author.

A cataloguing record for this book that includes the U.S. Library of Congress Classification number, the Library of Congress Call number and the Dewey Decimal cataloguing code is available from the National Library of Canada. The complete cataloguing record can be obtained from the National Library's online database at:
www.nlc-bnc.ca/amicus/index-e.html

ISBN: 1-4120-1474-3

TRAFFORD

This book was published *on-demand* in cooperation with Trafford Publishing. On-demand publishing is a unique process and service of making a book available for retail sale to the public taking advantage of on-demand manufacturing and Internet marketing. **On-demand publishing** includes promotions, retail sales, manufacturing, order fulfilment, accounting and collecting royalties on behalf of the author.

Suite 6E, 2333 Government St., Victoria, B.C. V8T 4P4, CANADA
Phone   250-383-6864   Toll-free   1-888-232-4444 (Canada & US)
Fax   250-383-6804   E-mail   sales@trafford.com
Web site   www.trafford.com   TRAFFORD PUBLISHING IS A DIVISION OF TRAFFORD
                                HOLDINGS LTD.
Trafford Catalogue #03-1852   www.trafford.com/robots/03-1852.html

10   9   8   7   6   5   4

INDEX

Foreword

Chapter One – Dreams	1
Chapter Two - The Formative Years	4
Chapter Three - #3 AC&WU	8
Chapter Four - A Letter From Holland	30
Chapter Five - Moulding a Fighter Pilot	38
Chapter Six - Tales of the Bay	59
Chapter Seven - The Cold War Warriors	69
Chapter Eight- Supersonic Warriors	95
Chapter Nine - Ferry Flight to Cyprus	103
Chapter Ten - In-flight Refuelling	125
Chapter Eleven - The Interlude	130
Chapter Twelve - Refuelling - Cyprus	135
Chapter Thirteen - The Firebirds	151
Chapter Fourteen - Posting to Ottawa	162
Chapter Fifteen - The Desk Job	169
Chapter Sixteen - Pedagogy	195
Chapter Seventeen - A Canadian Icon	211
Chapter Eighteen - Desk Job Revisited	230
Chapter Nineteen - DMOC	245
Chapter Twenty - Royal Service Continues	276
Chapter Twenty-one - Evacuation - Iran	296
Chapter Twenty-two - Asian Refugees	314
Chapter Twenty-three - G-7 Summit '81	333
Chapter Twenty-four - The Future	362

FOREWORD

The letter I received from Holland in 1998 was my inspiration and once the idea caught on I couldn't put it away until I had finished the story. It was from Jan Van Rossum du Chattel, a fellow student on my NATO pilot training course in 1953/54.

I set about preparing my reply and as I toiled over my keyboard, other incidents in my air force career began to pop to mind. With the zest of an ageing fighter pilot who can no longer leap over tall buildings or across fast flowing rivers, I have approached the task of recording these stories with as much fervour as my first entry into an attack on the flag* from the high perch.

The stories have in fact been woven together to provide an account of my experiences as I remember them. But I think they are more than that.

They represent the experiences of an average Canadian youth of the day that intimately remembered the images of World War II. A prairie boy that grew up close to the farm and like the thousands of others from across Canada, responded to the nations need to rebuild a military capability that had briefly languished following WW II.

I think our stories are all similar and it would be a loss if some of them were not preserved for future generations. We joined the armed forces when only an unsteady peace existed. There was a war in far off Korea. Elsewhere there were wars and rumours of wars. The allies and the Soviet Union were engaged in nuclear weapons testing, threats and

---

* *A large banner towed by another aircraft used as a target for air to air gunnery training.*

posturing. The arms race was on in earnest and only the strong would survive.

Western governments encouraged their populations to build private nuclear shelters and issued plans and specifications to those who wished to attempt to survive a nuclear holocaust in their basements or backyards.

Governments built bunkers to protect legislators from nuclear attack, plans were put in place to re-establish social order following a nuclear exchange. The atmosphere of the western world was tense and democracy was tested regularly by those intent on world domination by any means.

Within this context the Canadian youth of the forties and fifties faced the escalating "Cold War". They were patriotic and intent on defending Canada and North America until the threat had been eliminated. They learned as they pushed the edges of technology steadily forward and society benefited through their efforts.

This book is really about a generation of young Canadians who took up arms where their older brothers, fathers and uncles had left off. They carried the torch for new generations that now face their own challenges. Since Korea thousands of young men and women have devoted their lives to the military, intent only on the preservation of peace in a tumultuous world. Many have paid the ultimate price.

They tried to make their government's impossible experiment with forces unification work and they failed. Perhaps the only major failure of Canadians in uniform ever recorded. They were the new age Warriors of the twentieth century.

It is these Warriors to whom this book is dedicated.

CHAPTER ONE
DREAMS

As I grow older I become more contemplative about the manner in which hi-tech has affected my life. These days I marvel at the young snowboarders and the gymnastic skills they exhibit in quest of perfection on the slopes. There are a significant number of sporting and recreational activities once open only to small-dedicated groups that are now easily accessible to those who wish to participate - all with scientifically designed equipment engineered to individual specifications.

Oh, we had good equipment in my day, or so we thought at the time. Cable harness and bamboo ski poles and a set of wooden boards were all you needed to fling yourself down the mountainside for an invigorating day on the slopes. That is, after you had first climbed the mountain.

Today, hi-tech equipment and advanced teaching practices make recreational sports more accessible to more people than ever before. In fact, it's difficult to name a recreational activity that isn't effected by the hi-tech revolution

I look back in wonderment at my own youthful dreams that with a little creativity could be turned into action. The satisfaction of having accomplished the seemingly impossible was the stuff of youthful dreams. It was in Medicine Hat that I began to discover the power of those dreams.

I wonder in retrospect at the spectre of my own youthful audacity, pretending I was Zorro with makeshift wooden sword in hand, running along the remnants of the concrete foundation of an old office building imagining I was defending the ramparts from the invading hordes

One clear memory of my youth was the proud accomplishment at the age of eight in the completion of my own self-designed home-built aircraft.

It was made of lath and whatever remnants of canvas I could find. Glue, bailing wire, old baby-carriage wheels and a modicum of string were used to hold the whole contraption together. I clearly remember the happy day when with the help of my co-designers and builders, we ceremoniously moved our prototype to the steep hill across from my house at the top of Second Avenue in preparation for its first flight.

Since it was my design and built in my basement, I was unanimously elected to be the test pilot. Final flight preparations complete, our beautiful craft was launched from the hilltop.

I performed a graceful initial roll downhill and then at last; the machine struggled to break free from the laws of gravity. Abruptly, with help from a bump on the hill, or perhaps a sudden gust of wind, I was airborne. I must have achieved an amazing altitude of one or two feet.

It lasted only a few seconds before our magnificent creation crashed unceremoniously into a willow along with it's erstwhile pilot. Satisfied that I was unhurt, we all cheered approvingly that indeed man had made his first flight. In keeping with boyhood attention spans for such major projects, the small group of new aviation experts departed, well satisfied that they had partaken in an historic event. Without hesitation, we moved on to other death defying projects.

Most boys of that era experienced many such events in the course of growing up. While fond memories undoubtedly dim over time, those were the most fulfilling days of any boy's life. Dreams and reality intermingled and nothing was impossible.

CHAPTER TWO
THE FORMATIVE YEARS

In 1943 we had been in Medicine Hat six or seven years. My father, who had established his career with the Bank of Montreal, was transferred to Whitewood, Saskatchewan. The branch there had run into some loan recovery difficulties and he was sent to clear them up. It seemed the manager who had preceded him had lost contact with his farming community clients, a problem that exists today throughout the charter banking community.

I can remember Dad setting up a visiting schedule shortly after our arrival in town. During a period of a few very busy months he managed to meet informally with every farmer and rancher who was indebted to the bank. Often he would take me with him.

The Bank of Montreal was justifiably proud of its well-earned reputation of never foreclosing on a farmer throughout the depression or during the war years. At the end of the war the B of M forgave most if not all of the accrued interest on farm loans and worked out repayment schedules related to the principal, a renegotiated rate of interest and a repayment structure that best suited the farmer's income. It might be said that the banks of the times truly helped to bring a faltering economy back to prosperity.

In 1945 we were transferred to Castor, Alberta, a robust farming community. Now in my teenage years, I quickly made friends in the town and in the surrounding farming community. I became a cowboy learning to herd cattle. I learned how to handle a team of horses on the plough, cutter and hay rake. I learned to drive a tractor, car and truck - all by the age of fourteen. It was during this period of my development that I discovered my own independence.

My eminent title in life as "The Son of the Bank Manager" seemed to follow me from the time I started school. For some reason, that gave me the status of a "city slicker" among my peers. It was a status I did not enjoy and I was quick to do battle with those who made the mistake of referring to me in what I considered to be a pejorative manner.

Coached by the farmers, for whom I worked when not in school, I developed the ability to improvise, an attribute that has served me well throughout my life. I finished my high school in Castor in 1950 and was venturing into the world with some trepidation.

My decision to enter the banking profession was not based on any burning desire to be a banker. I just wanted to get started on my future whatever it was to be. Asserting my blooming freedom, I joined the Bank of Nova Scotia, which didn't seem to bother my father a whit and he welcomed me to the club.

My father didn't like the direction banks were going but all he could do was to try to represent his customers to the bank. A principle that later was lost as he entered his retirement years and the chartered banks discovered the new vogue of retail banking services.

In the town of Stettler just forty miles west of Castor, I soon fell into the routine of banking at the junior level and it wasn't long before I began to analyse the situation in which I found myself. The high stool and the elevated sloping desk designed to hold the over-large ledgers of the time held little appeal.

Posting the ledger, as it was called in the bank, was done with India ink, by hand and with a straight pen. Many long hours were spent looking for an errant penny or two. Frequently the exercise would stretch well into the night

At the end of the day all the ledgers had to balance. It was possible to make up a balance by contributing a few cents from ones pocket but eventually, the bank inspectors would come and with sharp-eyed efficiency, find something suspicious and then all hell would break loose.

Six months of this had been enough to convince me that banking was a calling contrary to my adventuresome nature. I wanted to see more of the world. My experience was limited but I yearned for the adventure that travel was sure to bring.

I recall a warm spring day in early March 1951. The sun was shining, the winter ice was melting and water dripped from the icicles clinging to the eaves.

This was one of the few occasions that I managed to finish my duties early in the afternoon and during my walk along the main street, I happened upon a poster displayed in the post office window. It was a picture of jet pilot fully suited, hardhat under arm, standing beside his Sabre-jet and looking with reverence at the billowing sky ... I was sold.

At seven the next morning I called the manager of the bank at his home. "I'm leaving for Edmonton by train in half an hour Sir, I'm going to join the air force". A very sleepy, "call me when you get back" was the only response that was forthcoming and I proceeded on my way.

My reception at the Edmonton recruiting centre was straightforward and professional. I was subjected to all of the usual tests. The IQ ratings, the aptitude tests, psychoanalysis and the medical were all conducted with dispatch. Returning after lunch on the second day of the process, I was told that I had passed all of the tests and had been accepted for training as an officer candidate leading to aircrew selection and hopefully, pilot training.

In the peacetime air force, one was an officer first and a pilot second. There was however; "One small problem Mr. Thompson, our quotas for aircrew selection are booked until the fall. We will keep your name on our list and advise you when we have an opening for officer training".

No doubt the look of disappointment on my face was not uncommon to the Flight Lieutenant recruiting officer before whom I stood. "Mr. Thompson, as an intermediate step, you might want to consider entering as ground crew". He went on, "You would be provided with trades training that matches your qualifications and skills. When an opening for aircrew training becomes available, you will be automatically re-mustered to aircrew".

Many of us I found out later were given the same story only to fulfil the recruiting officer's quotas equitably and many of us waited patiently for the call to aircrew. For some it never came.

But, I wanted in and I didn't care what it took to do it. I accepted immediately and returned to Stettler a hero. The girls in the bank, who represented one of the major changes to banking as a result of the war looked at me differently, I was no longer the inky-fingered junior, I was a member of the air force.

The farewell parties were great and after fond farewells to my family and my friends, by early April 1951 I was on my way to RCAF Station St. Jean, PQ for my basic training.

CHAPTER THREE
#3 AC&WU - A NEW BEGINNING

The CN and CP railway companies were familiar with large military drafts. It was a mere five years since the cessation of WW II hostilities and railway staffs were accustomed to dealing with raw Canadian youth on their way to war.

Conductors and porters treated our fairly large draft of Alberta boys with some reverence and we were allowed more latitude in our behaviour than our civilian counterparts. We ignored the underage drinking restrictions that prevailed at the time, as did the conductors and porters assigned to see us safely to our destination. The anticipation and apprehension of what boot camp might hold soon replaced our self-importance as the new war heroes.

After four days and nights on the train we disembarked on the railway platform in St Jean PQ. What was left of our pretentious egos was instantly devastated. A gruff, smartly uniformed sergeant met us and immediately directed us to an isolated area of the platform. "Line up here you bums, no talking and listen up".

Our indoctrination into the air force had commenced. Beginning at the railway station, the process of reducing us all, physically and psychologically to one very low common denominator was underway.

Overnight we became pea brains, Harvey dumb shits and Ishcabibles. We were harassed by endless drills on and off the Parade Square. We were subjected to lectures on service law, service etiquette, service this and service that. We studied the Kings Orders and Regulations until we could recite them by heart. When we made a mistake, it was forty or fifty push-ups depending on the severity of the misdemeanour.

More often than not, the punishment was out of proportion to the transgression.

Marching drills, route marches, physical training to the point of exhaustion filled our days and by nightfall the barracks were silent as we collapsed on our crisply made military bunks and slept the sleep of the dead.

By early summer our course sergeant and disciplinarian began to lose his draconian persona. He even became somewhat friendly as our course of 100 or so began to take shape as a well disciplined military unit. We lost some along the way but those of us who survived would have given our lives for each other in a heartbeat.

As the three-month course came to an end, the bank clerk was gone. In his place there was strong healthy young man who had found pride in himself and had learned to do things he would never previously have been capable of accomplishing. He became a man. He had developed an esprit de corps beyond his high school class or the town hockey team. He was disciplined, ready and eager to go further.

Aptitude tests administered during basic training indicated a strong inclination for technical training and my assignment to RCAF Station Clinton, Ontario to attend a radar technician's course seemed natural.

The boot camp atmosphere eased but the cerebral activity assumed much larger proportions. Ohms, volts, amperes, waveguides, impedance measurement; output-input and echoes dominated our daily lives. Logarithms, algebraic equations and trigonometry, all subjects I hated in school, became a common vernacular among us.

The day before we were to graduate, I was called into the Chief Warrant Officer's office. "Thompson, we don't have a posting for you", he advised. "We would like you to take the Fighter Control Operator's course". This was somewhat disappointing to me as I was looking forward to my posting to an operational unit. As a qualified Radar Tech Ground, I had been promoted to Group 1 Aircraftsman First Class. This meant an increase in pay of around eight dollars a month and represented a significant milestone in my career progression. A new secondary technical qualification would have no effect on my pay rate.

Following the ceremonies marking the successful completion of one course, I began another. Fortunately, I was not to be subjected to the theory portion of the course as it was deemed that through my technical radar training I had assimilated all or more than the minimum basic radar theory that I needed.

The radar system of the day was the Air Ministry Experimental Station Mark 11C (AMES11C). The "C" denoting the fact that the unit was convoy (vehicle) mounted and that gave it an air of mobility unique to the times. The radar and its black boxes were mounted on a dozen or more three tonne wartime trucks. The AMES designation was chosen during the war in order to disguise the unit's actual role. The system was developed by the RAF during WW II and was a follow-up of the Chain Home system used effectively along the East Coast of England during the Battle of Britain.

We were told that the unit was mobile and could be moved on very short notice. It could be readied for operations equally as quickly at a new location. We were not able to witness any of the mobility aspects of the AMES 11 convoy at Clinton since it had been integrated into the existing training establishment building structures in order to expedite the training program.

Within three or four weeks I had completed the Fighter Control Operators course and had learned how to vector aircraft and plot their movements. In due course I was on my way to my first operational, posting at RCAF Station Trenton.

The train trip from Clinton to Toronto was uneventful and we had an hour or so to wait for the connection with the next train east to Trenton and beyond. The Royal York Hotel was across the street from the old Union Station but could be reached through an underground pedestrian tunnel. All hotels had a beer parlour in those days and the Royal York had one of the best.

As I recall we missed several trains during what was to have been a brief pause for refreshment and at some point in the evening I went off in search of a washroom. Somehow, I mistakenly took an elevator to get back to the scene of revelry and was standing alone as the conveyance seemed to move on its own in the opposite direction to the one I had selected.

Suddenly, the door opened and there not twenty feet away strolling along a red roped pathway casually chatting to the crowds, their Royal Highnesses, Princess Elizabeth and the Duke of Edinburgh. They were coming straight toward me and I didn't know who was more surprised, the Royal Couple, their security cadre or me.

Standing there in full uniform and in a rather dishevelled state, I didn't know what to do with myself other than performing an act of magic and disappearing in a puff of smoke. Fortunately, one of the security officers calmly reached in and sent me back to the lower floors where I belonged. I had wandered inadvertently into a formal reception for the Royal couple who were performing their first official visit to

Canada. In later years I was moved to refer to the incident as my private "Royal Visit".

We finally caught our train around ten o'clock that night and I arrived in Trenton just before mid-night, barely the worse for wear. My companions were all proceeding on to Montreal and Quebec City.

The bus meeting the train dropped me bag and baggage in front of the guardhouse at the base at Trenton. They were expecting me and sent me off suitcase and kit bag to my assigned quarters on the base where I would spend the first year of my career as a fully trained airman.

The next morning I was collected by a van and transported out to the unit on the edge of the airfield. I was impressed and proud to be reporting to my first operational employment in the air force and was looking forward to becoming a productive member of the service.

Although we all lived in the barracks on base, the AMES convoy could have been used as a home on wheels. One vehicle contained the large foldout antennae that measured thirty feet in diameter. It rotated through 360 degrees on its pedestal and was mounted on the vehicle. There was a maintenance vehicle and other vehicles that housed all of the many transmitters and receivers and other assorted equipment that made radar work. Several other electrical generation and support vehicles made up the unit. Once set in place the empty vehicles could be used as sleeping and eating quarters if required.

At the heart of the whole operation were the two operations vehicles that when joined together housed the controllers, the radar operators and the plotters who provided full defensive radar coverage of our designated area twenty-four hours a day - seven days a week. A small cadre of three officers provided the command and supervision under a Flight Lieutenant who was nearer to God than we minions.

We numbered about fifty on the unit and held a special relationship within the base organisation. The base was owned by Training Command and all of the base support systems and structures were designed to support training operations. We were the only operational unit on the base and reported to Air Defence Command located in St. Hubert PQ. Although tenants on a training base we were deemed ready for war.

Our unit was designated as # 3 Aircraft Control and Warning Unit (#3 AC&WU) and was dubbed "Three Ack and Woo". We were located in an open area just to the east of the runway complex on the far fringes of the airfield. Surrounded by low trees that had been cut back so as not to interfere with our radar waves, we were isolated from the rest of the base. Hidden from the main roads, those that knew we were there suspected some sort of top secret operation in progress.

We operated happily in our isolation and when asked by others on the base what we did out there, our response was usually, "Sorry, I really can't talk about it". This saved endless explanations of what #3 AC&WU was all about.

However, our mission was essentially that of providing early detection and warning of unknown or hostile aircraft, identify them by use of the fighter aircraft that would be scrambled for that purpose and then dealt with accordingly.

I was on duty the night that the invasion of North America began. A blip appeared of on the B-scan at fifty-eight miles. A quick strobe of the plan position indicator placed it on an easterly bearing. It was very strong indicating a large formation of multiple targets. I watched expectantly for a few minutes and noted that there was no movement whatsoever in the target. It was stationary on a bearing of about 090 degrees at fifty-eight miles.

The officers on call were alerted and began heading out to the unit to take up their operational roles. After some confusion and a lot of discussion between the Air Defence Command operations centre and ourselves, it was decided that we were to maintain a close watch on this target pending further developments. All other radar traffic that was being monitored on the radar network was accounted for. We then completed a rapid performance check of the radar systems to ensure that the equipment was operating at its optimum capability.

It was a clear summer's night and one could see for miles. As we maintained our watch someone burst through the door exclaiming excitedly that there was a strange light in the eastern sky and it looked to be quite close. Our two officers on duty were also qualified pilots and they immediately burst into action. One grabbed a shotgun and a handful of shells that we kept handy to control rats and other pests around the site and they both headed out the door in a flurry. Within minutes they had commandeered a C-45 Expeditor, a light twin engine communications aircraft and were off to save the nation from the enemy.

We vectored our C-45 interceptor into the close proximity of our target blip and they found nothing. They merged with the blip several times as they flew their pattern back and forth through the vicinity of the unidentified target and still nothing. Except – they were over the city of Kingston roughly fifty-eight miles to the east. From their position they could also see a strange light low in the eastern sky.

The weary warriors returned to the unit having not fired a shot and the gun and shells were returned to their rack and shelf. A lengthy debriefing ensued and an explanation for the evening's phenomena soon became apparent. There was an inversion lying over the east end of Lake Ontario that night. Inversions occurring at the lower levels of the atmosphere are not uncommon and tend to bend radar waves.

We had become the victims of circumstance. The planet Mars was particularly bright that night and astronomical conditions had conspired to place it on an easterly bearing from Trenton. The inversion that formed to the east had bent our radar waves downward to illuminate the man-made topography of the city of Kingston. As a final coincidence Kingston was on a bearing of about 090 degrees from our location at Trenton.

#3 AC&WU, having established itself as a stalwart defender of North America, continued to maintain its heroic vigilance for several more months at Trenton. The motto of the times was, "Sleep well Canada, your Air Force is awake".

We had developed a four-shift operating system whereby we worked four day shifts, four evening, four midnight shifts and then four days off. It was a happy schedule and suited everyone on the unit. Some of the troops moonlighted working on a part time basis for La Palm the mover in Trenton. Many of us took advantage of our situation and made a little extra cash on the side. I managed to put together enough money to buy an old '38 Oldsmobile that became the pride of the unit. It was a dignified four-door sedan with a nicely appointed interior. It was used on many occasions by various swains on the unit to impress the local belles who enjoyed the company of the airforce blue uniform.

It was about this time that my friend Jim Lucas and I set up our loan sharking business. Comparing notes one day we discovered that we were two of a very few who on occasion still had bit left over a few days before pay day. There were always those who would give blood (and some did) to pick up a few extra bucks to tide them over until the twice-monthly distribution of pay.

We decided to let it be quietly known that we would lend five bucks for the return of ten following the next pay parade. This was loan sharking and highly illegal of course but we managed to keep our operations under ground and happily provided what we considered to be an essential service for our fellow man. We made a few dollars but our un-collectables began to mount and we retired from the scam before we got carried away.

The pleasant routine that we had established ended for me one day as I was preparing to take some leave. "Your leave has been cancelled", I was told, "Report to the CO immediately".

"Thompson you are being assigned to Northern Electric in Belleville and will be part of the testing team for the new radar systems that are soon to begin production". All of the technical training that I thought had been wasted on me had come fully to the fore. I would not only participate in the operational trials of the new FPS 3 search radar and the ISG 98 height finder but, would also participate in the preliminary systems testing and the development of servicing and maintenance standards.

The new radar systems were destined for the NORAD Pinetree and Dewline bases that were nearing the completion of construction. Following an intense testing program that lasted three or so months, I returned to #3 AC&WU looking for other challenges.

It was at about this time that I remarked to the group as we sat around outside the command vehicle drinking our morning coffee that I had applied for and was accepted as aircrew during my recruiting procedure. I went on to wonder out loud just when they would call me into the aircrew selection process. It was then that I realised my own naivete. Our shift sergeant nearly fell out of his chair laughing at my innocence even after over a year in the service to my country.

To his credit he called me into his office the next day and coached me through the completion of a form called, "Application for Remuster to Aircrew". Once completed and duly signed by the unit commander it was sent off into the ethereal world of the air force hierarchy and was forgotten for a time.

I didn't have to wait long for new adventures with #3AC&WU as in the late summer of 1952, our orders came in to pack up and move with all due dispatch to RCAF Station Foymount near Arnprior Ontario. It was my first involvement in an operational move and I was surprised at how quickly everything was taken down, packed up and readied for the road.

We had never practised the moving procedure because of the priority of our role in the defence of Canada system. A few of the troops on the unit had participated in the earlier move-in and set up at Trenton but never a complete move from one location to another.

As it turned out, it was a holiday, or at least we all treated it as such. It was a new and welcome diversion from the routine of radar surveillance and the inevitable boring exercises designed to keep us on our toes. The unit was ready for the road in less than two days. The engines on our fifteen or so vehicles had not been run for a couple of years and most of our time was spent on engine tune-ups and catching up on neglected maintenance.

We packed our personal kit aboard the vehicles and set off early one morning. Those not assigned to truck driving duties rode in the several administrative vehicles that were part of our inventory. None of us had convoy-driving experience but that didn't seem to bother anyone. We just headed out for the highway and followed the vehicle ahead.

The old British army trucks once destined for the war in North Africa now sported a kitchen yellow colour scheme that was more a preservative than paint job. It was quite a sight to see fifteen brightly coloured yellow vehicles heading down the road at a top speed of about thirty miles per hour. I felt some sympathy for those faced with travelling behind us as there was not much opportunity to pass and we were only able to maintain a snail's pace in comparison to other vehicles on the highway.

Strangely, there were no outward signs of frustration from those forced to follow slowly behind for long periods. It was clear evidence that the air force was doing its job in defending the country and our convoy was accepted without question.

It took us most of the day to cover the one hundred and fifty miles or so to Foymount and we arrived in the early evening. We were ushered to our shiny new quarters and then to dinner in a brand new airmen and airwomen's mess. Everything was new. The site had been located, surveyed and construction including access roads had commenced a year or two before. The new radar site was on the verge of becoming operational and so little reliance was placed on #3 AC&WU to fill the gap.

This era marked the end of the AMES convoy. It was developed too late to be used extensively during the later stages of WW II but its value was immeasurable in the training of post-war radar technicians and operators. It did indeed fill a gap in the early stages of the development of the complex early warning and control system that was to become NORAD.

For some reason the mysteries of the air force came into play and a small group of eight of us were transferred within days of our arrival to RCAF Station Uplands just outside of Ottawa. We were shipped out one night after supper and transported by bus to our new base. On arrival we were directed to an airmen's barrack block close to the airmen's mess and the canteen.

As it turned out the location was very convenient as we discovered the next day that we were to be misemployed outside our respective trades on the base. At that time the base was experiencing a shortage of security guards and administrative personnel. Seven of our group of eight opted for the security role and were promptly made acting security guards under the direction the base service police.

I on the other hand had tired of shift work and chose one of the few administrative positions that were open. I was immediately assigned to the Warrant Officer 1st Class in charge of the base recreation centre. It occurred to me that this might be a good boondoggle and I reported to the WO1 fully turned out shaved, pressed and shined.

He welcomed me with open arms and we spent the remainder of my first day reviewing the operations of the recreation centre. I quickly discovered that my job was to be more than doling out sports equipment to the officers and other ranks using the facility.

It became obvious that the WO enjoyed more than just a little nip once in a while. The first few days we opened up the Rec Hall together. After a few more days of my apprenticeship, I was issued keys to the building, the sports stores and the cash box.

The WO's hours began to shorten at both ends of the daily spectrum. I had become used to expecting him in time for coffee and would have it ready for him by 10:00 AM. However, his arrival time crept up the clock to eleven and then to just a few minutes before lunch and the opening time for the bar at the Senior NCO's mess. I soon had the Rec Hall all to myself and the user clients. After a few weeks his appearances became sporadic and I learned to operate without him.

Unfortunately, the Station Adjutant began calling daily and I would make up some excuse indicating that the warrant officer was running an errand or some other plausible reason why he wasn't available. After a week or so the Adj called and I mumbled yet another lame excuse for his absence. It was not long before the WO stopped making his brief appearances altogether and I could only assume he was whisked off to some place to dry out. I became the Leading Aircraftsman in charge of the Rec Hall and found myself reporting directly to the Station Adjutant.

This period of my early career was beneficial to me in learning the finer points of basketball, volleyball and other team sports that I had missed because of the dearth of gyms during my school days on the prairies. I was always being asked to fill in on one team or another as the various house leagues came up short of players at game time. Although I was far from being considered a jock, I managed to perform well enough to be asked to play with most of the teams whenever they needed a spare.

I also re-established myself as a passable hockey player. I had played junior hockey back in Castor and my experience was entirely on open rinks. It was not uncommon to be required to clean the ice between periods and this was particularly onerous during intervals of snow. Playing hockey in the arenas on the base and around Ottawa represented a luxury for which I was not accustomed but I quickly acclimatised.

It was an idyllic existence and I began to enjoy the responsibilities that came with operating a large recreational centre. I found that I could maintain a fairly active social life and this generated some jealousy among my peers who worked the shift schedules required for twenty-four hour station security. Their places of employment were the security checkpoints scattered around the perimeter of the base. Armed with rifles they manned the network of guard posts that were intended to keep spies and other unwanted trespassers out. My job was viewed as cushy and I was treated to a daily barrage from my friends related to how good I was having it.

The F – 86 Sabre was being introduced into the RCAF at the time and as squadrons formed at RCAF Station Uplands and reached their full compliment of officers, men and aircraft they were dispatched to their assigned bases in the Air Division in Europe. I witnessed at least two squadrons depart for the RCAF Wings overseas before my own tour at Uplands came to a sudden end.

It ended abruptly only because I didn't see it coming. I was beginning to enjoy the freedom that being my own boss gave me. Halloween parties came and went followed by Sadie Hawkins Day parties at RCAF Station Rockcliffe. Then as the Christmas party season was about to commence, I was told to report to the Station Adjutant's office for pre-selection interviews as an officer candidate.

I had been reading Time Magazine cover to cover every week as well as several other good current affairs publications recommended to me by others. While the world outside the air force held little interest for me at the time, I managed to retain enough current affairs information through my reading to get me past the review board. I was told that I would be contacted in due course and to continue about my business.

In early December I realised that I hadn't saved anything for Christmas and found myself in front of the manager of the Bank of Nova Scotia near the streetcar loop in the Glebe in Ottawa. I guess the manager took pity on me as a former employee and I left the bank with a hundred dollars in my pocket leaving behind only the promise to repay my loan at the rate of ten dollars a month until the debt was retired. Repayment was a somewhat burdensome task severely challenging my gross monthly income of around ninety bucks but somehow I managed it.

Having completed my weighty banking transaction, I dispatched a letter to my father enclosing a money order for seventy-five dollars requesting that he take care of the shopping for my mother and sister and to get something nice for himself. I am rather embarrassed when I think about it now but my father seemed to take it in stride and after a spirited thank you note, he never mentioned it again.

Don Tomchick and I then made our last minute preparations to journey to Timmins for Christmas. Don and I had become close friends. He was a most agreeable young man and had a good family upbringing. Unfortunately, he and I sparked off one another, occasionally raising the eyebrows of those in authority. Particularly after we had consumed a beer or two.

His mother had invited the two of us to come for Christmas and on the 23rd of December we set off on our journey. Airforce bus to the Glebe, street car to Bank and Wellington with a change of cars for the onward trip to Britannia Beach and the western end of the streetcar line. Darkness was closing in as we hitched our first ride that took us as far as Deep River. After some food and several beers at the local hotel we made ourselves comfortable in the lobby where we spent the night.

We were travelling light with only our toothbrushes in our battle dress jackets. Don carried the toothpaste and I the cigarettes. The next morning suitably refreshed, we let breakfast slide and were on the road at first light reaching North Bay around noon. It was a freezing cold day but we didn't seem to spend too much time standing on the roadside waiting for a lift. We arrived at Timmins at about suppertime and were welcomed enthusiastically by the whole Tomchick family. Don's sister and brothers had come home for Christmas and to my delight, I became part of the family. The Polish food was wonderful and I was introduced for the first time to Pirogues made in the traditional Polish style. The Christmas turkey with all of the fixings was one of the best that I have ever had.

The Yuletide was a blur of good food, lots to drink and Christmas carolling throughout the large Timmins Polish community. I was just another member of the Tomchick household. Our every need was taken care of from freshly laundered clothes to daily shaving equipment and whatever else might have been required.

Tired and happy we made the return trip to Ottawa in one day following the reverse path of that we had travelled a few days earlier. We boarded the streetcar at Britannia Beach, the last leg of our homeward journey back to the reality of air force life.

We arrived back at work on December 27th and there was message waiting for me to report to the Station Adjutant. This was it I thought; I'm off to become an officer and a pilot. I was shattered as he told me that I was transferred to RCAF Station Edgar, a mountaintop radar site near Barrie in south-western Ontario. I was to be on the train at Ottawa Station departing at mid-night on December 29, 1952.

"But what about my remuster", I croaked. "Not to worry son", intoned the Adj, "your re-muster will be along soon enough".

Needless to say I was disappointed. How were they ever going to catch up with me if they kept moving me around the country so damn much? I boarded the train at the appointed time quite depressed. It was a small compensation that the eight of us who had been transferred from Foymount a few months before were all going as a group to Edgar.

Evidently, our social lives had preceded us and as we arrived at our new station we were dubbed the "Terrible Eight". I'm not sure what we had done to deserve that title but we became a revered club once established on the base. We had only been at Edgar a week or two when all eight of us were banished to the old Piggot Construction barracks at the foot of the mountain. These so called barracks were pretty austere living quarters intended for the construction crews at the radar station and they had long since moved into more tolerable quarters for the winter.

The construction barracks boasted only the bare necessities that today would be considered unfit for human habitation, particularly in the winter months. We took this all in stride however and found that our location, remote from the station proper, allowed us to enjoy our private accommodation to the fullest. It soon became obvious that many of the other junior ranks living in the luxury of the new quarters up on the mountain envied us for the freedom we enjoyed. A freedom that was not readily apparent to the senior NCOs and officers. We were for the most part, "out of sight, out of mind".

I recall a few good parties in the "Gulag" as it became known. When the weather wasn't too extreme we managed to throw some of the better unofficial station affairs and we managed to turn what should have been a disciplinary exercise into a rather frivolous affair. Somehow, the more enjoyable of our experiences while living in this hell hole escaped the notice of our superiors.

The cause of the banishment was nothing more than a rather foolish prank. The eight of us were qualified Fighter Control Operators with experience on the FPS 3 radar and the ISG 98 Height Finder, the new radar soon to be operational on the site. The training centre at Clinton was graduating all female courses trained on the AMES 11 radar. But Clinton at the time had neither the equipment or the experience to train recruits on the new installation. We, "The Terrible Eight" with our "trials" experience on the new radar systems were it.

As the courses of WD's graduated at Clinton, they were whisked down to Edgar and were subjected to a three week course on the new radar and associated systems. The syllabus for the course was designed and taught by the newly famous Terrible Eight. A female sergeant was assigned to us to provide the disciplinary link to the young impressionable airwomen who had become our student charges. This lady became our good friend and mentor as she provided us with the professional instruction on feminine hygiene that allowed us to more accurately assess whether Mazey was experiencing "that time of the month" or was just goofing off. It didn't take the girls long to realise that the Terrible Eight could not be hoodwinked and another notch was added to the holster of our repertoire. Many a teary eyed young damsel was sent back unceremoniously to her place in class after trying to swindle an afternoon off.

I have unfortunately made this sound worse that it really was. Yes, there were a few that made life tough for the rest of us but fundamentally we found the gals to be great students. They learned easily and cheerfully retained almost everything we threw their way. The only one complaint that I ever heard was that we had been desperately trying to hold one stag night a week in the Airmen's & Airwomen's Mess. Each time it was put to a vote at a mess meeting, the gals who outnumbered us by at least twenty to one, voted us down. Stag parties were therefore not allowed in the mess but it applied both ways.

After two weeks or so our "banishment to Siberia" was withdrawn. It couldn't be proven beyond reasonable doubt that the eight sets of ladies panties found flying from the station Flagstaff one Sunday morning was the work of the Terrible Eight. The esteem in which we were now held by all junior ranks on the base, both male and female, was extraordinary. We began to enjoy a very high status among our peers.

The mystery of the ladies panties or how they came to be flying at full staff was never solved.

I was about halfway through my second course teaching the gals when I found myself along with my good friend "AJ" Holmes dispatched to the Institute of Aviation Medicine in Toronto. As Leading Aircraftsmen, we were accustomed to the bus and train. For this trip however, we were assigned a car and driver. Cheers went up from the rather large group of junior ranks who showed up early on a cold winter morning to wish us well on our way.

The let down for us all came that evening when we returned in our chauffeur driven staff car to explain that, yes we had undergone all of the tests. We had been stuffed in the high altitude chamber and passed out so that we could experience the effects of anoxia. We were whirled around in a machine to test our "G" tolerance and subjected to a myriad of IQ and medical examinations. But no, we knew nothing more than when we had departed that morning.

A few days later amid much jubilation, AJ and I were posted to the officer candidate selection school at RCAF Station Crumlin near London Ontario. Our compatriots at Edgar were sorry to see us go but happy to wish us well in this new stage of our careers.

This event marked the end of the Terrible Eight saga and it is said that the Commanding Officer of RCAF Station Edgar did a dance of thanksgiving around his desk first thing every morning for several days following our departure.

AJ Holmes and I had made it through the selection process and now the officer training qualification loomed as the next challenge. We had spent much of our very short careers in the air force together. AJ hailed from Dartmouth Nova Scotia and was a Maritimer through and through. Our friendship was not unusual. The prairie boys and those from "down home" seemed to share a common outlook on life and identified themselves separately from those of central Canadian heritage.

There was an easy camaraderie among all Canadians of all races, religions and colours. It just seemed that those of us from the less financially fortunate provinces of the times shared similar values and national outlook.

AJ and I were considered to be the old men on the course and since we were the only two re-musters from ground-crew among the ninety or so candidates fresh out of school we became the barrack room advisors for the group. One young man in particular was shamefully innocent and really not well prepared for the big bad world. AJ and I took him under our wing showing him how to make his bed and take care of all of the other domestic activities that had never previously been of any concern to him.

He was socially immature and attempted to join in all of the many events that most of his new found friends took for granted. His first night at the cadet's canteen was a disaster. After a few beers he became quite boisterous and within about half an hour had gone through most of the stages leading to drunkenness. AJ and I escorted him back to the barracks and saw him safely off to bed.

He was very quiet for the first part of the next day and wasn't until mid-afternoon we discovered that he had no memory whatsoever of the night before. Furthermore, he couldn't quite grasp what had happened to him. By the end of officer training, Stew Pollock had become a man. The transformation was complete in every respect and Stew went on to pilot training at RCAF Station Claresholm, AFS at Portage La Prairie and then to an F-86 squadron in Air Division. He retired recently as a senior captain for a major airline.

This once again highlights the innocence of Canadian youth entering the armed forces. Not much had changed since the war and many immature young men were fast-tracked into adulthood.

AJ and I celebrated the night before our departure. We were now full fledged flight cadets and were pleased to be assigned to pilot training.

A new world was opening before us as we closed the door on a memorable period of our lives.

CHAPTER FOUR
A LETTER FROM HOLLAND

It was late February 1953. A bitter cold prairie evening and we had just disembarked at the railway station in Red Deer. There were fifty of us in all, representing five NATO countries.

21 Canadians, 10 Brits, 7 Italians, 7 French and 5 Dutch made up our motley group all preparing for flying training under the auspices of the NATO Air Training Program. This was one of the many new NATO member programs that provided the basis for the international military initiatives opposing the spread of communism throughout the European continent.

We Canadians were the latest graduates of the Aircrew Selection and Officer Candidate School at London, Ontario. Of the one hundred or so entering the selection process, there were about sixty graduates.

As we moved into the next phase of our training we took on a cosmopolitan flavour. Our horizons expanded immeasurably as westerners, Maritimers and those from central Canada became just "Canadians" as we were thrown together with our NATO air force counterparts.

The selection process had determined that we would be split roughly between twenty to the navigator-training course at Winnipeg and twenty or so to each Penhold and Claresholm in Alberta for pilot training. Our new NATO friends had all completed a similar selection process in their own countries and were assigned to the training bases proportionately.

We first came into contact with our NATO compatriots as we boarded the train out of Toronto. We travelled as a military draft and were assigned to cars on the train that had been reserved exclusively for military as was the custom of the day.

It was natural that under the close quarters imposed by extended train travel, that there was ample opportunity for the development of an esprit des corps between our course members of all nationalities. There was a natural segregation between groups assigned to navigator training at Winnipeg and the two remaining contingents headed for pilot training further west at Claresholm and Penhold.

AJ and I were assigned to RCAF Station Penhold and our arrival in Red Deer was a release from the confines of the train. We were all eager to get settled at the base a few miles to the south and west of Red Deer. It was to be our new home for the next twelve months.

There was a group of media awaiting our arrival on the platform. As the only Alberta boy in the contingent I was selected as the RCAF representative to be interviewed by the media and photographed with members of the other air forces.

We were the first course that would complete the whole training program at Penhold. #4 Flying Training School was still officially located at McCall Field in Calgary and had a course or two to graduate before the final move of flying operations north to the new location.

Ground school began a day or two after our arrival. It was a unique beginning to learning how to be a pilot as we had no aircraft on the base.

While the base consisted of the old wartime hangars from the British Commonwealth Air Training Plan days, most of the support buildings, barracks, messes and ground school buildings were all spanking new.

One of the few exceptions was the officers mess that remained in the old wartime building assigned to it and presented a rather quaint contrast to the new buildings on the base. We, as officer cadets of course were not allowed to mingle socially with officers who for the most part were also our instructors. We were assigned to the newly built Flight Cadets mess.

Our barrack blocks were brand new and shined up beautifully for our arrival. Naturally, we were expected to keep them that way and many an evening was spent scrubbing and shining for the next day's inspection.

We had the base to ourselves. The quiet solitude of our small group provided for a perfect academic environment. Among us there developed a close and easy camaraderie. I formed a close friendship with a young Dutchman whose full name took some learning and he insisted on leaving nothing out. My friendship with Jan Jacobus Cornelius van Rossum du Chattel was to span many years.

It was an intrusion when in the early spring our pastoral setting was assailed as the first snarls of the Harvard Trainer announced its arrival. Our excitement soon overcame any misgivings we may have had about sharing "our" base with two pilot training courses both well advanced in their training programmes.

Within days the base was humming with new vigour. The expectations of young men dreaming of their future aviation careers climbed to new highs. The six AM wake-up call was easier to answer and the step became a swagger during the morning march to met briefing.

We were introduced to the Harvard aircraft that from our perspective was a large and imposing monster. We spent many hours in the cockpit in the hangar memorising our checklists and learning to find the various controls, handles and switches blindfolded.

Part of the learning process was the care and maintenance of the hangars. Their cleanliness was of equal importance to either the barracks or the mess kitchen. It seemed to us that a pristine shine to the hangar floor was a fundamental principle of air power and that total defeat was imminent should a speck of prairie dust intrude within the sterile hangar environment.

It is a mystery, in retrospect; how we managed to learn the fundamentals of aviation together with the hours preparing for each air-lesson plan, the airborne instruction followed by lengthy debriefings and yet maintain the hangars and barracks equal to a white glove inspection.

The first entry in my logbook reads, "June 8, 1953 – Commenced Flying Training". We had been in continuous ground school since our arrival in February. All fifty of us experienced Lesson Plan #1 within a few days of one another. Henceforth, we would all proceed at a pace dictated by the schedules developed by our instructors, weather factors and our individual abilities to absorb instruction.

Completion of the first solos was marked by a ridged tradition. Immediately after landing the black service necktie, part of our flying uniform of the era, was clipped with a pair of scissors just below the knot. This was a sacred ritual followed by a good dousing with a bucket of cold water. As I recall, most of us made it to the clipping and dousing phase. As training progressed, the attrition rate started to take its toll and the dreaded "Ceased Training" (CT'd) phrase entered our lexicon.

We were never privy to the developing training problems of those among us who were experiencing difficulty with the flying program. One day they would be there, the next they were gone. CT'd became the past tense reference to those individuals who were no longer with us.

Soon it became apparent that of those of us who were left after the second month of flying training, most would likely see it through. Morale among us became even higher than ever before and all of the nationalities blended together as one.

Many of these memories came rushing back not long ago as my youngest son, who had developed a friendship with a young lady visiting from Holland, mentioned the surname of a friend of hers, "van Rossum du Chattel". Could this be the daughter of the same person that I had known so many years before?

I explained to her that one of my best friends during my pilot training days was a Jan Jacobus, Cornelius van Rossum du Chattel. I asked that the next time she saw her friend, could she find out if her father had trained as a pilot in Canada.

From the beginning of our early friendship Jan and my paths had seemed to parallel. We roomed together, studied together, suffered the bad and enjoyed good times together. Jan had an aristocratic air about him. He was good looking; blond, tall and very physically fit. He was instantly liked and accepted by those around him. Girls would have fallen at his feet had he paid them any attention. He was a good student pilot and stood close to the top of the class.

We graduated as commissioned officers in February 1954. Most of us went on to Portage La Prairie and then to Macdonald for advanced training on the T-33. Some went on to multi-engine aircraft training to Saskatoon and the few Canadian reservists on the course returned to their sponsoring units.

It was a sad day for me when we completed our NATO training phase at RCAF Station McDonald, Manitoba. We Canadians went on to our respective operational training units and the other NATO member students returned home. Jan and I wished each other a fond farewell with all of the usual promises to keep in touch.

A dozen years later I was in Holland as a member of the Canadian government team that had been established to assist the RNLAF in the acquisition of the CF-5 aircraft. I asked after my old friend Jan and was told that there was a van Rossum Du Chattel in the RNLAF somewhere in Holland but I was never able to make contact with him.

Now nearly twenty years after I retired from the air force, a chance meeting by my son turned a coincidence into a reunion. Within a few weeks a letter arrived from Holland. "Mr. van Rossum Du Chattel" read the return address. It was astonishing; here after forty-six years I was renewing a friendship that had almost been forgotten. Now a husband, father and a grandfather, the following paragraph provides a capsule account of Jan's career that commenced with his NATO pilot training in Canada.

On his return to Holland in 1954 he converted onto jet fighter aircraft and served out a short service commission before leaving the air force. Following a brief tour with KLM Airlines, he resumed his career in the air force serving as an instructor, Aide de Camp to the Deputy Chief of the Air Staff, Commanding Officer of a helicopter squadron. Finally in 1977 he was appointed as Equerry to Her Majesty, Queen Juliana of Holland.

In his letter, reminiscing our days together, I was reminded of the hardships he had faced as a youth during the war years. His own words best tell his early story and his Canadian experience.

"Canada at the time, left a deep impression on all of us for its seemingly enormous wealth and prosperity, its vastness and beauty, such a well organised and orderly society. To me personally, this was even more impressive having spent the wartime years, 1942 to 45, in a Japanese concentration camp on the island of Java and coming to Holland penniless in 1946. To this day I feel privileged to have been trained in your country and have always been proud to wear on my tunic the RCAF wings that we earned".

So much has happened over the years since we were together at Penhold. The airfield has been turned over to the City of Red Deer. Some of the old hangars still remain and some smaller hangars have been added. The barrack blocks and messes remain in mute testimony to the young men who once studied there and learned to fly. Air traffic is sparse compared to the days of the "Yellow Peril". As one walks through the area, a sleepiness has swept over the remains of the base. But the memories are still there.

The crisp dark mornings as we formed up on parade for the march to the flight line return vividly to mind. You can almost smell the high-octane fuel guzzled by the Harvard aircraft. The summer brought the smell of fresh mown hay from the surrounding fields and then the smells of harvest and the smoke from burning straw piles in the fall.

The Penhold interlude will remain in the memories of the many NATO students who trained there. All of us went on to separate careers in our own air forces. Some lost their lives in the service of their countries. May they too be remembered in the tributes to those who flew for their country and for NATO.

Wherever they are, the ghosts of Course 5305 assemble in the memories of youthful carefree days. The days of pilot training that were so full of wonder and accomplishment. The Letter from Holland took me back.

CHAPTER FIVE
MOULDING A FIGHTER PILOT

During my Advanced Flying School training at Portage, I had accumulated around twenty-five hours more on the T-33 aircraft than my classmates. You see, I was deemed to be a slow learner. Somehow I was cursed with a sickly instructor during the pre-solo stage of my T 33 training. This gentleman, whom I will call Flying Officer Grump showed up on the flight line three or four times a week - if I was lucky. It seemed that every time I was fine-tuned for the solo check, F/O Grump would take sick and after a couple of long days sitting on the ground I would have to start all over again.

This had a very depressing effect on me and worse, in the eyes of my mates I was marching down CT (ceased training) alley.

Finally, one day a swashbuckling youngish instructor strode into the flight room and seeing me sitting gloomily in the corner shouted, "Thompson why the hell aren't you in the air". I stammered that I hadn't yet passed the solo check. Most of my course-mates had flown solo at around five hours and here was I with eight hours on type and not yet qualified to fly the T-33 on my own.

After a brief examination of my flying records, F/O Windover introduced himself and I was told to get ready to fly. In my insecure state, I wasn't sure whether he meant off the end of his flying boot or actually in an aircraft.

With a hurried but detailed briefing we completed our pre-flight checks and were airborne. "Take me to twenty thousand feet" said my fearless instructor. Once level I was told to "burn off the tips and then, show me your sequence". Burn off the tips meant using up the fuel in the tip-tanks before entering into any high "G" manoeuvres. We flew around for a while practising turns at different angles of bank while maintaining level flight. Finally, the tip-tanks were empty and our aerobatic phase could begin.

A loop was fairly straight forward, as was a roll. It was a different story when it came to the "show me your sequence" part. I had heard others talk about their sequences but with my rather hesitant beginning, I had not had the opportunity to develop and practice a consecutive sequence of aerobatics nor had I been shown any of the finer points of developing one.

F/O Windover I began to discover had a very gruff approach on terra firma but once in the air he inspired confidence in me and we began to get along amicably. "Show me your sequence" he said once again, as I completed a loop.

Not to admit I didn't know what I was doing, I put together a roll each way and then a loop followed by a lazy eight. "Show me a vertical eight", was the next instruction from the back seat. Once again I was in the dark, as I had never completed one of these manoeuvres in a T 33 before. However, relying on second hand information gleaned from bar conversations, I proceeded with macho confidence.

I entered the bottom of my vertical eight at ten thousand feet and at 350 knots. It went very smoothly at first and as I approached the top of the second loop I thought I had it made. Airspeed a bit low, 100 knots and decreasing rapidly but no sweat. That's when all hell broke loose. The nose of the aircraft pitched upward followed by a snap roll and then into a set of unrecognisable and uncontrollable gyrations.

I made several attempts to recover but I didn't really know what I was recovering from. After a few seconds when nothing seemed to work, I took my hands and feet off the controls and to my amazement after a few more flips the aircraft entered an upright spin which I did recognise and my subsequent recovery was uneventful. However, I felt certain that the peculiar gelandesprung at the top of my vertical eight had scotched my chances of ever becoming a fighter pilot.

"Take me back to base", was all I heard from the back seat and I headed straight home calling on the radio for a fighter break and landing. Since I expected this to be my last trip in the T-Bird, I was pleased that my circuit and landing had been by the book.

I completed the post landing check as I taxied in. I knew that all fighter pilots did that. I pulled off the high-pressure fuel cock as I turned into the line (all fighter pilots did that too) and came to a stop with the nose-wheel precisely where the marshaller indicated he wanted it.

We dismounted and walked wordlessly into the servicing shack. I stood quietly while Flying Office Windover signed in and as he completed the paper work, he turned to me and said, "you had better grab a quick coffee puke, because you are going solo".

Needless to say, I was surprised and overjoyed but I had no time to celebrate. We debriefed over coffee and I was told that the reason for the bizarre manoeuvre was that I had entered the base of the vertical eight at too high an altitude not allowing me to sustain sufficient airspeed over the top of the second loop to complete the tight sequence.

"But what was that thing at the top of the vertical eight", I asked. "Beats the hell out of me", he evaded sheepishly, "but your recovery technique was flawless". That was the only answer I had until several years later when a test pilot at Cold Lake experienced a very unusual gyration during a routine test flight on a T 33.

A test program was embarked upon immediately and identified my unique vertical eight experience as a "Tumble" and went into the history books as a recognisable manoeuvre. I never encountered it again after my initial experience but had I done so, I had the recovery down pat. Furthermore, all of my vertical eight manoeuvres thereafter were entered at a much lower altitude.

As mentioned earlier, I graduated the course with more flying time than any of my course-mates. It was as though all of the instructors were trying to make up for my lost time waiting to go solo. I couldn't sit quietly and work on my logbook or just simply hang out. Every time an instructor walked through our crew room I would hear, "Thompson, get your ass in the air" and away I would go again.

We lost only a few of our course members to "ceased training" as we progressed through AFS. On graduation we received our wings before proceeding to gunnery school training at RCAF Station MacDonald. It was sleepy little base just inland from the southern shore of Lake Manitoba. Now as full-fledged pilots we endured only limited ground school and flew multiple sorties a day. Each sortie was a different event. Air to air live ammo against the flag, ground strafing, air to ground rockets and bombing. We often flew four sorties a day on each of the different events.

Toward the end of the course we were having one of those dull days on the prairies. The kind of a day you can't see the sun. But at thirty thousand feet you can see one hundred miles to the horizon. A thick layer of high cirrus blanketed the whole of southern Manitoba and it was a good day for weapons training as there was no need to make allowances for the glare of the sun. It was a happy day as we neared the end of our weapons school training at RCAF Station Macdonald.

I had just landed following what turned out to be my last gunnery sortie on that base. My logbook reads July 14th - Flag Live, four plane, 30%. Not a bad score when one considers that 10% was about the average for most of us at this stage of our training. I hesitate to mention that it was the only above average score that I achieved during the whole course.

On entering the crew room I was told to report to the Flight Commander who advised me to pack my bags as I was to leave immediately for 3 All Weather Fighter Operational Training Unit at RCAF Station North Bay, Ontario.

It turned out there were four of us who had been selected for operational training on an aircraft that was the pride of Canadian aviation, the CF 100 All Weather Fighter. We were to become all weather pilots in the defence of North America. The four of us departed together for our new home at 3 AWF OTU, otherwise known as the "Witches Squadron". The OTU crest was a black witch riding her broom into a full orange moon

North Bay was a fine station recently designated as a key air defence base and a temporary training centre for CF 100 aircrew. New messes, new single quarters and new hangars and administrative facilities gave us all a sense of pride and a keen desire to get on with our operational training. The instructor staffs were mostly all seasoned veterans of the Second

World War and many had seen combat up close and personal.

We of course were in awe of these heroes who had gained so much distinction during the war and we clung to their every word and gesture. Our little group of four were part of the second course to have completed the advanced flying training on the T-33 and we all had close to 100 hours on the "T-Bird". It didn't take us long to discover that each of us had more time on type than the whole OTU instructor staff put together.

We were confronted by the CF-100 Mk II, or the Clunk as it was intimately called. An imposing aircraft that had been Jerry-rigged with dual controls and a baseball bat handle for a stick in the rear cockpit. After a few months they modified both cockpits by canting the stick off 15 degrees to the right so that one could read the instrument panel. This was deemed to be important in an all weather/night fighter aircraft and after the dual aircraft were modified with the canted stick the technical staffs went on to modify all succeeding marks.

The first day of the OTU course was called the wedding day. Equal numbers of pilots and AI (wartime talk for "Airborne Indicator") navigators were dumped into a room together and told to get on with it. "It" being that each pilot and navigator had to find each other before met briefing the next day. There were a few introductory classes during the first day together and by late afternoon there were a few "courtships" in progress. Two or three hours after the bar opened at 5:00 PM the ritual had reached frenetic proportions as pilots and navigators careened around the room beer in hand searching for like-minded souls.

I am sure that nowadays there are more scientific ways of matching pilots and navigators and making them into proficient all weather fighter crews. But this somewhat inhuman means was effective and many pilot/navigator relationships are still intact to this day. They have been "best man" at each other's weddings; some were godfathers to each other's children and in some instances their progeny intermarried thus extending the relationship over two generations. In many cases they became family.

Not all initial pairings were successful and mine was one that didn't work. Either I had a bad effect on navigators, or I was just too independent for the process. After three attempts at crewing up and each time with a navigator who was unable to complete the training satisfactorily, I went on to complete the course with staff navigators.

My initiation into the world of the all weather night fighter was somewhat sobering since we had all been trained on the prairies where the weather was generally good and if questionable at all, flying was postponed until the weather improved. At North Bay however, I experienced some of the blackest nights of my flying career. Most of our intercept training was done far to the north over vast areas devoid of habitation. There were few lights on the ground even if the weather was good. During the later stages of my training in the fall of 1954, good weather was merely a memory of a warm summer past.

USAF Strategic Air Command bombers often over-flew the area carrying out their own training exercises at night and welcomed our participation as interceptors so that they could exercise their built-in defensive systems against us. The mighty B-36 eight-engine pusher was being phased out as the faster, higher flying B-47 was being phased in to take its place. Both aircraft however, were well within the capabilities of the CF-100 and they made excellent targets for advanced interceptor training under all conditions.

The USAF Strategic Air Command training exercises that took them from their bases in the US far to the north, often to just off the north coast of Russia and then a return flight through our defence region to exercise our air defence capabilities.

Dark nights combined with the late fall weather systems provided a daunting challenge. Dense cloud from a few hundred feet above the surface to over forty thousand feet was not uncommon. Much of our interception training was carried out in darkness and in cloud. We couldn't be sure of the target aircraft type until we were able to manoeuvre to within a few yards. Sometimes the ring of the flame within the aircraft jet pipe was the only visual reference that could be seen from a few hundred yards astern. Often the pilot was only vaguely aware of a dim shape as he closed on the target only to find himself flying formation on one of the engines of a B-36.

While it never happened to me, there were stories of pilots who intercepted the B-36 in darkness and in cloud and were unable to identify more than the aircraft engine. Visibility was such that the interceptor pilot was unsure whether to move right or left to locate the fuselage of the target and backed away knowing only that it was a B-36.

An extraordinarily high level of realism in our training was experienced during the operational training phase. Many of our senior instructor pilots and navigators had flown Mosquitoes in the RAF and were accustomed to night fighter activity under combat conditions. Conditions that were much worse than those we were encountering with the exception perhaps of the problems associated with high altitude flight. In this respect we were all breaking new ground.

The pressurisation system in the early CF-100 marks was not too reliable above thirty-five thousand feet and creeping cabin pressures from what should have been a maximum of twenty-five thousand feet, often reached ambient altitudes of forty-thousand feet or more.

Complaints of the bends in knees and elbows echoed throughout the debriefing rooms after such sorties. We learned the hard way not to fly with even a minor case of sniffles. The decent from forty- thousand feet could cause excruciating pain throughout the sinus system during the later stages of the approach and landing. Aviation medicine was in its infancy and we forged ahead finding anecdotes as we encountered the obstacles.

We sometimes learned high altitude aviation physiology through new experiences in the high altitude arena. Many of our solutions found their way into the study of the science of aviation medicine. Many ideas developed on the OTU assisted in the development of environmental systems and training programs that today minimise the hazards of high altitude flight and space operations.

My own training process while challenging was slow. My navigator was whoever on staff happened to be available whenever I was scheduled to fly. Primary and secondary duties for the instructor staff being what they were on the OTU, my needs for operational training were accorded a very low priority.

To ensure that I didn't get bored sitting around, I was checked out on the twin engine C-45 or the "Bug Smasher" as it was fondly known. I became part of the target force and flew many a sortie alone day or night, fair weather or foul flying target for the B-25 radar trainers. As the OTU was short of instructors, my C-45 experience was followed by a check-out on the B-25, a WW II twin engine bomber made famous by Jimmy Doolittle in his carrier-borne attacks on Japan. By the time I graduated from the CF-100 OTU course, I was checked out and current on the T-33, the CF-100, the B-25 and the C-45.

On completion of my final night sortie marking the end of my OTU training I ambled over to the bar for a quiet beer. To my surprise there was one helluva party in progress. One of those wild celebrations that started for no apparent reason and continued on for as long as there were people standing and the bar remained open.

The CO, Wing Commander Bob Braham, a well decorated former RAF pilot during the war, turned to me as I approached the bar and asked "Whatchyer cock"? I guessed that it meant how are you and I replied "fine Sir" as I tried to ease in the direction of company more in keeping with my own modest rank level. But before I could move away, the WingCo who was bare from the waist up and wearing a shirt collar and tie around his neck with shirt cuffs around each wrist asked with great dignity, "I say cock, how'd you like to stay on at the OTU as an instructor". I was momentarily speechless but without much hesitation I managed to stammer that I would be delighted to become a genuine "Witch". For a fighter pilot to stay on as an instructor was heresy but I had good reason to be pleased with this possibility and was told to report to his office at 08:00 hours next morning.

Once again my confidence failed me and as I turned out the next morning fully pressed and polished for my appointment. I was sure that the WingCo had completely forgotten our brief discussion of the night before. What if he was to ask me why I was there? What the hell would I say?

As I walked into the Adj's outer office all I heard was, "Thompson, get your ass in here". As I saluted smartly, the WingCo, now sharply dressed in full uniform, barely acknowledged my presence as he snatched up the phone on his desk and called someone at Air Defence Command Headquarters in St. Hubert. A brief conversation ensued which seemed a bit one sided. It went something like, "Thompson is staying here on staff - get the paper work done" and that was it.

Pipeline pilots like myself were being trained and along with their navigators were streaming through to their assigned operational squadrons. Some of which had yet to take delivery of their shiny new CF 100 Mark IV aircraft. The graduating CF 100 squadron pilots, once established at their various units across Canada, maintained their currency by flying anything they could get their hands on but mostly it was a small fleet of two or three T-33's assigned to each base that provided for their interim flying needs.

Conversely, I was in pilot's heaven. There were four types on the base and I was checked out on all of them. It couldn't have been better training for a green young pilot and while I picked up a few bad habits from some of the old wartimers, my basic and advanced training at Penhold and Portage La Prairie provided me with a solid reference point.

They were great days at 3 AW OTU North Bay. Up at first light, met briefing and into the air. Finish flying in time for supper in the mess and after a few beers to bed to start all over again the next day. Weekends on the base were dull and those of us who were still single volunteered to fly anything anywhere, just to be in the air.

We were expected to fly cross-country missions on weekends and there were always a half a dozen aircraft away from Friday night to Sunday night. Whitehorse, Vancouver, Gander and all points in between were all on the agenda. We flew to any base in Canada and some in the US that had the appropriate servicing facilities for our aircraft. Our inventory of T-33, C-45 and B-25 aircraft never had a chance to cool down. We didn't take the CF-100 on away trips very often because of its unique servicing requirements. But we more than made up for it on the other types.

Training was stepped up and the course sizes were increased to feed the demands of the operational squadrons that were taking delivery of their CF 100s at an ever-increasing rate. We turned out operational all-weather fighter crews who were trained to carry out lights-out intercepts at night and in all weather. In the process we learned about jet engines, high-speed aerodynamics and aviation physiology. As we encountered technical problems, they were corrected. If procedures were found wanting, they were modified.

The Mark III CF-100 had been our front line fighter aircraft. It was equipped with an APG 33 fire control system that had relatively short-range radar and a rudimentary computer system that calculated a lead pursuit course to the target. The success of this system was dependent on the fighter having a speed advantage over the target and while it worked well on slower targets, those that cruised at higher mach numbers presented more difficult intercept problems.

The aircraft was equipped with eight 50-calibre machine guns mounted in a belly-pack that could be quickly removed and replaced. It presented many technical difficulties but we managed to maintain a reasonable air to ground gun firing capability on the small weapons range located just north of North Bay. Why it was considered necessary for all weather fighter interceptor crews to maintain an air to ground capability would likely escape the fighter pilot of today. The aircraft had the capability so why not use it, seemed to be sufficient justification. Although, it should be remembered that at that time air doctrine was still developing into what it is today. Air forces the world over were beginning to explore the parameters of the new arena in which jet-powered fighter aircraft would operate.

Prior to the Korean War a fighter aircraft had to be light in weight, manoeuvrable and fast. There was a separation, although not too well defined, between air combat fighters, air to ground fighters, night fighters and so on. But basically one fighter aircraft suitably equipped was more or less capable of performing all of the roles assigned to "fighter aircraft". As the jet engine and advances in high speed aerodynamics pushed fighter speeds into the supersonic realm, the age of specialisation and a new categorisation of fighter roles began.

High altitude air defence dictated by the highflying - supersonic bomber threat necessitated a specific design criteria for that role. Such an aircraft, tailored to the high-high arena were ineffective at lower altitudes and a specific air superiority capable aircraft design was required below thirty-five thousand feet. Even in the similar roles of reconnaissance, low level strike, and ground attack, engine airframe combinations were optimised for each of these roles.

There were many studies done beginning in the 1960's searching for a single all-purpose fighter aircraft that, with a quick change of weapons systems, could perform all of the roles required of the "fighter aircraft". These studies have continued to this day but in the final analysis, the cost of the design and manufacture of such an aircraft is prohibitive. Exotic metal alloys were developed to withstand the heat and energy demands on engine-airframes. Thrust and manoeuvrability at high altitudes and high supersonic mach numbers raised additional demands. Manoeuvrability at low level, ordnance-carrying capability, range, loiter times, all presented additional challenges to the designer. Finally, but not surprisingly, cost became a major consideration.

These are all factors that pull the designer in multiple directions and while technologically it is possible to produce such a multi-role aircraft today, the cost is exorbitant. Even if the cost were deemed acceptable, it is unlikely that a wing commander would risk such a high priced asset in a non-permissive environment? To expose sophisticated expensive aircraft is a strategic call that can only be made after all of the benefit/risk analysis has been completed

The advent of the smart bomb in today's tactical air arsenal has to some degree eased the ridged criteria in the low-level arena but specialisation of tactical air power is still a factor to be considered in defining the roles for the establishment of air power.

So, in North Bay we attempted to maintain a capability in any of the roles our aircraft was even remotely capable of performing. But we were not alone, other air forces were beginning to confront the same dilemma.

In January 1955, I completed what is referred to in my logbook as the MG 2 Flying Circus. This was a brief practical course on the MG 2 Fire Control System installed on the B 25 aircraft and the new Mark IV CF 100. The new system replaced the old APG 33 package and boasted a longer range and a lead collision computing attack capability that allowed the interceptor to engage targets with a speed advantage over the CF 100. It was the technological marvel of its era and allowed the CF 100 to maintain its effectiveness as an operational fighter for well over twenty years.

The MG 2 FCS allowed attacks on targets from near the head on and computed continuously an impact point between the weapons selected and the target. For the crews the initial exposure to the intercept equation was a bit hair raising. Early on in the attack, it would appear that target and fighter were on a true collision course. Beginning at about twenty miles and often less, the navigator held the radar contact on a constant bearing of about forty degrees to the right or left of the attack track. Once the radar had been locked on to the target by the navigator, the weapons system computer took over and began predicting the impact point between the air to air rockets and the target.

The CF-100 weapons system had been designed to optimise the capabilities of the 2,75 inch rockets. This rocket was one of the most effective weapons of the times. Rocket flight envelopes were based on a number of factors; burn time, rocket flight time, relative closing speeds were among the more important. In general, rocket release ranges varied between three hundred and six hundred yards. The higher the closing speed the greater the range of release. Since the Soviet bombers of the day boasted radar trained-tail mounted cannon, it was a wise crew that kept their attack course in the forward hemisphere of the target flight path.

Watching the attack visually, one could only conclude that death was near as target and fighter appeared to be on a collision course. It wasn't until the attack progressed down to about one thousand yards that the target would finally begin to alter from is constant angle off and break across the nose of the attacker at five to six hundred yards. In the final phases of the attack on dark moonless nights, both members of the crew had to execute maximum concentration on their radarscopes to detect the initial indications of the target breaking ahead of the fighter.

Occasionally, a crew would have to render an aircraft unserviceable due to the weapons system inadvertently computing a true collision course. This was never a pleasant scene and during training, the first practice intercept of the mission required additional intense monitoring by both members of the crew.

To my knowledge there were no mid-air collisions as result of lead collision practice interceptions.

We did however experience one close call on a dark night over Lake Temiskaming. Two student crews were practising visual identification intercepts on one another. They had each completed several runs and in accordance with their briefing they were each to do a minimum of two visual identification runs with the target's lights out. Following the initial sequence of intercepts, the first crew carried out two successful lights out intercepts on the target aircraft. Roles were exchanged as the fighter became the target and the target aircraft now became the hunter.

All went well in preparation for the first of the two intercepts that were to be accomplished. Ground radar put the target on an assigned heading and vectored the fighter into a position where the navigator in the intercepting aircraft acquired the target. Once acquired, the navigator advised the ground radar controller that he was now locked on the target and was taking control of the interception. He then guided his pilot toward a position from which the pilot could identify the target.

Everything so far had been accomplished according to established procedure. The navigator manoeuvred his pilot to a loose line astern position where the fighter aircraft could then creep in to the point where a visual identification could be accomplished. "Ten degrees port, ten above, two hundred yards, closing at ten knots", the navigator called as they approached the lights-out target. The closing angle, the elevation and the closing speed remained constant until the navigator had difficulty seeing the target blip in his short-range clutter. Suddenly both aircraft were rocked as they came together briefly and then separated as the two pilots took reflexive evasive action.

Fortunately, following the collision and with all lights blazing, it was determined that both aircraft were still flyable and both made precautionary recoveries back at base. It was found on landing that the target aircraft had a twenty-foot rip along the bottom of the fuselage and the fighter had sustained a significant amount of damage to it's fin and rudder.

During the debriefing following the mission, it was determined that the student navigator who was directing the last intercept had mistakenly understood that if the azimuth and elevation angles remained constant, that everything was OK. It took a while for it to dawn on him that with a constant azimuth and elevation combined with a closing speed, he had set up a true collision situation.

We had several fatal accidents during my ten months at the Bay. None of them related to the intercept role. All of them might have been prevented had we been equipped with today's knowledge of aerodynamics and aero-engine technology. Metal fatigue of a hydraulic flap mechanism was the cause of at least one fatality. Fatigue in high-pressure fuel and hydraulic lines, contributed to some, engine failure to others and finger trouble was predominant in others.

Finger trouble or pilot error was too often among the findings of accident review boards. Pilots who had lived through serious accidents were often branded with pilot error when they could not explain accurately what had happened – often they didn't know. Human engineering had yet to be invented and ergonomics was unheard of. The pilot was responsible for herding a collection of machinery through the air by sheer force of will, skill, sometimes brute force and a goodly dollop of luck.

My checkout on the B 25 was typical of the times. I had around two or three hours in the right hand seat and was comfortable in the relatively large cockpit. One day the RAF exchange officer on the OTU, F/L Paul Kent, scheduled me for the checkout. It was my first trip in the left-hand seat and off we went climbing to five or six thousand feet. We completed a couple of stalls, steep turns, climbs and descents. We then feathered an engine and I was allowed to fly around on one for a while to get the hang of it.

Suddenly, Kent announced that he had to get back to base fast as he had lost track of the time and had an appointment with his bank manager. We landed uneventfully and as we signed in, the servicing NCO, Sergeant Jones, announced that he had an air test on a B-25 that had to be done before lunch. To my surprise Kent turned to me and said, "No problem, Thompson can do the air test now, we'll do his single engine check-out after lunch".

I had developed a good rapport with "Jonesy" during my C-45 experience and it didn't seem to bother him that my checkout was incomplete. The air test was required on the feathering mechanism on the starboard engine in the air. The propeller stops were set to 89 degrees to the airflow when fully feathered and this engine wouldn't un-feather under certain conditions. Tests on the ground indicated that the mechanism now worked OK but it needed certification on an airborne test.

My second take-off in the B-25 aircraft went well with Jonesy in the right hand seat. We climbed to five thousand feet and once settled down I told him to go ahead with the feathering test. He was a highly qualified aero-engine technician and a qualified flight engineer. I monitored him as he completed a flawless feathering procedure and we flew along on one for a few minutes while Jonesy made some entries in the flight test checklist.

Then he prepared to un-feather which would put us back into normal flight conditions. It didn't work - no matter what we did, the prop stayed locked at 89 degrees streamlined to the airflow. We declared an emergency and headed back to base. "Do you think you can get us back on the ground" was Jonesy's only half question. "No sweat, there's nothing to it" I replied, sounding much more confident than I felt. I flew a very cautious straight-in approach and I was beginning to admire the great skill that I had exercised thus far.

My airspeed over the threshold was right on the numbers and as we came over the button of the runway, I eased the good engine back to idle. Then it began, in slow motion, the most panic stricken few seconds I had ever experienced. The aircraft, no longer affected by the torque from the good engine, yawed violently to the left. Every bit of confidence I had built up began to evaporate and it took all my strength to realign the aircraft with the runway.

For a few seconds I thought I had lost it, but sheer force and a lot of fear-generated adrenaline won in the end and as we touched down, I was able to steer down the centre line to the turn-off. As we shut down and deplaned, the WingCo arrived at the scene with Paul Kent in tow. "Well done" they said in unison. As we walked to the WingCo's car Kent said, "Well I guess that eliminates the need for a single engine check". I was now a qualified B-25 pilot while Jonesy stayed behind to direct the activities of his towing crew.

Our flight safety record by today's standards was abysmal but it was a learn as you go process. We sharpened our learning curve, found faults, recorded shortfalls and rectified danger areas. Our knowledge of jet operations improved exponentially as we gained knowledge from experience. In today's parlance, "we were pushing the edges of the envelope".

The OTU's existence at North Bay was to be short-lived. As my first winter of all weather flying over the dark expanses of northern

Ontario came to a close, a whole new era was to open before me as the "Witches" began preparations to move to RCAF Station Cold Lake in northern Alberta.

CHAPTER SIX
TALES OF THE BAY & CHILLY POND

We entered the thick grey cloud-base at around eight thousand feet in the climb and I settled down to some routine instrument flying. A few minutes later we broke out at twenty thousand feet into the brilliant early morning sunshine.

To my amazement, there stretching westward as far as the eye could see, the contrails from thirty CF 100s all enroute to Winnipeg, the only refuelling stop on our mass move. We continued our climb to thirty thousand feet and had little concern for other traffic. We had the sky to ourselves as commercial airlines had yet to make the transition into the jet world and normally operated below ten thousand feet.

We were on our way to our new base at RCAF Station Cold Lake. My navigator and I had been assigned to bring up the rear and we trailed a safe distance behind the aircraft ahead. The "Boss", W/C Bob Braham was in the lead and running about thirty minutes ahead of us as planned. The weather at Winnipeg was not bad, but a layer of cloud cover dictated prudence during our let down to the airfield.

Refuelled, we took off in the same order that we had established on our North Bay departure and took up the final leg to what was becoming fondly known as "Chilly Pond". We had all visited the base on earlier occasions and knew that we were heading into the northern Alberta wilderness. As its informal logo, the base had irreverently adopted the Palm Tree.

The airfield itself was located on what might have previously been a swamp. Everything was new from the runways, hangars, living quarters to the recreation and shopping facilities. So new was the base in fact, that the roads and sidewalks had not yet been finished and ground movement was slow and ponderous through seas of mud. Runways, taxiways and aircraft parking areas were the only concrete or paved areas on the whole base. Aircraft and ground handling equipment were not to be sullied by the same muddy conditions that mere humans endured.

Everyone on the base moved about in rubber boots. Officers and men, women and children in the schools and the married quarters, not to mention the school teachers and all of the other civilian staff that were required to run this new community seemingly dropped in the middle of nowhere.

The entryways to each of the brand new buildings were always clogged with muddy boots as people conducted their business inside in their stocking feet. Caution dictated that one's name was indelibly displayed inside the top of the boot as the statistics of size conspired to ensure that any unmarked boots left over were never an ideal fit or an identical pair.

The Base Commander, G/C Dick Stovel, was on hand to welcome us to the base and we were all transported off to the Officer's Mess for an early round of beer.

The base had transformed overnight from a sleepy, no rush - no fuss existence to a fully operational flying base. A course was already in residence and ready to start training immediately. Little time was wasted getting settled in and within a few days ground school was fully operational and flying training had commenced in earnest.

The domestic side of life suffered initially for some. Private married quarters were being constructed on a priority basis and as each house was completed it was filled with a newly arrived family. The school and base medical services were scrambling to keep up with the influx of people arriving daily.

The base hospital was opened to all base personnel, military or civilian it didn't matter. Air force nurses and orderlies became expert in the delivery of the new-born and the care of children and mothers. The whole medical spectrum expanded for the military medical service on the base. While the medical staff was severely taxed with the sudden influx of families, they performed remarkably well under the circumstances. Soon the base hospital was providing a medical service to a community of over four thousand people. Medical facilities and highly qualified military medical personnel had been plunked in the middle of nowhere and rivalled those found in larger centres in the western Canada.

There were about sixty of us witches, officers that were transferred with the squadron from North Bay. There were perhaps another five hundred ground crew and support personnel also transferred from the Bay many of who had to leave their families behind until suitable accommodation became available at Cold Lake. Housing construction was progressing at feverish pitch but strained to meet the demands of the heavy influx of personnel.

The OTU was divided into three separate flights. One for instrument and conversion which ensured that the pilots arriving for CF-100 training met a high standard of instrument flying on the T-33 before their conversion. Once all of the pilot standards were verified, the CF-100 Mk II dual aircraft were rolled out onto the line for the conversion portion of the course.

The student navigators arrived from Winnipeg at about the same time as the student pilots and after the usual "Wedding Ceremonies", began their ground school training together. Once the instrument and conversion phase was complete, the pilots joined their navigators in the B-25 Flight for the radar systems portion of their training.

On completion of their B-25 phase the crews moved to the CF 100 Mark IV Flight for their final phase of training. They flew day and night following a rigorous syllabus in preparation for assuming operational duties at their assigned squadrons. The course syllabus was tight but designed to ensure that the all weather crews required only a minimum amount of combat ready training on reaching their new units.

Throughout basic flying training the pipeline pilot was told that instrument flying was a full time job. Now he was told that he had to respond to the navigator's commands for the duration of an attack or an interception. Furthermore, he had to follow the visual indications on his front cockpit radar scope to press home his attack. Routine instrument flying took on an added dimension that pushed the inexperienced pilot to his limits. As more experience was gained the all weather pilot became highly proficient and handled the increased cockpit workload with ease.

The "lights-out" phase was even more stressful as lead collision intercepts now challenged the crews to the utmost. Targets crossing at five or six hundred yards in front of the fighter aircraft made for tense moments during the final phase of the practice intercepts.

Other pipeline pilots soon joined me on the OTU. Many had their squadron tours cut short to meet the OTU demands for instructors with operational experience. I continued to maintain currency on all of the OTU aircraft types and added the Otter on wheels and floats to my repertoire. I picked up a ski endorsement on the Otter later that year.

It was at about this time that I took some leave and headed back to North Bay to marry Joan Marjory Murray. I had met Joan at a nurse's Christmas party the year before and following an intense courtship we fell in love. I proposed in the upstairs lounge in the officer's mess at North Bay during one of my frequent weekend trips out of Cold Lake. I was nattily dressed in my drab grey-flying suit that seemed to be in a perpetual need of cleaning.

It was decided that we would be married in the Anglican Church in Gravenhurst Ontario on August 15th. Reverend Johnny Watson had moved into the parish a few years before and had been the Murray family chaplain for many years. On the wedding day we were confronted with a minor logistics problem in transporting families and bridal party to Gravenhurst some one hundred miles to the south. The biggest issue seemed to be keeping the bride and the groom from any contact with one another before meeting at the altar.

Formal ceremonies complete we proceeded to Niagara Falls for our honeymoon. The following day we began our leisurely journey west to our first home together.

Joan's arrival at Cold Lake was a major culture shock for her. While married quarters would be made available to us later in the fall; the only accommodation we could find was a small two-bedroom house on the edge of Grand Centre just few miles off base. The lack of plumbing and central heating added to the charm of this residence on the edge of the wilderness.

The base medical fraternity soon learned of Joan's arrival and she was conscripted immediately into a nursing position on the hospital staff. Her qualification as the only paediatric nurse on the base demanded much of her time. For the six weeks or so we camped in Grand Centre, Joan had access to the hospital laundry facilities. We both had access to showers at work and while our living conditions at our little home were rather sparse, we managed our routines to suit the situation.

By mid – November we were assigned a temporary married quarter on the base. For this we were charged thirty-two dollars a month, a sum we thought to be fairly reasonable under the circumstances. Our move-in from the cold was none too soon as we had been living under sub-arctic survival conditions with outside temperatures hovering near minus 20 degrees centigrade for a week or two. We began settling in to a Cold Lake winter.

The temporary quarters were nothing more than four single rooms in one of the officer's barrack blocks. A sink, a cabinet and a locker dominated one wall in each of the rooms. Bathrooms complete with multiple toilets, showers, sinks and bathtubs down the hall were shared with two other couples. A "Gender in residence sign" was crafted to identify the occupant of the facility.

While there were some drawbacks, in comparison to the deprivations of our first home in Grand Centre it was an experience in elegant living. All our neighbours were newly married couples with no children. If children were to arrive, then a move to private married quarters was mandatory. Some were so motivated.

We soon settled into a routine, Joan with her nursing duties while I became absorbed in operational flying training activities.

One day F/L Tony Gunter-Smith handed me a set of Aircraft Operating Instructions

(AOIs) for the F 86 Sabre. Tony was a good friend and former OTU instructor. He had been transferred to the Central Experimental and Proving Establishment on the base. "You had better read up on this", he advised, "I might be able to get you a quick trip".

A day or two later Tony called to tell me to get down to the CEPE right after lunch as I was scheduled to fly the "Sword". After an early lunch, I headed over to CEPE not totally convinced that I would get my Sabre trip but I was hopeful. I climbed into the cockpit of an aircraft in the hangar and with the AOI's provided by Tony nearby, I familiarised myself with my surroundings and ran through all of the cockpit checks several times.

After several minutes I looked up to see Tony peering over my shoulder. "Looks like you know where everything is", said he, "so let's get out to the flight line". The flight I was to take was an air-test.

Some modifications had been made to the armament system and the guns had to be test fired at altitude over Primrose Range. This added a new dimension to my first Sabre flight for which I was unprepared. But after a quick briefing on the armament panel, switch settings, range safety and firing procedures, I was all set.

Tony watched over my shoulder as I started the engine and then stepping away, he gave me a "thumbs up" and I was off.

The F 86 was a sports car compared to the CF 100 and I immediately began to enjoy the spacious cockpit and the easy access to all of the switches, knobs, levers and controls.

As I taxied out to the armament checkpoint, I marvelled at the visibility from the cockpit and the ease with which the pre-take off checks could be completed. A brief pause at the check-stop while the weapons technicians removed the safety pins on the guns and I was cleared for take off. The aircraft accelerated beautifully and I was airborne. Gear and flap up as scheduled in the checklist and I was ready for action.

The radar controller following my progress in the climb vectored me toward the range and assigned me to the pre-arranged test altitude of forty thousand feet. I made a few turns left and right of my assigned course just to get the feel of the aircraft during the climb. On reaching altitude the controller gave me a course alteration to centre me over the firing range and then the countdown to fire began.

I set the armament switches as I had been shown and then maintained my heading and altitude awaiting the clearance to fire from the ground controller. Ten seconds----- five, four, three, two, one – "FIRE" came the order from the ground and I squeezed the trigger. The sound of the guns firing and the mild vibration was exhilarating but far too short. There were only fifty rounds loaded for each gun and my firing experience was over in seconds. Time to head home.

My first all too brief encounter with the "Sword" was a great personal thrill and it would be several years before I once again had an opportunity to fly this delightful aircraft.

I had only one other experience flying as a test pilot for CEPE. The boffins (engineers) had a fully instrumented CF 100 Mk IV that was armed with fifty-eight 2.75-inch rockets that had to be test-fired over the range. The whole exercise would be monitored by telemetry and they only needed a pilot to fly the aircraft. They called to see if I could do it. I jumped at the chance and soon found myself being briefed on the details of the mission. Once airborne I checked in with the ground controller and then followed his instructions. A climb to forty thousand feet and vectors to the range had become the standard procedure. Then the countdown to "FIRE" and as I pulled the trigger, I disappeared into a huge but momentary ball of flame. All 58 rockets launching at once made for a rather spectacular few seconds in the darkening sky.

The post mission debriefing with the boffins was routine and as we finished up I asked what the approximate costs of the mission had been. Rockets alone, it came to about eight thousand 1956 dollars I was told. Over dinner that night I explained proudly to Joan, that my little exercise over the range that day had cost the price of a brand new Cadillac. She was not impressed.

The arrival of the Weapons Practice Unit (WPU) at Cold Lake signalled the beginning of a new era. The unit was formed to provide live weapons training to all of the All Weather Squadrons in Canada. The two to three week practice camps ran in succession a couple of weeks apart. Each CF-100 squadron in Canada and those forming in Europe dispatched two crews at a time to complete their rocket firing continuation training over the range at Primrose Lake. Inter-squadron rivalry was at the forefront both in the air and on the ground and all crews looked forward to their annual tour at "Weapons Camp".

The early years at RCAF Station Cold Lake were unforgettable for those who opened up the base to air operations beginning in 1955. The quality of leadership from the base commander to the line corporal was exemplary. Men and women toiled under the most extreme conditions to prove that flying operations could truly be carried out in all weather, day or night. Temperatures reaching minus 35 degrees centigrade were commonplace for at least four of the winter months each year.

Those who served at Cold Lake in the early days of the base history treated these conditions as normal. In the process a high standard of all weather operations was established; a standard that is recognised around the world. It was not long before other western air forces were bringing their new aircraft testing programs to the base to complete their cold weather testing trials. Today, the base continues to establish new benchmarks of excellence in air operations.

The small towns surrounding the base have prospered since it opened fifty years ago. Today the "City" of Cold Lake has become a major economic centre for the petroleum and tourist industries. The airport has a civilian component that provides for regularly scheduled airline communications with other major centres in the west.

The many Canadians who served in the air force during the fifties and sixties look back fondly on those lively years of their service at RCAF Station Chilly Pond. The outhouse has become obsolete, plumbing and central heating have at last found Grand Centre.

CHAPTER SEVEN
THE COLD WAR WARRIORS

In the fall of 1957 I was transferred to RCAF Station Comox, BC. I had "crewed up" with Squadron Leader Bruce Cameron who had been on a staff tour in Ottawa and was keen to get back into the air. Because of his background as an AI navigator during the war, he was not required to go through the whole training process.

I was assigned to assist with his refresher training and an instant friendship ensued. So it was that Bruce and I became a crew and were posted together to Comox.

The squadron was equipped with the Mark V CF-100 that boasted a three-foot extension to each wing. This allowed the aircraft more stability and manoeuvrability at higher altitudes. But had little effect on performance in the lower levels.

Bruce and I enjoyed the life of a line crew and completed our combat ready training in short order.

We flew together for a time but as Bruce began to take on more responsibilities as Navigation Radar Leader on the squadron our status as a crew grew more tenuous. Bruce, somewhat older than most of us on the squadron became fondly known as "Nav Rad Dad".

Once again I was assigned whatever navigator was available for the flying schedule. A situation I had become accustomed to back at North Bay a few years before. Bruce and I remained good friends and flew together whenever possible. Joan and Bruce's wife Jean, an English War Bride, had also established a sound friendship and our working and social relationships flourished.

In late March 1960 spring was definitely in the air. I had been rather discouraged a year earlier when the Arrow programme had been cancelled. We had been told in early 1959 that Bruce and I had been selected as one of the early crews to commence conversion training onto the CF-105 Arrow at Malton near Toronto. We were of course overjoyed but our exuberance was short lived as the program was cancelled shortly after our selection was announced. My disappointment was soon overshadowed by the concern over where they would post me next. Most All Weather aircrews were going to the DEW line after one operational tour and here I was completing my second tour. The prospects for another flying tour looked grim.

I had arrived home from a stint on "Q" earlier that spring morning to give my mother-in-law, Lila, a hand with our eighteen month old son. Joan had just had our second boy a few days before and we waited for the call to collect her together with our new-born from the hospital. I had been on Quick Reaction Alert or "Q" all night and had been scrambled twice from a deep sleep.

This was not unusual at 409 Squadron Comox. The bell clanged loudly and the number one crew pulled on flying suits and boots. By the time we were dressed, the Ops B had prepared two cups of cold orange juice that we gulped as we dashed by the Ops desk. It provided the sugar jolt needed to augment the adrenaline flow.

Our flying helmets and safety gear were previously installed in the aircraft cockpits on the tarmac below. The ground crew began a quick pre-flight check of our CF-100 MK V aircraft that was completed as we arrived on the run.

Climb up and in, Mae West on, helmets on, and start up. We'd strap in while taxiing out. Check the time, two minutes from the bell to wheels rolling. Not bad, we'd make it in under five minutes to wheels up. Airborne and established in the climb we double-checked each other to ensure that the strapping-in process was completed appropriately and then, it was time to wake up.

We had been operating on automatic up to this point and now we looked forward to the reality of the forward air controller briefing us on the unknown target that he was following on his radar screen. A sardonic "Vector 320 degrees, climb to angels 40" was not an unfamiliar initial direction from ground. We would be briefed in more detail as we went along. The height, speed, and approximate track information was followed by an estimate of the number of aircraft comprising the target. Once level at forty thousand feet the interception would begin in earnest.

This whole procedure had become old hat after three years on 409 Squadron and I always enjoyed the thrill of the scramble. The sudden burst of activity from a dead sleep in your assigned bunk, sweeping through the ops room and a skip down the stairs and out onto the tarmac always got the juices flowing. The excitement and challenge of the chase was invariably exhilarating and occasionally frightening. Particularly when the weather was marginal and the possibility of a difficult recovery after the intercept loomed in one's mind.

We had little time to ponder whether we would identify the leading edge of the invading Russian bomber force or some other unknown target. Sometimes a commercial airliner would wander off course or his estimated entry times into North American air space might be out by a few minutes. A commercial airliner that was outside of NORAD correlation had to be positively identified. Frequently it was a formation of USAF B52s from Strategic Air Command. SAC routinely conducted mock attacks on the North American continent. Occasionally, it would be a lost soul over the mountains that needed guidance to a safe landing.

We always planned for the worst. Our "Q" aircraft were perpetually fully armed. We only had one shot but our 58, 2.75-inch air to air rockets would obliterate anything they hit.

Tonight, our unknown came on the screen in the rear cockpit. "Contact 20 degrees port sixty miles" the calm statement from the back seat. This was followed by a series of commands as the navigator had now taken over from the forward air controller on the ground.

The running commentary would continue interspersed with directions. "Port ten degrees ---- harder -- hold – steady, starboard five degrees ---- steeeeady". Then, the final moments of truth - "Fifteen port, ten above, 400 yards overtake ten knots". My response, "no visual". From the rear, "Ten port, ten above, 300 yards closing, five knots overtake". Now the commentary would get urgent and continuous. "Ten port, ten up 200 yards closing at five". Flying the aircraft on instruments with the mental picture provided by the navigator's running commentary, I began the visual search in earnest taking care to keep one eye on the instrument panel. "Ten port, ten up, 100 yards". "Still no visual".

Then at last, "got him" was my exuberant shout as I sighted the quarry and now the identification process would begin. Not much to see on a dark night, often in cloud.

Sometimes you could pick up the ring of exhaust fire from the engines, if you were lucky. If the target was not showing any running lights the target was either enemy or possibly a USAF Strategic Air Command bomber testing NORAD defences. Without lights the pilot had only a vague awareness of a shadow that lurked there in the darkness a few feet away and travelling in unison at 450 knots. The navigator carried a large flashlight in the back seat and as the fighter closed on the intruder he would switch on and hopefully illuminate the tail numbers of the target aircraft.

On this occasion we had come upon a Super Constellation enroute to Seattle from Alaska. The running lights had been turned off to prevent the reflection of the glare off the cloud from distracting the pilots. We were now in close formation and could make out the white ghost of an aircraft within the misty bowl of our world. The lights were quickly flashed on when the pilot became aware of a strange light beam sweeping his aircraft as we searched for an identification number.

Many an airline pilot was surprised and sometimes humiliated that he had been caught "out of correlation". While the airlines usually had their running lights on and if they were aware of our presence they would turn on their whole array and could be seen for miles around.

To satisfy NORAD though we still had to close to a position from which we could identify the type of aircraft and provide a tail number so that officials on the ground could determine why the aircraft was out of correlation. This usually meant a lengthy debriefing for the airline captain once on the ground at his destination and of course a full explanation of his navigation techniques. To their credit, most airline crews of the day navigated their aircraft with remarkable precision over great distances and across wide expanses of ocean with very limited navigation aids.

So it was on this night. Identified, one friendly airliner out of correlation and a few hours later a second scramble on a formation of B 52's from USAF Strategic Air Command. They were heading home after probing Soviet defences on the far side of the North Pole.

Not a bad night's work followed by a steaming breakfast back on the ground at 6:00 AM, the formal hand over to the daytime standby crews and then the reward; a hot shower. Another shift on "Q" had been completed and it was home to the quieter life.

I hadn't been in the house more than ten minutes when the phone rang. It was Joan calling from the hospital and impatient to get home. She had been released earlier than expected. So after packing Lila and small noisy child into the car, off we went to retrieve the new mother and the newest addition to the family. As we drove, Lila asked casually how my shift had gone and I responded, "routine". Like most close family, she was unaware of what "Q" was all about and was reluctant to ask.

Once we were all safely home and family introductions were complete our conversation turned to the future. I was due for a posting in the coming summer and was convinced that I was destined for the DEW line, the chain of northern radar stations along the Arctic Circle. With the cancellation of the Arrow program all the good flying jobs seemed to have been taken. As we were discussing this dismal prospect, my Squadron Commander, WingCo Hal Bridges called.

"How's Joan and the new addition" he asked. I knew he hadn't called just for that purpose and had a sense of foreboding. "Everything is fine thank you Sir" I replied trying not to let the tremor in my voice sound too obvious. "Well, I have some more good news for you, you have been selected for an exchange position with the RAF".

I don't think my mother-in-law had been danced around the house so boisterously since she was a young girl. Even Joan in her barely serviceable post-natal condition got a turn around the living room. Then, rather sheepishly, "uh, hello Sir, are you still there? "Wouldn't have missed it for the world", words I could just hear above the din going on around me.

It turned out that I had been assigned to 56 Squadron, Royal Air Force at Wattisham, Suffolk. The squadron was equipped with the Hunter MK VI, a sleek and highly manoeuvrable day fighter. I was advised that in a few months the squadron would be converting to the single seat English Electric Lightning, the new Mach 2 RAF all weather fighter.

It was expected that the squadron would undergo conversion early in the New Year. The aircraft was often referred to as the P-1. The designation P-1 however, stood for prototype one, a single aircraft. But the P-1 designation was used extensively throughout the aviation community to refer to all RAF Lightning aircraft. I was not to learn this distinction until after my arrival at Wattisham.

It took a day or two for the news of my new posting to sink in and I went about my duties on the squadron under the envious eyes of my peers. As the reality of the situation was finally accepted we decided that Joan and the kids should go ahead to North Bay to spend some time with her folks before we departed on our UK tour. By the end of June we had completed the planning arrangements for the move and had booked airline reservations for one adult and two kids under two.

I drove the family to Vancouver where Joan spent the night with Frank and Kay Augusta, old friends of ours from North Bay and Cold Lake days. I returned to Comox that night and Frank and Kay saw my family safely off on a TCA Super Constellation the following morning.

On my return to Comox I had arranged for our furniture to go into long term storage. I settled somewhat reluctantly into single officer's quarters for the month or so before my embarkation leave was to commence. The day of Joan's departure from Vancouver I spent watching the clock and trying to imagine where my little family was in time and space. Toward the end of the day I began calling North Bay and then Toronto as Joan's Dad and Mum were to pick her up there. Joan's folks had already departed by car for Toronto. My calls to Malton provided me with little information. Nobody seemed to know the whereabouts of my Super Connie flight and I was starting to get concerned enough to demand whatever information I could get from the airline over the phone.

Finally after several long distance telephone calls, I was able to determine that the flight that Joan and the kids were on had been detained in Regina, one of the several routine stops enroute. The mystery became clear the next day when Joan and kids arrived safely in Toronto after a long delay at Regina.

Evidently, the cusp of the kook era had appeared over the horizon. Shortly after take off from Regina enroute to Winnipeg, it was reported that there was a bomb on board the flight. The aircraft turned around immediately and performed an emergency landing back at Regina.

This was a very unusual situation for which airlines and airport terminals were unprepared. As Joan related later, no one was quite sure about how to handle this disturbing state of affairs. It was finally determined that the aircraft should be parked out on the airfield some distance from the terminal. Passengers were unloaded, supposedly women and children first, but businessmen travelling light managed to be the first to hit the tarmac. Joan waited patiently for everyone to disembark and then was ably assisted by the cabin crew out into fresh air and safety.

Baggage was all off-loaded and each piece had to be identified by its owner and then opened in front of the security officials who had little experience in such matters. The whole process took hours and when not identifying personal belongings the passengers were all locked in a room in the terminal waiting their turn to expose their personal effects to the prying eyes of the officials.

Nothing even vaguely sinister was found but the process took about six hours before the passengers were loaded back on the aircraft, fed and provided tender loving care for the remainder of the trip to Toronto.

My very irritated father-in-law now waiting in Toronto was quite naturally furious at the lack of information on the whereabouts of his daughter and grandchildren. He and Lila spent the evening pacing the terminal at Malton making sure they were available for each new bit of information as it came in.

Knowing my father-in-law, I'm sure that no one was happier to see the safe landing of this Super Connie than the airport staff who had no option but to withstand his wrath for a period of several hours on that fateful night.

Following their five-hour drive from Toronto to North Bay, my family had finally made it safely to their destination and I was so advised by phone the next day. For the most part this had all transpired without my knowledge. Information coming westbound was sketchy and eventually, having been assured that there was no cause for concern, I assumed that all had arrived safely in Toronto and they had decided to spend the night before setting out for North Bay in the morning.

I was only partially right in that the decision was not theirs and it only goes to prove that the wives and families of the fighter pilots of the day were not immune from the dangers of service life.

As the weeks rolled by prior to my departure, I found myself being left off the flying schedule more often that not. Sometimes if I insisted on participating in the flying program I could manage the odd trip. But for the most part the flight commanders were, quite rightly, concentrating on ensuring that the newer less experienced crews were assigned priority on the flying schedule.

One memorable night I had volunteered to fill in the flying programme for another pilot who had taken ill. The weather was not great but it was flyable. A large system had moved in and parked itself over the West Coast. There was cloud from five hundred feet up to forty thousand and there was no moon.

We launched in darkness and climbed to our assigned altitude of forty thousand feet and began our training exercise. We had completed two intercepts on our partner and were comfortably flying target when my navigator, Gary Hodgins, announced that he was noticing strange alternator readings. This was no major problem since there was an alternator on each engine and should there be trouble with one; there was a relay system that would automatically fail-safe to the other. We had just finished our second run as target when we faded to black. We had experienced a complete AC failure that wiped out our radar, our running lights, radios, avionics and most of the flight instruments.

This was the stuff of any pilot's nightmare and the problem we faced had no easy solution. We tried resetting the alternator several times and nothing would bring back our AC. I set up a left-hand triangle flying one minute on each leg. This was the international distress pattern and we hoped that the ground radar would see this on their scope and would vector another aircraft on to us and lead us back to base.

We flew several of these patterns using up valuable fuel in the process. Finally I said to Gary that we would have to recover ourselves since nobody seemed to be paying any attention to our problem.

Our AC power supply was irretrievable. We had some battery power that was dependent on how well charged the battery had been when we developed our electrical failure. It would run the radio compass, the sole means of navigation and a small but inadequate cockpit light for as long as the battery would hold out.

I set up a heading toward base flying on my needle ball and airspeed. The needle provided an indication of whether the aircraft was turning left or right. The pilot had to maintain the ball displayed under the needle in the centre to ensure that the turns were co-ordinated. A constant airspeed indicated straight and level flight, airspeed increasing meant descending and a decreasing airspeed meant climb. Heading was maintained by the use of the standby compass similar to one you might find in a car and was never too reliable. The altimeter, a barostatic instrument functioned without a power source. The pilot using audio signals from a beacon accomplished the navigation.

By manipulating the directional antennae the pilot could determine the bearing that was being emitted from the beacon. Once this bearing had been determined, there remained a one hundred and eighty-degree ambiguity check to determine the direction to the beacon. This was resolved only by assessing the increase or decrease in the volume of the tone as the aircraft flew toward or away from the beacon. Station passage was ascertained as the aircraft passed through the null or cone of silence directly overhead the radio beacon.

We managed to achieve the first station passage just above cloud at about forty thousand feet. It mattered little that we were above cloud, as it was pitch black out despite the minimal ambient light from the stars. Whatever battery power we started out with was beginning to dwindle and I had my flashlight arranged in my strapping so that it shone approximately on the only instruments that were of use to me.

I set up racetrack pattern letting down ten thousand feet on each of three outbound legs. On the fourth outbound leg I dropped another five thousand feet hoping all the while that some miracle would bring our AC power back to life. We were now at five thousand feet as we passed overhead the beacon for the fourth time and I advised Gary that if he heard me say eject once, the second time would be an echo. He seemed reasonably calm sitting there in the back seat and I wondered if he fully appreciated the fix that we were in. As we turned outbound once more we were over the Strait of Georgia and it was darker than the inside of an unlit coal mine.

We executed another racetrack pattern and were now crossing the beacon at two thousand feet just above the final approach to the runway. Still black outside the cockpit and I wondered how much longer I could hold it together. "Gary, I'm going to turn outbound and let down to one thousand feet, if we don't see anything, we're out, do you understand". At this point I hesitated to use the word eject fearing that if I did he would be gone and me with him. A night ejection over water was not among my favourite activities.

I levelled off at one thousand feet and I knew I had no more than a few minutes flying on a north-westerly heading before I would be running into trouble as the mainland and the island land masses more or less converged at the Northwest end of the Strait. "Gary, we're at one-thousand feet and I'm going to drop down to six-hundred feet briefly, if we don't break out we'll be swimming, understand?" "Roger", was the only reply. This usually very talkative navigator was thankfully for once silent.

Suddenly, as I peered out ahead I could see the phosphorous white caps on the water below. I dropped lower and as I looked back over my left shoulder, I could see the lights from the base intermittently through the low hanging cloud. I dropped right down on the water now in visual flight and turned toward the base. The airfield at Comox was only eighty feet above sea level and at times I was looking up at it from my position low on the water. I had to climb slightly as I positioned myself on final approach, dropped the gear using the emergency system and landed without flaps or speed brakes. Fortunately the wheel brakes worked well and I proceeded to taxi in to an abandoned ramp.

As I pulled into the line and parked, the doors of the servicing shack burst open and the servicing crews came tumbling out to a now still aircraft sitting in the darkness on the flight line. After shutting the engines down and opening the canopy to the fresh sea air, I sat quietly taking in deep breaths for several minutes before I finally recognised the face that appeared at the top of the ladder beside me. "You OK?" said the corporal. I acknowledged that we were fine. "The tower didn't call and we didn't see you taxi in", he said apologetically.

Under the startlingly bright lights inside the servicing shack I explained my problem to the servicing officer who immediately ordered the aircraft into maintenance. I then proceeded upstairs to the squadron crew room where everyone gave me a casual look as if to say, "What are you doing here?" I stormed into WingCo's office and threw my hard hat on his desk.

"You have a problem, Terry?" he asked. Well that was it, I let it all hang out and proceeded to tell him that the ground radar controllers were a bunch of Harveydumbshits, my squadron colleagues were from Mars for not coming to my rescue at forty thousand feet and the radar operators all needed to have their credentials checked. I finally got it all out of my system and started to think that even if another aircraft had found me, it would have been doubtful that the visibility in cloud that dark night would have permitted a safe formation let-down.

I had expected that radar would have tracked me through the ordeal and I was surprised to find after landing that no one knew of our predicament. With our electrics out our transponder did not show up on any of the radarscopes nor were we presenting any raw echoes of significance. Since we were well within our sortie duration, there was no reason to consider us overdue and so we were wandering around over Georgia Strait and no one knew we were there. We had no running lights and the tower did not even know we had landed.

Somehow by sheer luck there were no other aircraft on final approach at that time. We had landed undetected and taxied in without notice. The ground crews had not been alerted by the tower of our arrival and were busy inside with other activities.

Hal Bridges let me rave until I finally ran out of nasty adjectives. He finally decided that my outburst called for strong measures and said, "Let's go over to the bar and talk about it". The beer went down pretty good that night and I noticed that Gary, who was not a heavy drinker, managed to put away a few himself. A short while later our servicing officer arrived at the bar. He advised me that the alternator relay out of our aircraft had bench-tested serviceable on the initial tests. "The damn thing operated as it should and automatically switched back and forth from one alternator to another with ease, on the seventy-eighth cycle it failed at top dead centre and wouldn't move either way".

I was relieved that the problem we had experienced had been explained and went to bed that night thinking that all of those needle ball and airspeed exercises that seemed silly to me during my training had paid off. From that day on I became a proponent of the necessity to practice needle ball and airspeed otherwise known as limited panel instrument flying frequently enough to be proficient should it ever be needed.

With only a few weeks left to go on the squadron I began to get impatient to get on with my future and I contemplated the few months ahead.

My posting to the RAF was a dream come true. My father was born and raised in Ealing and he still had family over there, although I had never met them before. My posting to England delighted my father and carried the promise of many new personal experiences in my life.

I had chosen to travel to North Bay by train from Vancouver. My good friend Bruce Inrig flew me to Sea Island in a C-45. This would be my last ride for a while in this little aircraft and I felt rather nostalgic as I was allowed to do most of the flying including the landing at Sea Island. A staff car waited on the tarmac that saw me safely to the railway station. In the dining car over the supper hour I bade farewell to the West Coast for a number of years. I had opted for the train since I felt it would give me time to rest for a few days and catch up on the reading that I had allowed to lapse over the summer months.

The reunion with my family in North Bay was wonderful and I realised how much I had missed them all. My father-in-law and I did some hunting and fishing. We both enjoyed a good shot of whisky and spent many hours telling each other wild tales of the wilderness. We were both Leaf fans and the season had just begun in earnest. We were perpetually in the doghouse as the channel selector was ceremoniously set on the Leafs game wherever it was being played.

Toward the end of my leave Joan and I were both invited to proceed to AFHQ in Ottawa for briefings on how an exchange officer and his wife should behave while serving their country with a foreign air force. Not much to it really, we arrived in the capital by train and were put up in the Lord Elgin Hotel, a very pleasant, elegant hotel in those days. It was right across the street from the headquarters and convenient for our overnight stay. I am not sure why Joan was invited along but it was a nice touch and gave the two us a short holiday time together.

The only downside of the trip was my introduction to some Group Captain who asked my escorting officer who the dumb bastard was that selected a CF-100 jock for an exchange posting to an RAF fighter squadron. Needless to say I was flabbergasted and concerned that perhaps my prize posting would not materialise after all. Later on in the day I was assured, to my relief, that the Group Captain had a thing against CF-100 pilots, mainly because he had never flown the aircraft and had a tendency to disparage those who did.

On our return to North Bay we began the frenzy of packing our personal belongings that were to see us through three years in England. We had been collecting kids' stuff at an ever-increasing rate since our departure from Comox and the numerous child-related items became a logistic nightmare. Carriages, cribs, bathinettes, children's apparel and associated paraphernalia assumed mountainous proportions. And this did not even include our own personal gear.

After farewells to Joan's folks we journeyed by train to Montreal. The air force had made reservations for us at the Laurentian Hotel and we were all jammed into a room for two. Once the cribs had been installed for the children it became an obstacle course to get from one side of the room to the other. The kids were twenty-three and six months of age respectively and behaved like all children of that age. They hated disruption from their norm and let us know about it. After a fitful night we arrived at dockside to find that most of the baggage we shipped ahead had been placed in the ship's hold. Not to worry we were told the ship would not be sailing for a few days as there was a longshoreman's strike and we would remain alongside until the strike was settled.

Under any other circumstances we would have rejoiced. But with a busy toddler and a babe in arms we were not predisposed to enjoying the bright lights and clubs of Montreal while living in luxury aboard ship. Nevertheless, it gave us the opportunity to retrieve the priority pieces of luggage from the hold that had been misdirected there earlier.

We were sailing on the Italia of the Home Lines. She was a beautiful luxury cruise ship that spent the summers plying the waters of the Caribbean Sea and had been contracted to pick up a draft of RCAF personnel on posting to Europe. The Italia was returning to it's home port for a winter refit at its company base in Genoa. The timing suited both the Home Lines and the RCAF travel organisers beautifully. There were only four military officers on board and I was the senior of the lot. It fell to me to take charge of the draft while at sea and I had some misgivings as Joan had previously been prone to motion sickness and I was concerned that I may be "it" when it came to looking after the kids.

After a day or two the strike was finally settled and we slipped our berth and headed down the St. Lawrence. I was now in charge of the draft consisting of two hundred and eighty five servicemen, wives and children during our passage.

We sailed from Montreal to Southampton in the last days of September with an estimated time at sea of six days. The passage down the St Lawrence provided a fabulous view of the fall colours along the shore. As we exited through the Cabot Strait into the open Atlantic we got our first taste of the vicious character of the North Atlantic Ocean.

As it turned out Joan was a good sailor as were the kids. The motion of the ship ensured excellent childhood sleeping habits. We were assigned one of two first class cabins designated rather appropriately, P-1.

A delightful middle–aged lady doctor of philosophy from Washington State University occupied the other, P-2. She was also enroute to the UK and had opted for an ocean passage on the Italia for sentimental reasons. She and her husband, who had passed away a few years before, had been for a cruise on the ship just after they were married. She enjoyed a drink or two and we became good friends for the duration of the voyage.

The ship pitched and rolled throughout the crossing despite the stabilisers that had been installed to smooth the ride. That she was a great ship went unnoticed by many that did not leave their cabins for the entire crossing. As I moved about the various decks, I became aware that it was not only the passengers who were suffering. The Ship's Hostess, who was also a good sailor, informed me that over 65% of the crew had succumbed to seasickness and the Captain was beginning to worry about the welfare of his human cargo.

Both Joan and I ate hearty breakfasts each morning followed at noon by whatever was being served for lunch. The kids when not eating spent most of their time asleep as the rocking of the ship lulled them into a natural comatose state. The quality and quantity of food did not suffer because of the rough weather and the evening meal was the treat of the day. Our newly found doctor of philosophy friend joined us each night in the near empty dining room. Most times we were ushered to the Captain's table who never did make an appearance due to the demands of his duties on the bridge. Following dinner we played cards and enjoyed our brandy and coffee before finishing the evening off with a tour of the bars on board.

A few times Joan and I attempted to dance to one of the popular bands on the ship that didn't seem to mind the rough weather. It was very difficult for the dancers though as the small crowd on the floor hastened in two-step from one side of the dance floor to the other following the ship's tilt as it rock and rolled its way through the night. Only rarely did either Luigi or Marta summon us. They were our loyal cabin stewards, who kept a sharp eye out for the kids whenever we moved about the ship.

Many of the military personnel and their wives on the draft did not fare so well. Seasickness was epidemic on the decks below and there was a shortage of diapers for the babies. We carried with us a substantial stock of disposable diapers sufficient to last us a month or so. As other mothers on the ship ran short we provided reinforcements from our own stock. This was soon depleted and we were reduced to using the standard cotton diaper.

The ship's laundry had no experience with diaper washing and following their first attempt proudly presented us with freshly laundered, starched and ironed cotton diapers. We were reduced to washing diapers in our bathtub in the cabin until Joan had completed her delivery of a crash course indoctrinating the laundry staff on the finer points of proper diaper washing.

At about mid-Atlantic we were advised that because our progress over the stormy seas was so slow, we would not be docking in Southampton as scheduled but instead would be proceeding directly to Le Havre. We had been at sea for six days at this point and still had three more days to go. While many on board accepted this news with much dread, we had been enjoying ourselves and were happy to have the extra time being treated so royally by those members of the crew who were still capable of performing their duties.

Finally we arrived in Le Havre and after a layover lasting several hours, we boarded the British Railway Ferry for an overnight voyage back across the channel to Southampton.

Our stay in Le Havre was somewhat taxing. For the first time during our voyage the children went through a cranky patch. The travel organisers had arranged for a bus tour of this historical port and it would have been an outstanding diversion had it not been for the kids who were in no mood to be cooped up on a bus for hours. Following my rather forceful protests we were billeted in one of the local hotels that provided us with first class accommodations and service throughout our daylong stay.

We were booked on an overnight ferry that was to sail at mid-night. Once on board, we were assigned to a very small cabin with four very narrow single bunks. While Joan settled the kids down I wandered about the ship and found a cosy lounge. As I checked the clock I discovered to my delight that we were heading back into an earlier time zone. I quickly made my way back to the cabin, paid the steward to listen for the kids who were now fast asleep and invited Joan out for a night-cap.

As the waiter placed our brandies in front of us, I pointed to the clock. It came as pleasant surprise to Joan to find that we had been given an extra hour that we hadn't expected. Tired and harassed from a very disquieting day, it was probably one of the most special hours of our whole Trans-Atlantic voyage.

As we docked in Southampton early the next morning a telegram from my aunt awaited us. In typical English custom she welcomed us home with an invitation to tea on our arrival in London. We stayed at a hotel opposite Hyde Park Gate and to our delight, the baby sitting service provided by the hotel granted us a respite from our parental duties. We spent hours walking Oxford Street and the labyrinth of streets around Hyde Park. Herrods, Fortnum and Masons and many other premium stores were taken in on our tour of wonder.

On our first night in London we loaded everyone into a London cab and proceeded to Ealing and my aunt's house for tea. I had never met my aunt and uncle or their daughter Mary, my cousin. We spent a delightful evening getting to know one another.

My Uncle, Sir Cyril Flower was a philatelist and had sent me numerous stamps for my stamp collection during the war years. He was knighted by King George VI immediately after the war. Following a distinguished career in the army during WW I, Uncle Cyril had worked as a registrar in the British Records Office. On the declaration of war in 1939 he immediately moved all of the British records out of their permanent location in the centre of London. He scattered them all over England storing them in barns, warehouses, and wherever he could find secure space for them. This would keep them from being destroyed in the bombing. But most importantly, it would keep them out of the hands of the Nazis in the event of an invasion.

At the end of the war, Uncle Cyril through his meticulously kept inventory recovered all of the British records to their rightful place in the central records registry in London. A process that took only a few weeks to accomplish and the machinery of government was unaffected by the change. For this he was honoured by his King.

Family duties completed, we set off the next day by train for RAF Station Wattisham. The commanding officer of 56 Squadron met us at the Ipswich Station and transported us to his married quarter on the base where we were invited to stay until suitable accommodation became available. We soon found a house as I divided my time between house hunting and a quick check-out on the Hunter VI on the squadron, it was deemed by Fighter Command that I should attend the Hunter Operational Conversion Unit (OCU) at RAF Station Chivenor in Devon. "To learn the language", you know.

The crates that contained our shipped belongings had been held in storage for us and arrived on a Saturday morning. I spent most of the day opening boxes, setting up cribs and generally getting Joan reasonably settled prior to my departure the next day for Chivenor.

It was good thing that Joan came from a hardy stock as neither of us had ever had to contend with coke and coal fired heating appliances, at least not in the English manner. My initial attempts to get the fires going were filled with frustration and Joan learned the choice expletives one must use when confronting the challenges of antiquated heating systems. On my return three weeks later I discovered that my wife had become an expert in the manipulation of British home heating.

The flying was good at Chivenor and I completed not only the OCU, but the gunnery course was thrown in for good measure. Soon I was back at Wattisham taking my place on "Q". The principles were the same as those in Canada but the manner in which we worked our shift was somewhat different. I made the assumption it was because we were closer to the enemy.

There was no going to bed while on "Q" with an RAF fighter squadron. Two hours on cockpit readiness and then two hours off. You couldn't go anywhere during your off time but you could snooze if it suited you. Usually there was a card game on the go and pilots cycled between the cockpit and the card game throughout a normal twelve-hour shift.

While the Hunter aircraft was an excellent day fighter, it had limitations when it came to operations at night. We maintained our day fighter flying proficiency but frequently, our group headquarters would exercise us beyond the limits of the day fighter role.

We were scrambled day and night as Fighter Command insisted that our conversion to all weather fighter interceptors should be realistic. Many an hour we spent out over the bleak expanses of the North Sea in our single engine Hunters. The aircraft were ill equipped for night flying but we made do because we were, "training to be all weather fighter pilots".

In early December we were removed from the Order of Battle and began our ground school training for conversion to the Lightning. Amidst great excitement, the first of our assigned aircraft began to arrive. One by one these large impressive aircraft were delivered to the squadron and by the middle of January we had six of them in various stages of acceptance testing. By the end of January we had completed our simulator training and each of us in turn experienced our first flight in the Lightning.

As I lined up on the end of the runway ready for take off on my first encounter with this supersonic fighter, my knees were shaking as the hand-brake held against 100% RPM. As I released brakes and selected full reheat I became a passenger. I began to coach myself, "keep straight, keep straight, nose up, my God 170 knots already. Airborne, get the gear up quick so as not to over-speed. 360 knots, pull nose up to 20 degrees angle of climb". I felt as though I was lying on my back and the aircraft seemed headed for orbit.

Two minutes from brake release I levelled off at thirty six thousand feet and throttled back taking a well-deserved breather. How did I get here so fast? It seemed unbelievable after all of those years on the CF 100. Years that now seemed like ancient history. I proceeded to make a few turns in accordance with the prescribed profile for my first flight and was delighted at the response. Only light pressures on the control column were required and I found that I had to be careful not to over control. After a few minutes I was ready for the next exhilarating experience -- supersonic!

Gingerly at first I advanced the throttles to 100% thrust. The way the aircraft responded I didn't think I would need the reheat to blast me out into supersonic flight. I began to react instinctively to my simulator training. Last check of all instruments at 100% power then slam, I'm in max reheat. (In North America we call this full afterburner).

I felt like I had been hit in the back by a Mack truck. I now have a bull by the tail and ignoring the airspeed indicator, I focused on the Mach meter. Point 96 mach -- .98 -- a slight hesitation. The acceleration seems to have slowed. But only momentarily.

With a surge, the aircraft slides easily through. Mach 1.1 – Mach 1.2 out to Mach 1.5. I'm really moving and as the aircraft tightens around me there is almost total silence. Little noise is evident other than the hum of cockpit sounds and the beat of my own heart. I reduce reheat to avoid exceeding Mach 1.65, which is the limit for this flight.

I've done it. Faster than most pilots have flown and it all seemed too simple. There would be other times when operationally I would fly out to Mach 2 and beyond. The Plexiglas canopy goes opaque above Mach 2, as I was to discover later over Germany.

Within a month the squadron was declared combat ready in the all weather fighter role and we were re-instated on the NATO Air Order of Battle. We were soon back into the routine of endless training day and night and the generally boring but occasionally exciting shifts on "Q". We had now become a fully operational squadron on one of the fastest fighter aircraft in the world. Nothing much had changed but our fighting arena had expanded considerably and the time it took us to accomplish our task was halved.

CHAPTER 8
SUPERSONIC WARRIORS

In the winter of 1962 the President of the Soviet Union, Nikita Sergievich Krushev, spoke to the Security Council at the UN Headquarters in New York.

During a heated part of his speech he removed his shoe and pounding it on the podium for emphasis, stated that communism would dominate the world by any means necessary. Following this rather angry outburst, behind the scenes activity intensified and there were hints that the Soviets might forcefully close western access to the city of Berlin.

Following WW II such access was limited to rail and the three air corridors that had been established to provide air supply to the beleaguered city. Check points virtually closed East Germany to the west and access to Berlin was severely limited. Berlin, the island of freedom in a sea of communism could not survive without western support and the supply lines were crucial.

British preparations began immediately at Air Ministry in London. The RAF developed contingency plans for consideration by Joint Chiefs of Staff and the British government. A range of options were prepared and the planners made ready to respond effectively to government decisions effecting the RAF participation in any resulting military response.

Air Ministry planners determined that a positive answer to the Soviet threat was required and developed a plan involving the despatch of an RAF Comet transport aircraft to make a daily flight into Tempelhof airport near Berlin. This airport had been reconstructed immediately following the war and was expanded to handle the Berlin airlift that kept the vital supply lines open until a suitable east/west compromise was achieved. The Comet would carry a priority cargo of food and emergency medical supplies for the citizens of Berlin.

In addition it was determined that, while somewhat provocative, the Comet would be escorted through the central air corridor to Berlin by Lightning aircraft. It was the consensus of western nations that the Soviets should not be allowed to threaten the UN and the free world. Such a challenge could not be ignored.

As the only supersonic fighter squadron operational in Europe at the time, 56 Squadron having only just achieved it's operational status was called to the fore. Warning orders were issued and the squadron prepared for immediate deployment to RAF Station Gutersloh in West Germany. It was ideally situated at about one hundred miles outside the entrance to the central air corridor leading to Tempelhof.

It was decided that four aircraft and a small ground support group would be deployed for the duration of the operation. Re-enforcement's if required would be assigned in due course. However, intelligence indicated that frequently there were observers positioned in the woods surrounding the base. It was speculated that they were recording base activity and in particular were taking special note of tail numbers of aircraft visiting the base.

After some contemplation, Fighter Command decided that the simple solution would be to replace the four aircraft assigned on a daily basis. When they ran out of squadron tail numbers they would borrow aircraft from the other squadrons not yet operationally ready. Every day four new aircraft would be ferried to Gutersloh and four returned to the UK. This gave us all a bit of a chuckle knowing that whoever would be collecting the information on the other side would have difficulty assessing the meaning of all this activity and a small deception was established.

The day following the receipt of the warning order, the order to deploy arrived. On the following day we launched our first four aircraft for Gutersloh just over an hour's flying time away. On our arrival we were given an up to date intelligence briefing on the situation including a short description of the local spy hiding (not undetected) in the woods. The Comet would begin its routine flights the next day and we made preparations for the escort operation.

We launched at noon the first day of the operation and completed the rendezvous with one large white Comet. The mission was carried out as planned with our four aircraft providing escort into the Tempelhof control zone following which we made our way for home flying down the centreline of the corridor at Mach 1.65. We had been advised not to violate the limits of the corridor either in-bound or on our way home. Coming out, however, we were to accelerate out to Mach 1.65, where the red line on the Mach meter indicated the arbitrary limiting Mach. We were to maintain this speed until safely into West Germany.

Our airspeed limit was established at Mach 1.65 mainly because the aircraft had tendency to enter what was called a roll yaw coupling at high Mach numbers. This simply meant that aircraft could change ends much like a dumb-bell with catastrophic results. If the pilot was very careful not to induce too high a rate of roll, higher Mach numbers were achievable. But extreme caution had to be exercised. During our ground-school training we had been told about the English Electric test pilot who had experienced roll-yaw coupling at a high Mach number. The aircraft began to oscillate during a fairly rapid roll as it approached Mach 2. The oscillations increased uncontrollably to the point where the aircraft began to tumble through the air end over end and broke up as the violent stresses exceeded the integrity of the airframe.

The test pilot was blown clear and while he sustained serious injuries during his inadvertent supersonic ejection, he survived to fly again. He was fortunate that the automatic system on his parachute functioned perfectly dropping him gently into the North Sea in a semi-conscious state. He was rescued a short time later.

The first day or two of our escort duties went off without a hitch and the routine was almost becoming boring. On the third day however, we were advised by intelligence that the Soviets had scrambled fighters to intercept us.

For the next mission or two we could clearly see the Migs streaming contrails just outside the corridor on either side. But they made no threatening moves. Our aircraft were much faster and during our departure out of East Germany we left them well behind.

Things seemed to get more tense each day until finally we were advised that negotiations at the UN had taken a positive turn and the operation would be terminated after the next day's sortie.

That night we had a bit of a celebration in the officer's mess. Not much had been done in the way of renovations to the buildings on the base since the war. Gutersloh had been the headquarters of Herman Goring's Luftwaffe bomber force and in a small room above the mess, Goring enjoyed listening to the tales told by his aircrews as they returned from their bombing missions over the UK. In the centre of the room there was a large table around which the crews sat to enjoy their post-flight pints of ale. Goring had a small table attached to the wall off to one side. The table was equipped with mysterious looking lever that was not visible to the casual onlooker.

There is a German saying that loosely translated means, "If I lie, may the sky fall on my head" and the younger crews used this expression frequently when excitedly relating stories of their bombing missions over England. The hidden lever was connected to a heavy oak beam in the ceiling that ran the length of the large table. As Herr Goring became bored with the saying used perhaps once too often, he would activate the lever dropping the beam onto the centre of the table.

Naturally the newer pilots on the base were quite startled by the crashing beam that tended to scatter pilots and beer glasses in every direction. With the beam carefully restored and re-armed the hero stories continued well into the night. But it is said that the old sayings were notably absent from the vocabulary for the rest of the evening.

We enjoyed the atmosphere of this room during our turn at the story telling but carefully avoided the mechanisms that we knew to be lurking in the shadows. We also avoided the use of any worn out proverbs or dictums that might trigger the sky falling on our heads and our beers.

The briefing the following morning revealed that our Comet inbound from the UK enroute to Tempelhof would be right on time. There was tense note in the air however as the Commander in Chief (CinC) of Fighter Command, Sir Hector MacGregor appeared at the briefing. Intelligence advised us that they expected that at least two squadrons of Migs would rise to monitor our progress from just outside the boundaries of the corridor.

Furthermore, it had been noted that several of the Eastern Block ground to air missile sites had been ordered to increase their launch readiness times. No one was sure what might happen but we felt that it wouldn't be unlike the Russians to make our last mission as escorts as unpleasant as possible.

Following the operational briefing the CinC stood and with a fierce look in his eye said, "There you have it chaps, we are unsure of the reception you will get today, however for this mission you may ignore the red lines on your Mach meters on your way out".

This was it. The moment of truth for all of us had arrived. The formation briefing was routine and we were quietly subdued. We walked wordlessly out to our aircraft and strapped in. As our start-up time approached all eyes turned to the leader and on his hand signal we fired up our engines. The brisk radio transmissions between us and between our leader and the tower were methodical revealing nothing of the mission ahead. We taxied out and utilising the wide runways at Gutersloh, we performed a four-plane take-off. There was no time to contemplate the task ahead. We set a heading that would take us to our rendezvous point as we climbed to altitude.

Once level we assumed battle formation and began to search our radar scopes for the first signs of our white Comet that under ideal conditions could be seen by the naked eye at twenty to twenty-five miles. Within a few minutes the call came from one of the formation; "Five degrees port at twenty eight miles". We all began to search our scopes in that vicinity. Soon we were all painting the Comet on our radar scopes and the leader began to manoeuvre us into position to escort the larger aircraft. We soon closed up and stationed ourselves two on either wing of the Comet aircraft and settled into our routine run into Tempelhof.

To our surprise we arrived over the airport without incident. The Comet had descended rapidly on entering the Berlin control zone as we maintained our altitude and circled overhead until the Comet was safely on final approach. Our clearance from radar control was a standard; "You are cleared for your return flight to Gutersloh".

We took up a heading that would take us down the centre line of the corridor and accelerated to Mach 1.65. On reaching our desired Mach number we barely had time to throttle back when the leader called for us split into two sections of two and accelerate out on either side of the corridor. This placed our two sections about twenty miles apart both accelerating rapidly. Our navigation systems were not that accurate and the Migs orbiting just outside the corridor looked perilously close. We watched our rear view mirrors expectantly for surface to air missiles but none were to be observed.

As my Mach meter eased up to Mach 2, I began to throttle back slightly to maintain a speed of just over Mach 2. We had learned in ground-school that kinetic heating build-up on the airframe as speeds exceed Mach 2.2 could cause damage to the skin of the aircraft or burn the canopy. As I was contemplating this disturbing fact, I heard the call from one the pilots in the formation. "My canopy has just gone opaque".

We were only seconds from clearing the corridor into West Germany and the leader immediately called for us to reduce speed to below Mach 2 and then to below Mach 1. We closed back into our four plane close formation for the recovery to find that one of our members indeed had an opaque canopy and was immediately assigned to the box position in the formation. While he couldn't see out the sides of his canopy, the one-inch thick bullet-proof windscreen was intact and he could fly the line astern position with ease.

A new canopy had to be flown over the next day to replace its battle-scarred predecessor and we all flew happily back to Wattisham – mission accomplished.

To the Cold War Warriors none of this makes much sense today. But during the fifties and sixties it was real. The threat of nuclear annihilation was ever present. There was an enemy and he was readily identifiable.

One more cat and mouse exercise had been completed successfully and Mr Krushev never again openly threatened to dominate the world.

CHAPTER NINE
FERRY FLIGHT TO CYPRUS

We were "coasting in" over the north of France and the formation leader called; "Natter frequency go", a signal that we were all to switch to a pre-selected discrete channel that would allow us to chat or "natter" with each other as we went along.

At forty thousand feet we pretty much had the airspace to ourselves. The canopies on our Hunter VI aircraft glistened in the morning sun as we cruised in the smooth air mass along our first leg to the French Air Force base at Orange in the south of France. An RAF radar station was a lodger unit there and it was to be our first refuelling stop on our way to Akrotiri on the Island of Cyprus.

The weather was splendid and the scattered white cumulus cloud well below reflected the bright sunshine. We had been dispatched from RAF Wattisham to deliver four Hunter aircraft to the RAF base at Akrotiri. The aircraft would be picked up later by the Jordanian Air Force as part of a bilateral defence agreement between Great Britain and King Hussein of Jordan.

Our recent conversion to the Lightning aircraft had left us somewhat nostalgic for the Hunter Mk VI as this could perhaps be one of our last trips in this stalwart day fighter aircraft.

"Noddy, Flight Lieutenant Nodwell McEwen, was the squadron wit and could always be counted on to make light of the most serious of situations.

As we were completing our night checkout on the Lightning aircraft several months earlier, Noddy, who was preparing to take off on his second sortie of the evening, was becoming impatient waiting just short of the runway for the last of the recovering aircraft. As each aircraft from the first wave of the evening turned onto final approach, Noddy whispered through his radio into the blackness of the night, "you're going to die". Most of the pilots were seasoned fighter pilots and took little heed of these chilling remarks other than to chuckle to themselves that Noddy was at it again.

Now as we swept across northern France we carried on a conversation on the radio to pass the time. At one point, Noddy at his entertaining finest put on his best Yorkshire accent and related a story about the Vicar and the housemaid. Evidently, the Vicar had been sampling the forbidden fruit and was caught red handed when the housemaid's errant trews were seen to dangle out of his sleeve as he gestured grandly during one of his thundering homilies.

As the story came to an end, we were startled by a very English but strange voice breaking into the squadron radio channel. "Glad to find you chaps. Hope the Vicar survived his ordeal" The voice continued; "French air traffic control is raising merry old hell because they can't contact you". It was the pilot of an RAF Victor bomber out of a Bomber Command base enroute to somewhere in the Middle East. He had been asked if he could raise us on any of the discreet RAF frequencies.

"Bugger the French"' our fearless leader replied. Wing Commander Bill Howard was our WingCo Flying and had decided that he would lead this the last of the Hunter VI ferry flights to Cyprus. The WingCo had joined the airforce just prior to the declaration of World War II and was among those Englishmen who still held the

French responsible for those who collaborated with the Boch during the Second World War.

Reluctantly, we changed to the frequency passed to us by our bomber friends and more or less cleaned up our radio act. Only a minor admonishment from the controller and we were directed to a new heading to take us to a point from where we would begin our descent into Orange.

The letdown was uneventful and as there was a resident French Air Force wing of F-100 fighter aircraft on the base, the WingCo decided that we would perform one of our best death-defying fighter breaks. A manoeuvre none of us had practised since we had relinquished our combat ready status as a day fighter squadron several months earlier.

Skimming the fence at over 400 knots at the approach end to the runway, we maintained a tight echelon right. Just short of the button of the runway the WingCo called, "At one second intervals breaking now". On the imperative "now", he eased his throttle to idle while simultaneously selecting his airbrakes out and pulling about four "G" as he described an upward arc toward the downwind leg of the landing pattern.

Each pilot in turn performed the same manoeuvre one second apart and all four aircraft arrived in the downwind leg in a line astern formation with about one hundred yards spacing between aircraft. Following the leader during the tight turn to final each pilot paced himself and alternating left and right of the runway centre line, carried out a flawless fighter landing.

The French Wing Commander met us as we shut down on the tarmac and there was jovial, emotional raving as only the French can achieve about how wonderful our landing performance had been. Several of the pilots representing different squadrons on the wing joined us and as comrades in arms we were all loaded on a small bus and driven to the officer's mess.

In the washroom as we cleaned up for lunch, the WingCo gave us the most important briefing of the day. He had experienced French Air Force hospitality before. "They will try to fill us in", he said. "Watch yourselves carefully as I want us all to make Valletta before nightfall". RAF Station Luqa, not far from the city of Valletta on the Island of Malta was one of Britain's strategic air bases in the Middle East and our next refuelling stop.

Now I had enough experience with the RAF by now to know that the Brits could drink gallons of beer without much affect on their English composure. Hard liquor was another matter and I have seen staid Englishmen approach a state of madness after a few stiff shots.

Wine though, the French staple, was another matter. The Brits enjoyed a glass of wine with a meal but tended to look on it as a ladies drink when taken at other times. It was thought that wine was not strong enough to be a man's drink and it did not really count on the restricted list of drinks not to be consumed before flight.

Our hosts having placed us at intervals between our French counterparts around the long dinner table proposed a toast with the first pouring of wine. "To our English brothers and trusted allies". We all politely sipped a toast while our hosts to a man downed the contents of their glasses in a single gulp. Wineglasses freshened, our WingCo responded in kind and once again the sipping, and gulping ritual ensued.

The formalities accomplished, we sat down and serious conversation commenced as we engaged with our hosts in stories of various feats of aviation supremacy and miscellaneous iterations of macho pilot excellence. The appetiser was served along with the requisite draft of white wine. The two wine stewards assigned to our table were well trained and as the diners sipped, the glasses were topped up immediately they were set back on the table. The food was good and we ate ravenously as the first course was completed and the entree served.

The stories grew more outrageous as the meal progressed, the French trying to outdo the English and the English, consuming smaller quantities of wine, tried to keep the conversation in perspective.

Finally, the WingCo rose and soberly thanked our hosts for their splendid hospitality and we made our way back to the flight line. Several cups of the bitter black French coffee were consumed as we worked out our flight plan and briefed. By the time we were ready to walk out to the aircraft we had worn off whatever residual effects remained from our modest exposure to the lunchtime wine.

Our formation take off was performed without hitch and we climbed to altitude in loose "Finger Left" formation. In order to visualise the formation, lay your left hand, palm down on a table and the tips of your fingers will approximate, the "Finger Left" positions of the aircraft in a four-plane formation. The finger right formation conforms to the same rule of thumb.

As we levelled off at our cruising altitude the WingCo called us into "Battle" formation. This allowed a two to three hundred yard separation between aircraft and its purpose was to allow each of the formation members to watch out for other aircraft. A three hundred and sixty-degree surveillance was possible in this formation and no enemy aircraft could approach the formation without being picked up by at least one member of the group. We used it to our advantage – sightseeing the Med from thirty-five thousand feet.

My first view of the azure blue waters of the Mediterranean filled me with awe as we passed to the west of Corsica and across the island of Sardinia. Further on we paralleled the West Coast of the island of Sicily and could just make out the city of Palermo in the distance to the east. The island of Malta lay dead ahead as we began our descent toward Luqa.

Once again the WingCo called for a fighter break and landing. The venerable Hunter VI would go out of RAF service in fine style as one of our last acts as day fighter pilots. Once again we performed our arrival manoeuvre with polish and taxied in to the flight line through throngs of women dressed in long black cloaks that covered most of their faces and bodies. It took me few minutes to figure out that they were labourers working on airfield repair. They were handling large concrete blocks about a foot or more square and about eight inches thick. They were shaping and then laying them to repair faulty taxiways.

An RAF servicing crew detached to Luqa marshalled us into the line and began refuelling and servicing our aircraft as we made our way to the officer's quarters for a well deserved shower and change into civvies.

We had some time to kill before the dinner hour and some of us took the opportunity for a leisurely stroll around the base. It was one of the smaller RAF bases in the Middle East and was now primarily a staging base for fighter aircraft enroute to other RAF defence establishments throughout the near and far east. The quarters and grounds were well maintained by the local civilian employees most of it by hard bull, or more properly - Maltese women's labour.

Outside the confines of the base the countryside was desert like and stood in stark contrast to the lush green of the well-landscaped base properties.

Following our brief sight seeing tour, it was time to gather in the mess for quick pint and to make our plans for the evening. It was decided that "The Colonial" (me) having never been to Malta should be introduced to a dinner at Charlie's Bar followed by whatever downtown Valletta had to offer.

The Maltese are a friendly people and didn't often miss an opportunity to express their gratitude to the British and Canadians for their resolute defence of Malta during the Second World War.

Charlie, the story went, was a Canadian and had been in the RAF during the war. At the end of hostilities he decided that he liked Malta and Valletta in particular so he settled into business for himself and had apparently become quite prosperous. Needless to say I was intrigued to meet a fellow Canadian in this far away place and looked forward to my introduction to the now infamous Charlie.

The cab we called to take us to town was late forties vintage north American and was equipped with the latest phonographic apparatus. It consisted of a turntable upon which the driver installed an eight-inch long-playing record for the enjoyment of his passengers. Placing the head holding the needle over the record and gently lowering it onto the record face the cabby would smile proudly as the music filled the cab with the big band sounds of the forties. This seemed to work quite well when the cab was stationary, but the playing arm was prone to skipping all over the record face as the car took motion. The roads, being what they were in Malta at the time, did nothing to improve the fidelity of the sound. Loud shrieking and scratching noises interspersed with occasional melody intruded on what otherwise might have been a pleasant drive to town.

Presently we arrived at the front door to Charlie's Bar. An imposing edifice on the outside with garish flashing neon signage that belied the necessity for address numbers on the building. A Maltese concierge met us cheerfully at the door and in response to his question, we indicated that we had not made reservations. This perturbed him little and he ushered us with European grace to a magnificently set table in the dining room. As we were seated we could see the notorious bar through an entryway that we had not noticed on our arrival.

Bill Howard began to look a bit nervous as we perused our menus. The prices were higher than he had experienced during his previous tour at the RAF Middle East Headquarters on the island some years before. After a brief discussion to ensure that we weren't going to deprive anyone's kids of shoes or food, it was decided that we would allow ourselves some extravagance at this stage of our trip. After all, we had enjoyed a free lunch on the French earlier.

The WingCo now satisfied that there would be no surprises for anyone when the bill came disappeared for few minutes in search of Charlie.

On his return the food arrived and we dined in style on Charlie's special, an excellent

Lobster Thermadore unlike any other that I had previously enjoyed. As we finished our dessert and were about to order coffee the waiter announced, "Gentlemen if you are finished would you please follow me to the bar for coffee and liqueurs".

Thinking that this was a tradition of Charlie's Bar, we dutifully followed our attendant into the beautifully finished oak panelled bar. The shelves at the back were lined with every possible drink known to mankind and as we took our seats at the bar, a casually dressed gentleman of medium build approached us with an outstretched hand and a giant smile on his face.

Bill Howard had had a word with Charlie during his brief absence from the dining table earlier and after renewing his hearty greeting for the WingCo Charlie said, "I hear you have a Canuck with you". I was introduced and welcomed to the restaurant, the bar, the City of Valletta and Malta. For the second time that day the spirits of our group turned into a joyful camaraderie. Charlie regaled us with tales of wartime Malta and was genuinely curious about the new jet-age RAF.

We exchanged stories for several hours and although Charlie found out everything there was to know about me, I never did find out from where in Canada Charlie had hailed. In fact I became suspicious about his true nationality as his accent was unlike any I had heard in Canada, the USA or the UK.

Perhaps he wasn't a Canadian at all, but with his reputation throughout the Middle East I expect that his Canadian connections were genuine. Something in his past was preventing him from divulging the details of his background or perhaps it was just a reluctance to talk about himself. Some said it was because he had once been MI5 and was still in their employ part-time. I never did find out the truth. Charlie will always remain a mystery but we were grateful to him as he insisted that the evenings feast and drinks were on him.

As it turned out our day was not yet complete as we exited Charlie's Bar and headed for the Gut a short block away. The Gut, known to sailors around the world, is a canyon of eighteenth century buildings that run from the top of the escarpment above the harbour to dockside in the Port of Valletta. The upper levels of the buildings, mostly not more than two stories high, were adorned with giant speakers that emitted stereophonic sound at maximum volume. The bars are side by side bordering the street itself and present the pleasure seeker with a literal bazaar of drinking establishments from which to sample the fine beer, wines and other beverages that are available throughout the Middle East.

It became readily apparent that drinks were not the only items for sale in the Gut as mothers peddled daughters and women of all ages, sizes and shapes eagerly hawked their feminine wares to the visitors to this seamier side of this otherwise beautiful island.

At the beginning of our descent into the Gut we had determined that one beer in each bar would be our limit and we would attempt to make it all the way to the bottom by the evening's end. Unfortunately the expectations of our own fortitude were somewhat inflated and we hadn't made our way through more than five or six establishments as we moved down the Gut toward the sea when our evening came to an abrupt end. We had succumbed to the limits of our own stamina.

The climb back up the very steep street to Charlie's Bar was an imposing ordeal but all four of us gamely made it to the top and hailed a taxi for our return to the base. It was a different cab that saw us home but one equipped with the same remarkable sound system as we had witnessed during our trip into town.

We rock and rolled our way home to the base happy, well fed, well inebriated and satisfied that we had indeed seen all of the Gut in Malta that we needed for some time to come.

Surprisingly, the next morning we all appeared in the mess for breakfast at about the same time and in equally fine, healthy spirits. We were none the worse for the wear that we had imposed on ourselves the night before and eager to get on with rest of our journey.

The weather was excellent over the whole Mediterranean region, which was unusual only to those of us coming from the grey dampness of a late British spring. Once again our four-plane formation take off was completed without flaw. We were rapidly getting back to the old familiar Hunter day fighter standards that had been second nature to us prior to our conversion to the all-weather night-fighter role.

We levelled off at thirty thousand feet without a cloud visible in any direction. Established on course for RAF Station El Adam, Libya, we settled down to some station keeping in our battle formation. For a time things bordered on boring as we hung seemingly suspended in space and time.

There was no other air traffic for miles around and except for the occasional navigational check with a radar controller somewhere in the "Med"; we had the world pretty much to ourselves, or at least our small portion of it.

It wasn't spectacular at first but I did notice a slight flicker in my oil pressure gauge as I completed one of my cockpit checks. The flicker remained fairly stable for fifteen or twenty minutes and then it slowly became a more pronounced fluctuation. With at least another forty minutes or so to go before landing at El Adam, I began to take a serious interest in my gyrating oil pressure. In a single engine aircraft over water, any engine trouble is a cause for concern and I decided that I would give my leader an early heads up about my potential problem.

I did this with some hesitation as I recalled similar situations in the past. Being pestered by others outside of my cockpit who where ready to offer copious advice on what to do and what not to do does not sit well with a fighter pilot. Often this can be distracting. Other pilots in the formation, radar controllers and any others who are within radio range are sometimes quick to offer expert advice not knowing the full scope of the problem with which a pilot is attempting to contend.

All pilots have their own system of approaching a potential emergency. Managing a bad situation can be catalogued and simply described in the step by step procedure outlined in the emergency checklists. The approach to the problem and the attitude of the pilot in trouble play a greater role in problem solving emergencies than can be outlined in a simple check-list.

A non-committal acknowledgement from the WingCo told me all that I wanted to hear for the time being. The "roger" meant basically, "received and understood, call if you need help". Thankfully, I was then left alone to monitor my now rapidly deteriorating situation. The oil pressure had been fluctuating wildly for a while had now settled at the bottom of the gauge. Only occasionally did it show any life with a slight twitch toward the positive pressure scale.

We were now about one hundred nautical miles out from El Adam and I gained some comfort in the thought that if my engine should fail I could probably at least glide to the shores of Libya. I was pressed to recall whether the Mediterranean harboured sharks and was pleased that there was a good possibility of keeping my feet dry.

The minutes passed in silence and my team-mates left me to manage my situation on my own. The WingCo called to ask me if I would be OK for a formation letdown. I replied that I would providing I moved from number three to the number four or tail end Charley position which would allow me manoeuvre flexibility should I experience engine failure. I was made more comfortable as the WingCo announced that we would be making a slightly higher approach with additional airspeed to allow me room for an engine out landing should my situation deteriorate further.

As it turned out, we performed our fighter break for the last time as a four-plane formation. The circuit and landing were uneventful and we taxied in and shut down on the line. The technicians quickly determined that I had experienced a catastrophic oil pump failure and had pumped most of the oil overboard in the last minutes of my flight. Furthermore, metal fragments from the oil pump disintegration had contaminated the engine bearings and an engine change would be required.

This news was taken rather sadly by all of us as we had looked forward to a triumphant arrival at RAF Station Akrotiri on the island of Cyprus later that day. It was particularly sad for me, as I would be staying with my sick aircraft until it was repaired. This entailed the fly-in of a mobile repair party from the UK and could be a rather lengthy delay. A message was sent off to RAF Fighter Command in the UK and the Thompson recovery process had begun.

Following refuelling, I waved to my team mates as they departed on their last leg to Cyprus and I turned to take stock of my situation. Studying the wall charts in the flight-planning centre, I realised that the ancient city of Tobruk lay just to the north. Monty of Al Alamien had held off Rommel's Desert Rats here two decades earlier. He routed the Afrika Corps sending them back into Tunisia and eventual defeat. I decided that in order to make the best use of my time while I waited for the repair party, I would try to visit the area and explore the local culture.

I had a solitary dinner in the mess that evening feeling sorry for myself and my misfortune at being stuck in this far off, strange place. I could imagine my mates living it up over at Akrotiri a mere hour or so across the eastern Mediterranean.

The prime roast of beef that I selected from the menu was quite passable even though it was cooked longer than I like. After a leisurely dessert and coffee, I made my way to the bar where I could detect signs of revelry coming from the few technical and administrative officers that kept this Godforsaken base humming. I was readily welcomed into the group and soon we were all comrades in arms fully engaged in the common bar-talk of military men that is universal.

It wasn't long before I discovered why I had been the lone occupant of the dining room. I was told that this was the fourth night in a row that Yak, cleverly disguised as roast prime rib of beef, had been at the top of the menu and my new-found friends had had their fill. I found out much later that the Yak is a native of Tibet and the species is not found anywhere in Africa. Perhaps it was camel but at the time I was ignorant of the basis for the various food-groups in this strange country.

Next morning I rose bright and early and after a good breakfast of what I hoped were fresh chicken eggs and something resembling ham, I proceeded to the flight line to check on the progress of the repair party. To my surprise and tremendous relief, I was told that the repair crew would be arriving later in the day with a new engine for my ailing craft.

I called the base motor pool and within minutes a Land Rover was delivered to the flight line. I now had wheels and a road map of the area to assist me in my cultural tour of north east Libya.

I managed to spend a good part of the remainder of the day touring the base perimeter of El Adam and then on north a few miles to Tobruk. The town lies on the shores of the Mediterranean and compared to other smaller centres away from the seashore, it was fairly modern for the times. I drove east and west of the town for a few miles along the main road between Tripoli and Cairo. It was not difficult to recall the newsreel images from my youth as General Montgomery and his armoured corps battled with the mass of German armour assigned to General Rommel in order to occupy North Africa.

Unfortunately, I had little contact with the local inhabitants other than a native waiter who spoke no English or any other language that I could make out and he addressed me with large smiles and expansive gestures of friendship. I in turn put on a similar demonstration supporting my gyrations with my best British accent. After a few minutes of what must have looked to others as some kind of a pantomime, I found that my waiter and I had developed an excellent understanding. Later I discovered that I had dined on some sort of goat meat cooked in thick gravy. It is probably just as well that I didn't know what was on the menu at the time.

As I toured Tobruk I didn't find anyone who understood English but I found out later that once one becomes familiar with the people and their customs, the English language suddenly becomes understood and spoken by most people in the hospitality industry, such as it was in the early sixties.

I arrived back at the RAF Station at El Adam just prior to the dinner hour and was told that my new engine and the repair crew would be arriving later that night. I was pleased that action was soon to happen and looked forward to departing for Akrotiri the next day.

My euphoria was short lived however; when after a good night's sleep I arrived at the flight line to meet my repair crew. They had indeed arrived late the previous evening and gone straight to work. The old engine had been removed overnight and they were about halfway along in the installation of its replacement. Once installed, I was informed that engine tests would need to be accomplished on the ground followed by an air test before the aircraft could be certified for the completion of the final leg of the journey to Cyprus. Providing that the tests went well, I would be authorised to leave the following day.

Later that afternoon I was called to the line to perform the test flight. It was a simple test and required the exercise of all of the engine controls under all flight conditions. I decided that after take off I would remain in the local area while I tried various throttle settings at various speeds and filled out all of the appropriate information demanded by the test card. If all went well I would proceed out to some isolated area and perform a few aerobatic manoeuvres to check the effects of "G", on the operation of the new engine.

The take off was normal and the engine performed flawlessly as I flew around at various throttle settings close to the airfield and inside the control zone. Satisfied that all was well, I called for a vector to a practice aerobatic area. Taking up a heading of due south as I climbed to altitude I marvelled at the sudden change from the occasional green vegetation along the coast to the stark vastness of the Western Desert. The North Africa escarpment rising several hundreds of feet from the coastal plain passed below and while the Sahara lay some distance to the south, it was different only in name from the desolate desert terrain over which I now found myself.

I climbed to thirty-five thousand feet on my southerly heading jotting pressure and temperature readings on the test card as I went along. On reaching altitude, I performed a few steep turns and then rolled the aircraft inverted and held it for about thirty seconds all the while carefully watching my engine instruments.

Well done! My new engine was performing beautifully and I advised my air controller with whom I had been chatting as I went along that I was descending to a lower altitude to perform some aeros. "Roger" came the casual reply as I rolled the aircraft onto its back and pulled it into a vertical dive. At full throttle I scanned the instruments, everything OK. Mach .98, Mach .99, Mach 1.0. The aircraft slid easily through the sound barrier to just over mach 1.2 and then it was time to recover to level, subsonic flight.

No sweat, so far everything seemed to be in good working order. I was now at about five thousand feet above sea level and only a few thousand feet above ground. There had been nothing to see but desert for miles in any direction and I was startled to notice a line of specks on the white sands about ten miles to the east. Curious, I headed over to investigate.

It was a train of about twenty camels plodding methodically through the sand. A band of Bedouins, not uncommon in the area, were making their way north across the desert from some unknown origin to an unknown destination. Some were riding in style while others trudged alongside the camels through the sand.

These nomads roamed the desert as a way of life and they respected no boundaries. Those I had met at El Adam had been a simple friendly folk who enjoyed their own privacy and respected that of others. This group waved heartily at my aircraft as I flew over and I gave them a bit of an airshow before I set course back to El Adam.

My recovery was uneventful and I was beginning to look forward to my departure the next day and a reunion with my crew at Akrotiri.

That evening I enjoyed a few farewell beers with my new-found friends stationed on the base. They were stuck in this place and would be there until their tours ended. They were envious of me and my prospects of shish kebab and wine on the streets of Limmassol. To them it seemed like heaven compared to the dish they called Yak in the officer's mess at El Adam.

Next morning I was up at five. It was still dark as I breakfasted and carried my small suitcase now filled with dirty laundry down to the flight line. My aircraft was declared serviceable by the repair party who were also departing that morning on their return to the UK. I wanted to take off ahead of them in the event that some little thing might go wrong with my aircraft before I got airborne, otherwise I would have no one around qualified to fix it for me.

I was airborne by 07:30 AM and my wheels had just retracted when the tower called to tell me that a group of Bedouins had set up camp off the end of one of the runways. Apparently it was the custom to scare them off with a low pass or two and when they realised that they might be in a dangerous location, they would move on. It was better than leaving them alone until some itinerant aircraft either undershot the final approach or failed to stop following the landing role and ran them over.

I made one pass with the gear down simulating final approach and as I went by their camp, I could see them all out waving heartily. I wondered if they were the same band of nomads that I had seen out on the desert the day before. I overshot, cleaned up the aircraft and making a wide turn I accelerated to around four hundred and fifty knots. I came over their heads at a few feet and pulled the aircraft up sharply into a vertical climb. As I rolled over and looked back all I could see was a cloud of dust as my jet wake had swept the ground during the initial pull-up and sent their tents flying. Having accomplished my mission, I was cleared to proceed on course to Akrotiri.

On the radio, I could hear the pilot of the transport aircraft carrying my mobile repair crew as he called the tower for take off clearance. Taxiing past the end of the runway, the pilot advised the tower that from his much closer position, it appeared that the tribesmen had received the message loud and clear and were in the process of vacating the vicinity of the airfield. The tower thanked me for my assistance and transferred me to an enroute radio frequency.

I had a tail wind and was making good time. Radar positioned me on course outbound from El Adam and at once I was out over the Mediterranean and the broad expanse of open sea that gives a single engine fighter pilot pause for reflection. From this point on I was at the mercy of the elements. I was unable to do much navigating other than to hold my heading and cross check my standby compass to ensure that my main compass readings were accurate. Occasionally a controller would call up to give me a radar position. This meant little to me over the sea but I appreciated the human contact nonetheless. Sporadically, I would get a more helpful bearing and distance to my point of departure and then at about halfway this changed to a bearing and distance to my destination.

It wasn't long before the controller at Akrotiri called to say that he had me on his radar and Akrotiri lay dead ahead at one hundred miles. I sighted land appearing on the horizon through my windscreen and began matching land-shapes to those on my map of Cyprus. I had made it and after a brief but memorable few days at El Adam, I was pleased to be getting on with my interrupted program.

My welcoming committee was a bit larger that I had expected. Not only was I met by my team-mates who had been patiently waiting for me to catch up with them, but the four Jordanian pilots who had come to Akrotiri to ferry "their" Hunters back to Jordan. I hated to part with my faithful aircraft and my new engine hardly had time to cool down before the Jordanians took possession of our Hunters and headed for home.

That evening, we were all invited by the base commander and his lovely wife to Arife's for a shish kebab dinner.

Now, Arife was well known and well liked by all of the British who were serving in various capacities on the Island. His restaurant in downtown Limmassol provided a fine dining experience and was situated across the street from the only ESSO Station in town. There was no dining room in his establishment, just a kitchen. Sharp on the dot of six PM the gas station closed for the day, Arife and his staff hustled the tables and chairs out into the parking area adjacent to the gas pumps.

Arife also made his own wine and it was served in large earthenware crocks that were covered in wicker. The shish kebab was second to none and the wine made in Arife's cellars complimented the fine meal. The only distractions to our feast were the stray cats that perched on the tall stone wall to one side and the baying of the hounds that circled the wall hoping for a hand out.

We followed the custom of the regular diners and threw our small bones up in the air to the cats on the wall. Whatever they missed usually generated a growling and snarling session among the hounds fighting over the morsels that were missed by the cats on the wall above.

We all ate heartily and following this most satisfying meal we returned to the officer's mess on the base for coffee and liqueurs. It was an enjoyable evening and we finally retired in the early morning hours feeling smug that our trip to Cyprus had been a success.

The next morning gave us some cause for concern as we picked up the morning papers for our breakfast-time reading. Arife, it seemed, had been arrested late the night before for serving cat meat in his shish kebab. We wondered which if any of the cats we had seen hanging over the stone wall had become part of the menu. We also discussed the possibility that we may have also been treated to a morsel or two of hound.

Thus ended our short stay at Akrotiri. As the RAF transport aircraft sped us home in our unaccustomed role as passenger's, we acknowledged that we had enjoyed a unique experience. I liked the Island of Cyprus and enjoyed the people whom I had so briefly met. The feast at Arife's was something else and I would remember the experience vividly as it blended into my memories.

It would be another year before I returned to this otherwise delightful island in the Med.

CHAPTER TEN
THE EVOLUTION OF IN-FLIGHT REFUELLING

For the second time early in my exchange tour, we were about to be removed from the ORBAT, the Order of Battle for the British Armed Forces in the defence of the U.K. The first time it occurred as we began our conversion to the English Electric Lightning in January 1961. Our second withdrawal from the ORBAT came about early the following year as we began preparations for the Lightning in-flight refuelling trails.

The in-flight refuelling concept had been well developed by US forces. The strategic mobility and flexibility that this procedure afforded to both bomber and fighter operations was becoming universally recognised and RAF Bomber Command had spearheaded the adoption of an in-flight refuelling capability for British forces. It provided both a strategic and tactical advantage to bomber and fighter operations.

The Meteor and Javelin aircraft had previously proven themselves in the flight-refuelling role. Now it was time for the Lightning to do the same and 56 Squadron had been assigned the task of conducting the trials. The aircraft internal fuel system was designed for the flight refuelling capability but our aircraft required some modifications involving the addition of the external plumbing to equip us for the role.

Internal modifications to the aircraft were straightforward and minimal. However, the changes were more obvious externally with the installation of a long in-flight refuelling probe attached about mid-fuselage on the port side of the aircraft. It extended forward to a point that was just within the pilot's peripheral vision about four feet to the left and slightly forward of the cockpit.

None of us had any experience in the in-flight refuelling role and we embarked on the technical studies necessary for us to understand and manipulate the systems once aircraft modifications were complete. The modification program was such that only three or four aircraft could be in the process at any one time so we were able to sustain a minimal flying program that allowed us to maintain our flying proficiency on the aircraft.

As the first modifications were completed, the aircraft required air testing to re-certify airworthiness. Testing began as we completed our ground school training on the new fuel system. Four of us were selected to proceed to one of the RAF Bomber Command bases for familiarisation flights in the Valiant bomber. We were briefed on Bomber Command flight refuelling procedures and were given live demonstrations on training missions in the Valiant tanker aircraft out over the North Sea.

Through a friendly contact I had at USAF Base Wethersfield, just down the road from Wattisham, we arranged for in-flight refuelling familiarisation flights for four of us in the F-100 aircraft. We four would form the nucleus of the training program on the Lightning. Within days we had completed our familiarisation training on the F-100/C130 combination and returned to Wattisham only slightly more enlightened on aerial re-fuelling procedures.

We were at last ready to undertake in-flight refuelling on our own aircraft. Our tanker was to be the Valiant bomber refitted as a tanker. It was a relatively small aircraft by today's standards but could carry well over one hundred thousand pounds of transferable fuel.

There was little difference in the flight refuelling procedures other than the fact that the Valiant had only one centre line refuelling point compared to three for the C-130. The Valiant cruising speed was not an ideal match for the Lightning, but its performance was more compatible and much preferable to a Lightning/C-130 combination. Flight planning for both aircraft was adjusted accordingly and a suitable compromise between both flight envelopes was achieved.

Our in-flight refuelling training consisted of establishing a rendezvous with the tanker over the North Sea. The initial encounters with the tanker could be somewhat intimidating. The tanker itself appeared to be quite huge compared to the fighter aircraft with which we were more accustomed to flying in formation. The drogue or basket as it was sometimes called was less than three feet in diameter and looked very small hanging out there in space.

We practised dry hook-ups initially and once we became comfortable with inserting the probe into the trailing drogue and disconnecting cleanly, were we then permitted to take on fuel. Usually, after about thirty minutes our internal fuel levels were low enough that we were able to experience the sudden changes in the centre of gravity and the aircraft trim as the fuel flowed randomly through the lines and into the tanks located in the wings.

This was the most interesting phase of our training as we always had lots to do. Pre-positioning at fifty feet back of the drogue was no problem. Once the receiver aircraft was stabilised in this position, the technician in the tanker switched on the amber light on an array of signal lights protruding from below the tanker's aft fuselage. The amber meant proceed with caution as the fighter was cleared to approach and make contact with the drogue. Keeping one eye on the tanker aircraft and one eye on the drogue, the pilot established a closing rate on the drogue until the probe connected with a satisfying thud.

Sensors in the tanker aircraft indicated to the tanker refuelling technician that a clean contact had been made and the light signal changed to green allowing the fighter to close in to about twenty or twenty-five feet, the position at which fuel flow would commence. In the refuelling position the receiving aircraft was stabilised just below the tail of the tanker.

The sound of the fuel flowing under pressure was quite audible above all of the other normal sounds in the cockpit. Automatic pressure valves, non-return valves and shut off valves could be heard doing their job and the pilot had no control over the flow of fuel once hooked up to the tanker and the process had begun. He only had to ensure that he flew a steady formation position while fighting the constant changes in the centre of gravity.

Within three or four minutes refuelling was complete signalled by a fairly positive thump as the fuel flow from the tanker sensors picked up the stopped flow signals through the lines and the tanker pumps shut down. Tanker signal lights turned to red directing the receiving aircraft to terminate the exercise and the pilot had only to ease the throttle back a notch and the probe disconnected automatically from the drogue as the aircraft dropped back to safe distance behind the tanker.

High-level turbulence was the source of an additional problem for the refuelling pilot. Achieving a successful, clean contact with a drogue oscillating wildly behind the tanker that itself was being affected by the turbulence is an exciting experience. Under these conditions the pilot's only fear was the possibility that he may not be able to take on fuel during the refuelling bracket far from an alternate recovery airfield. During normal air operations, once successfully refuelled another happy customer could depart for other events on his tactical agenda.

Early on we adopted the "Accompanied Tanker Technique". This increased our specific fuel consumption marginally but negated the potential for delays during rendezvous. It had the added feature of relieving the receiver pilots of the responsibility for navigation, although most of us kept a close eye on our progress.

The UK based Lightning in-flight refuelling trials culminated with a five-hour circumnavigation of the British Isles. We flew four fighters in loose formation with the tanker refuelling us at predetermined flight refuelling brackets.

We planned our exercise well out to sea but ensured that we arranged our refuelling brackets within thirty minutes flying time to a suitable alternate aerodrome in the event of a failure to take on fuel. Such failures were relatively isolated and were usually the result of a probe breaking off inside the drogue denying any further use of the effected drogue assembly. While the Valiant carried a spare hose and drogue it was still prudent to err on the safe side when planning the refuelling brackets.

We completed our trials well ahead of schedule and were anxious to demonstrate our new capability in an operational environment. We had completed classroom exercises planning refuelling missions to the Middle and Far East. We conducted a classroom navigation exercise to South Africa. We announced to all that we were prepared to go anywhere and were told that Cyprus would be our first operational deployment.

CHAPTER ELEVEN
THE INTERLUDE

Our deployment planning had reached a final phase and we had little to do until the launch of our refuelling operation to the Middle East. I had the occasion to do some visiting in one of our remaining Hunter aircraft and landed at RAF Duxford as part of my tour.

The Commander in Chief of Fighter Command, Sir Hector MacGregor, who I had met the year before at Gutersloh, was also visiting the base to officiate in the opening of the station outdoor swimming pool. I was invited to the ceremony and joined the gathering of base personnel, officers, men and their dependants as the formalities began. The CinC made a short speech declaring the pool open. He cut the ribbon, turned smartly and marched down the length of the pool to the three-meter diving board. With full military dignity he mounted the ladder and climbed to the top whereupon he executed a perfect swan dive in full military regalia into the pool - flat hat firmly in place on his head. Sir Hector had endeared himself to all base personnel who would remember that with all of his imposing titles, he still had a human touch to add to the office he held.

There was one other incident involving the CinC that showed his remarkable ability to mix easily with his personnel and invite the loyalty of all who came under his command. It was a day that King Hussein of Jordan paid us a visit to Wattisham.

In his early military days the monarch had completed his flying training with the RAF as a young officer following his graduation from the Royal Air Force College at Cranwell.

He visited England frequently and on this occasion indicated a desire to the Air

Ministry to fly in the Lightning aircraft. With little delay, a visit to Wattisham was arranged for that purpose. It was decided that since this Royal visit involved an overnight stay, a mess dinner would be held in the King's honour.

King Hussein's afternoon trip in the Lightning two-seat trainer went off without a hitch despite the difficulty encountered in finding an over-sized flying helmet to fit him. He came into the squadron crew room following his trip visibly excited that he had flown at 1.5 Mach and had actually landed the aircraft at the end of the sortie. A short while later the CinC, Air Marshal Sir Hector MacGregor as the senior RAF representative arrived on the scene and after coffee everyone headed off to prepare for the evening function.

According to custom we sipped sherry before dinner and I had an opportunity to meet King Hussein and enjoyed a few minutes of conversation with him. Smoking was not allowed during the pre-dinner drinks and I was taken by surprise when he asked me if I smoked. I replied that I did and he promptly asked me what kind. I had access to duty free Dumauriers and told him so. He seemed pleased with that and moved on to greet the next person at hand.

After the dinner we adjourned to the anti-room where I found myself standing beside the His Royal Highness as I opened my cigarette pack. The reason for his interest in my smoking habits became clear as he told me that Canadian Dumaurier cigarettes were his favourite and he had been unable to get any for some time. I had a friend for the evening. As the meal had a chance to settle and the mess dinner format progressed into more energetic activities, I seemed to have the King immediately at my side every time I pulled out my cigarette pack. Soon the formal demeanour of dinner degenerated into a series of mess games that made little sense but required a high degree of skill mixed with an equal level of inebriation.

I found myself standing back watching the melee with some detachment. The game in progress seemed to involve frequent flying tackles, the purpose of which was somewhat obscure. There were bodies flying everywhere while in the middle of it all King Hussein stood, drink and cigarette proudly in hand enjoying the scene.

As had all of the other officers, he had removed his tunic to reveal a wide set of fire engine red suspenders. It was too much for the CinC who had also removed his tunic. Sir Hector had been watching the scene himself and seemed focussed on the Royal guest.

As the debauchery intensified, the CinC having exhausted his self-control, launched himself from the back of a chesterfield and tackled the King waste high. A momentary hush came over the crowd as the Air Marshal clutching tightly to the King slid down from waist to ankle, stretching the red suspenders to their limit. Suddenly there was a loud snap as the fasteners let go and there before us stood the King with his pants down around his ankles in his boxer shorts with an Air Marshal lying prone at his feet.

I was immediately summoned to the Royal presence to administer Dumaurier cigarettes to the combatants. After a few minutes of amicable conversation, the Air Marshal decided it was time for him to depart. His Aide had ordered his staff car to the front door, an order that was immediately countermanded by the Station Commander,

Group Captain Peter Horsely. Instead, he ordered a bus to be positioned out front.

It was a fifty-passenger bus but that limitation did not inhibit anyone by this stage of the evening. We all wanted to see the C in C to his waiting aircraft including the King of Jordan who escorted a rather wobbly Air Marshal out the door. Both led the parade, shoes in hand, mess dress tunics and pants neatly folded over their free arms as they marched arm in arm out the door and to the bus. Meanwhile, two very nervous Aides des Camp scurried along picking up shoes and bits and pieces of clothing as they desperately tried to find dignity in the whole, rather amusing affair.

The last to board the bus was the Base Commander who assumed control from the startled driver and proceeded to drive the bus himself. The thrash now mobile, lurched merrily from the mess to the flight line where the C in C's aircraft awaited engines running for its imposing passenger. All one hundred or so participants didn't miss a beat in their hearty rendition of North Atlantic Squadron as they formed a dishevelled escort for Air Marshal from bus to aircraft. The C in C was assisted into the aircraft by his aide and as the doors closed behind them the aircraft taxied hurriedly out of harm's way. King, Base Commander and motley crew returned to the mess for night-caps on a bus now driven by a rather nervous driver.

It was rare that we had a mess dinner on a week-night but this was obviously an exception and we were expected to be present at met briefing promptly at seven-thirty the next morning.

In accordance with normal morning met briefing protocol, all the pilots on the wing were seated and the WingCo Flying and briefing officers stood expectantly near the podium. At the stroke of the half-hour, Group Captain Horsely appeared at the entry and strode purposefully to the front of the room. All rose as he entered and stood at attention in silence as he made his way forward. On reaching the podium he turned to face those gathered.

As he glared out from under the peak of his flat-hat he gave forth with a very simple statement. "There was a drunken party in the mess last night, which in-itself is inexcusable, but the more serious offence was the theft of a base bus. For a short period the stolen vehicle was seen making its way from the mess to the flight-line and back in small hours of the morning. This behaviour is inexcusable and if I catch the officer responsible, he shall be severely disciplined".

My appreciation and respect for the RAF leadership had been advanced by another significant notch. They knew their officers and enjoyed the camaraderie of the mess party. They not only enjoyed it but they were active participants and often lead the shenanigans to the enjoyment of all. On the other hand they were deadly serious in the performance of their duties and expected those under their command to act accordingly. It was a lesson in leadership and the young fighter pilots on the base learned their lessons well.

What of the Royal visitor? The Arab King and his coterie stole away in the night, but not without leaving a message of good will and the pledge to entertain every single officer in attendance that evening to an equal fete should they ever have occasion to visit Jordan. It is disappointing to me that I never had the opportunity to accept this reciprocal hospitality and with the news of King Hussein of Jordan's passing in 1999, it is an opportunity sadly missed.

CHAPTER TWELVE
FLIGHT REFUELLING OPERATIONS
CYPRUS

In early 1962 the historic claims for the Island of Cyprus rose to a new level on the international stage. The Turks on one hand claimed sovereignty over the island while the Greeks claimed it for themselves. The history of this beautiful island in the eastern Mediterranean is traced back to before seven thousand BC.

Remains of the oldest known settlement in Cyprus dating from this period can be seen in Khirokitia and Kalavassos (Tenta) off the Nicosia-Limmassol road. This civilisation had developed along the North and South coasts.

During the Roman Period (58 BC - 330 AD), Cyprus became part of the Roman Empire, first as part of the province of Syria, then as a separate province under a proconsul. During the missionary journeys by Saints Paul and Barnabas, the Proconsul, Sergius Paulus was converted to Christianity and Cyprus became the first country to be governed by a Christian.

Massive, destructive earthquakes occurred during the 1st century BC and the 1st century AD causing extensive damage to all the major cities. These were rebuilt but there was a great loss of life when the Jews who lived in Salamis rebelled in 116 AD. This was followed by the plague in 164 AD. In 313 AD the Edict of Milan granted freedom of worship to Christians and Cypriot bishops attended the Council of Nicaea in 325 AD.

There followed a lengthy period of unsettled strife as one faction after another seized power and was overthrown.

The late sixteenth century brought about the Ottoman Period. In 1570 Ottoman troops attacked Cyprus, captured Nicosia, slaughtered the population of 20,000 and lay siege to Famagusta. After a brave defence by Venetian commander Marc Antonio Bragadin, Famagusta capitulated to the Ottoman commander Lala Mustafa, who first gave free passage to the besieged. However when he saw how few they were, he ordered the flaying, drawing and quartering of Bragadin and put the others to death.

On annexation to the Ottoman Empire, the Latin hierarchy were expelled or converted to Islam and the Greek Orthodox faith was restored. In time, the Archbishop as leader of the Greek Orthodox, became their representative to the Porte (The Ottoman court). When the Greek War of Independence broke out in 1821, the Archbishop of Cyprus, three bishops and hundreds of civic leaders were executed and the situation remained unsettled for the next half century.

Under the 1878 Cyprus Convention, Britain assumed administration of the Island, which remained formally part of the Ottoman Empire until 1914. Britain annexed Cyprus, after the Ottoman Empire entered the First World War on the side of Germany. In 1923 under the Treaty of Lausanne, Turkey renounced any claim to Cyprus. In 1925 Cyprus was declared a Crown colony. The British continued to maintain a strategic presence on the island until the conflict between the Greeks and the Turks made it necessary for UN intervention.

Cyprus became an independent republic on 16th August 1960 and went on to become a member of the United Nations, the Council of Europe and the Commonwealth. According to the Treaty, Great Britain retains on the island two sovereign bases at Dhekelia and Akrotiri-Episkopi.

It was into this ancient and rich culture that we were to be deployed on our first operational flight-refuelling mission. The Turkish factions disputing ownership of the island since medieval times once again indicated willingness to master control of the island - if necessary by the use of force.

The British Foreign Service and the Ministry of Defence had determined that a show of British resolve was required in order to keep the Turkish and Greek elements from going to war. Ground troops might be required later but it would take some time to assemble and transport them into the theatre ... we were it.

The floor of our crew lounge was soon covered with maps and charts. A navigator from Bomber Command came aboard to insert the necessary Valiant aircraft parameters into our preliminary planning sessions. We identified our preferred refuelling brackets taking care that they were positioned close to a suitable diversion airfield should an emergency occur.

Options and alternatives were examined and re-examined until we had established our list of potential diversion bases. This was duly forwarded to MOD and the Ministry of Foreign Affairs. Diplomatic over-flight and landing clearances were required even with only a slim possibility that they might ever be used. Our Squadron Commander, Squadron Leader Dave Seward, was to lead a flight of four and would be in charge of our fighter operations while abroad. I was included as one of the four pilots to deploy.

It was at this point that I was forced to confront a rather sticky situation brought about by my position as a Canadian exchange officer.

There were only eighteen squadron pilots and I had noticed that taking into account sickness, courses and other temporary duties, our squadron strength of able and willing pilots had little margin. If I was to pull my weight as a member of 56 Squadron, I had to be available. On the other hand, I had been cautioned and had signed a statement before leaving Canada, that I would do nothing to embarrass my country.

Canada had played an important role in the settlement of the Suez crisis a few years before but I couldn't relate this to a possible clash on the Island of Cyprus. I had no idea what position Canada might take in the event of a conflict and I was concerned that if I called the Canadian Defence Liaison staff in London, they would arbitrarily exclude me from the exercise, an exercise in which I dearly wanted to participate.

One evening over a glass of scotch, I made my dilemma known to Group Captain Peter Horsley, our station commander. He heard me out with little comment and we ended the evening with the Group Captain telling me to leave it with him. I had no idea where this might lead but I felt better that I had at least confided in someone.

The next morning the Station Adjutant called to tell me that the Station Commander wanted to see me and that I should bring along my passport and a sports jacket. I didn't even try to understand what this could be all about but showed up at the appointed time in full uniform with my Harris Tweed over my arm. "Let me see your passport", said the Group Captain without preamble. I handed it to him and he immediately slipped it into his desk drawer without a glance in my direction.

I was dismissed and the adjutant escorted me down the hall to a waiting photographer who snapped my portrait picture in the sports jacket that had temporarily replaced my tunic. I was told to get on with the rest of my day. At around four o'clock that afternoon I was again summoned by the Station Commander who, with a large grin on his face, presented me with my passport. It was not a Canadian passport, it was British and my occupation read British Government Official. The Group Captain had solved the problem and I went on my way with only a few minor misgivings about this seemingly small piece of fraud. The Canada flashes came off my uniform and I was ready to rumble.

It did have some significance to me though as I was still in the reproductive phase of my life and I wanted to keep it that way. We heard that we were to be issued what were colloquially called "Ghoulie Chits". RAF pilots flying over unfriendly Arab territory carried them. It was explained to me that the Arabs had a penchant for castrating those not sympathetic to their cause. Sewing the infidel's testicles inside their mouths, they would leave them to die on the desert.

In the event of an emergency landing or an ejection over territory controlled by unfriendly Arab forces, the Ghoulie Chit guaranteed compensation for the return of the bearer alive and in good health. They bore a picture of the Queen of England and proclaimed in several Arab dialects that the Queen would pay one hundred Guineas for the safe return of the bearer. I was told later that the Sheikhs of some of the tribes were outbidding the Queen so it seemed prudent to avoid problems over unfriendly territory. Most certainly it was necessary to avoid capture if one had the misfortune to come down in a hostile region. In retrospect I would likely have been better off proclaiming myself to be a Canadian.

This all became somewhat academic when in 1964 Canada became a major contributor to the United Nations Peacekeeping Force In Cyprus (UNFICYP) and continues albeit with a much reduced presence to this day.

Back at the squadron, the Lightning in-flight refuelling planning process having identified all of our deployment requirements, was transferred to the tanker force and to the squadron that would be providing the in-flight refuelling enroute. While flight-refuelling brackets would be strictly adhered to, fuel would be immediately available as a contingency for emergency purposes along the way.

At long last the final preparations were complete, clearances were in place and the weather forecast for the departure was excellent. We rendezvoused with our tanker just to the south of England right on track for our first refuelling point. Since our flight time was to be close to six hours, we received strict medical briefings on the diet we were to follow the day before and for breakfast the day of our departure. No coffee, one small glass of juice, no water on the morning before our take off.

We were not well equipped for the basic human needs for an extended period in the air. We had no toilet facilities on board nor did we have an autopilot that would allow some respite from the simple task of flying the aircraft. To make matters worse, the cruising speed we were forced to fly at was a compromise between the Valiant and the Lightning best cruising speeds. Faster for them and slower for us which placed us in a lower speed range requiring constant attention to the business of keeping the aircraft straight and level.

So there we were. Flying a large heavy aircraft at a less than an ideal cruising speed and unable to relieve nature if she were to call. We had been given the option of wearing a specially designed diaper but this solution somehow did not seem appropriate to a hardened fighter pilot.

To my knowledge there were no accidents on this first trip although I later heard of a pilot who having been caught short on another operation, filled his flying boot which he balanced carefully on his lap for the remainder of his flight.

Little can be said for the journey itself other than the normal boredom experienced by air travellers today. About once an hour, the adrenaline would begin to pump as we neared the pre-planned refuelling brackets. One by one each aircraft closed on the drogue, plug in and within three or four minutes the three other watchful pilots would breath a sigh of relief as another successful connect and disconnect was completed smoothly. The last man in experienced the biggest pucker factor. With one eye on the refuelling operation outside his cockpit and the other on his diminishing fuel readings inside the cockpit, he would be forced to wait patiently for those ahead to successfully take on fuel.

The process was repeated over the Island of Sicily and then just north of Crete. Landfall rose suddenly shortly after our final refuelling bracket. There, about one hundred miles before us lay the Island of Cyprus, the birthplace of Aphrodite. With a tip of the hat to our tanker following our final gulp of fuel, we made a beeline for the base and its waiting latrines. We formed up in tight box formation for the descent and our leader called for a fighter break and landing.

Akrotiri was a major British base manned by RAF personnel. Most of those who had been stationed at Akrotiri for a while had never seen a Lightning aircraft before and our arrival caused a degree of excitement throughout the base. There was a small welcoming party on hand as we taxied in. They were surprised and somewhat disappointed as four Lightning pilots who, despite their stiffened state imposed by six hours strapped into a tight cockpit, leapt from their aircraft and proceeded to the hangar and the beckoning latrines at Olympic speed. Once the cause for this rather obvious snub was understood, knowing winks and smiles abounded and the welcoming proceeded at a leisurely pace.

Akrotiri hadn't changed since my visit the year before although at that time it was in the early spring and the weather had been quite pleasant. This visit was another matter. The temperatures at high noon hovered in the low to mid-forties Celsius. Runway temperatures where in the high forties and often higher. Aircraft parked in the sun were equipped with tents that covered the canopies while allowing the air to circulate underneath. At the high temperatures being experienced, there was a danger of cracks or breaks in the Plexiglas canopies due to heat expansion. Those who thought the tents were to provide comfort for the pilot were badly mistaken. Although in extreme conditions it would be impossible for a pilot to enter an uncovered cockpit due to the heat of the metal levers and other controls that he would need to handle within.

Our support crew had arrived shortly after us and although in a slower aircraft they had departed Wattisham much earlier that morning. We had flown through three time zones non-stop and were all set to call it a day when we were advised that we were invited to a base welcoming party in less than two hours. Needless to say that some of us, both aircrew and ground crew, overcorrected as we tried to compensate for our fatigue with a touch of John Barleycorn.

The next day was a recovery day and we spent some time on the beach at Dhekelia a short distance from the base. Coming directly from England we couldn't spend too much time in the sun and some of us took up scuba diving. There was an excellent school on the base run by volunteers who were all qualified scuba divers and before we knew it we were cruising the bottom of Limmassol Harbour.

An overwhelming treasure of pottery and other artefacts that over many a millennium had been deposited there by accident or dumped as the trade cycles fluctuated. It is illegal to bring any artefacts found in the ocean in the vicinity of the island to the surface. Pottery in particular tends to disintegrate into dust as it dries when exposed to the hot dry air. Still, it was fascinating to descend to the ocean floor and hold in one's hand, pieces of pottery that were perhaps as ancient as civilisation itself.

We spent many of our off hours over the course of the next few weeks investigating the many stimulating points of interest along the south coast of the Island. We explored the historic town of Pafos to the west where Aphrodite emerged from the sea. Then a short distance east to Dhekelia where one can visit the most important ancient city Kingdoms with architectural remains dating back to the 13th century BC.

Our first few days were spent mostly relaxing, acclimatising and enjoying the local ambience. However, our idyllic existence was interspersed with the more important business of "showing the flag".

Our tanker friends had departed the day after our arrival and had been dispatched to wherever they were needed by the British bomber force. There were a couple of rag tag Canberra aircraft on the airfield and the odd Meteor. But apart from that we were the only game on the Island at the time.

Intelligence had confirmed that there was little danger of hostilities. We were assured that we could fly anywhere on the island without fear of drawing fire from anyone. It was also made clear that a sortie or two just off the coast of Turkey would do little to tip local sensitivities one way or the other. It was further decreed that there would be no need for us to fly armed aircraft.

As it turned out, our show the flag assignment was nothing more than that. We had a wonderful time exploring the island from the air often locating places that we would later visit on the ground for a more detailed adventure of discovery.

Remarkably, we were advised that Arife's restaurant, the fine food establishment that I had visited on a previous trip, was still in business. After we had been assured that Arife had learned his lesson and no longer served cat meat with his shish kebab, we returned on several occasions to enjoy the delights of Arife's Middle Eastern cuisine.

Our last few days before our departure back to the UK were filled with operational preparations. Flight plans had to be finalised, diplomatic clearances confirmed and we prepared to welcome our tanker that would shepherd us back to England. Ground crews worked hurriedly to ensure that all aircraft systems were in top order.

The Valiant tanker that would deliver us home arrived the day before and a joint crew briefing was held to ensure that everyone knew their roles, procedures and individual responsibilities. A small farewell party that evening completed our social activity on the base. The tanker crew was the first to retire since they would be airborne well ahead of us in the pre-dawn hours. Runway temperatures were forecast to be so high as to limit the ability of the fully loaded tanker to get airborne within the length of the runway during daylight. The tanker's departure was planned during the cooler pre-dawn period.

Temperatures affected us as well but not to the same extent. The take off run for the Lightning was extended significantly under such conditions but while longer than usual, it was well within the limits of the runway.

The sun came up about six AM and hot turned to very hot quite suddenly. We had a hurried breakfast, being careful to limit ourselves to one glass of juice, no coffee, no water. On the flight line the aircraft and ground crew were idle but ready in the shade. Metal ladders were too hot to touch with the bare hands, as were the cockpit rails and many of the controls, even though the overhead canopies were taken down only as we mounted the aircraft.

Little time was wasted starting engines, the canopy's were closed and the cockpit air-conditioning systems were set at full cold. The cockpit temperature was slow to cool but just perceptibly the temperature began to drop, checks were completed and chocks waved away. We taxied out and took off in a four-plane formation, which we held until we made the rendezvous with our tanker one hundred and fifty miles to the west.

We completed our first three refuelling brackets without incident and began to think ahead to our arrival home. The welcome home reception and celebrations at RAF Wattisham following our first long range Lighting in-flight refuelling exercise was about to experience a twenty four-hour delay.

The weather forecast for the U.K. prior to our departure from Cyprus had been for scattered to broken sky conditions with good ceilings and visibility. It was with disbelief that we received the news from our tanker that the weather over England was deteriorating rapidly and that there was good possibility that we would need to divert to another suitable airfield. The tanker had direct contact with the Bomber Command operations centre via single sideband radio. Bomber Command in turn were in contact with the operations centre at Fighter Command. We were being watched by Air Marshals and Air Vice-Marshals as we innocently made our way northward across France.

We had no cause to panic and were quite comfortable with the fact that while our tanker was running low on fuel, another had been scrambled from one of the bomber bases in the UK and could take us back to the Middle East if necessary. We were now airborne just over five hours and had become accustomed to the numbness that accompanies long periods of sitting in one position. We avoided any discussion of the state of the human bladder preferring not to draw attention to a problem that we were all beginning to experience. The option of returning to Cyprus was not even a consideration as far as we were concerned.

Weather conditions all over England were deteriorating quickly and most airfields were below limits. Closing darkness, low weather and the length of time we had been airborne were all major factors being considered by those on the ground who were grappling for a solution to our dilemma. As we approached the UK, Squadron Leader Dave Seward was now conducting communications with those on the ground. Of all of us, he suffered the most from inadequate bladder retention and we could begin to hear a new tone to his voice indicating that his condition as well as his patience was approaching the limits of his endurance.

As the situation approached emergency proportions, a new voice came on the air. An air traffic controller provided an encouraging weather report for an airfield on the West Coast of the UK. RAF Warton, near Blackpool was expected to be at or above minimum landing weather criteria for the next hour or so.

The Boss's decision was instantaneous. He wasn't thinking with his bladder but he had had enough of the indecision that lingered in the air. We took a last fill up from the tanker that had been scrambled to our aid and headed straight for Warton.

Because of the weather we had split into pairs for the descent, approach and landing. The hand over to Warton aerodrome control from air traffic control was routine and we were greeted with a welcome home from our assigned ground approach controller.

The first pair commenced descent right away and we followed a few miles behind. Radar directed us to the initial point where we began our final descent to the runway. The boss and his wingman were turning off the runway as we in the second section were touching down. Together we taxied in to the line.

We were astonished at the reception committee we could see waiting out of the rain in the lee of the hangar. Warton was the location of the English Electric factory where the Lightning had been designed and built. Employees worked diligently to manufacture aircraft for the RAF but had rarely seen a Lightning land at their airfield. The runways at the base were somewhat short and not suitable for test purposes so that once the aircraft took off on its first flight, it landed at a more suitable airfield nearby. Most were never seen again at Warton.

As we taxied into the line and shut down, the reception committee led by company presidents, vice presidents and assorted local media advanced on our aircraft as we hurriedly dismounted. There followed a repeat performance of the rush to the latrine escapade that had been rehearsed a few weeks earlier at Akrotiri.

Needless to say that our dignified welcoming committee was somewhat chagrined by our unorthodox and rude behaviour, the reasons for which became clear to them once four relaxed and smiling pilots returned from the relief of their very urgent human discomfort.

Formal welcoming rituals completed we were advised that there would be a late dinner in our honour that evening and we were whisked off to a local hotel to freshen up. It was explained to our hosts that all of our kit was on a support aircraft following a day behind us. Unfazed, our sizes were duly noted and we were told to expect suitable clothing and other accoutrements in time for the evening's entertainment.

The suit that had been selected for me was two sizes too large. The shirt fit reasonably well but the tie that was supplied was no match for anything that one could have dreamed up as a sartorial ensemble suitable for an officer and a gentleman. The others were no better off and we all wore our flying boots adding the finishing touches to a look that could have been a model for a Beverly Hillbillies costume wardrobe.

After a few drinks our lack of sartorial elegance didn't seem to matter that much anymore and we proceeded to avail ourselves of the hospitality so generously provided by our hosts. The dinner was excellent and the speeches were short and to the point. The development batch of the Lightning aircraft as it was referred to by the manufacturer had proven that the Lightning was indeed an aircraft worth its salt and the decision to mass produce future Marks was once again confirmed as the right one.

Needless to say, we were all a bit shaky the next morning as we boarded the small bus that had been dispatched to deliver us back to the flight line. Fortunately, the front that had stalled over the British Isles the day before had moved on to the east and continental Europe. We would have clear skies for our entire route home.

Our flight planning complete, we made our way to our waiting aircraft on the flight line. The company had turned out all employees to see us off and while our arrival reception was a pleasant surprise, the farewell was nothing short of spectacular. We weren't quite sure whether they were pleased to get rid of us or they just wanted to see a four-plane take-off as a departure from an otherwise dull routine aerodrome activity.

As a change to our normal take-off procedure, the boss decided that we would perform our take-off at one-second intervals in full reheat. On reaching one hundred and seventy-five knots just after lift-off, each pilot pulled four "G" until the aircraft had reached a near vertical climb. On reaching five thousand feet each pilot performed a wing over and we joined up in a tight box formation. Our farewell to our hosts consisted of a high-speed pass down the flight line at two hundred feet and just under Mach 1.

Our flight time back to Wattisham was only of about forty minutes duration and Dave Seward decided that we would do another low pass announcing our arrival. Once again, the whole base including wives and families turned out to welcome back the warriors from the Middle East.

The mission had been accomplished to everyone's satisfaction. Everything we had been tasked to do had been completed successfully and without a hitch. Aircrews and ground crews had added yet another dimension to the growing array of modern fighter tactics. The capabilities of the Lightning aircraft could now be used to the fullest extent.

Within a few days, the ORBAT once again beckoned and the squadron resumed its combat ready status in defence of the UK. The glamour of foreign travel was replaced once again by the dull drudgery of "Q", interspersed with the high drama of frequent operational exercises that ensured an elevated adrenaline flow during dark nights and inclement weather.

CHAPTER THIRTEEN
THE FIREBIRDS

We were not to be on the ORBAT for long. Now, four months later during the New Years Eve celebrations at the officer's mess, the Station Commander mounted the small stage and seized the microphone just before the midnight countdown began. With great solemnity he announced to the surprise of all, that #56 Squadron RAF had been selected as the official RAF aerobatic team for 1963. The Bandmaster commenced the countdown to mid-night as the crowd erupted with cheers and enthusiastic revelry.

The next morning our two flight commanders and myself were invited for "coffee" at the Squadron Commander's, home We had all been taken by surprise with the station commander's announcement the night before and were somewhat stunned at the turn of events. Dave Seward had been provided with the additional information that the Russians were planning to display a Mach 2 aerobatic team at the Paris Air Show in June. This of course provided us with all the incentive that was needed to get on with the task at hand.

We immediately rolled up our sleeves and began sketching out an initial plan for formation aerobatic training and revised our combat ready training schedules accordingly. We were to remain on the ORBAT for the initial work-up period and therefore we had to ensure that our operational training continued at a level that enabled us to maintain our combat ready status.

We decided as a group that we would begin training with a modest four-plane programme and bring the whole squadron up to each increased level of complexity as our skills increased. Our squadron inventory of twelve aircraft would be fully utilised in the aerobatic role as our training entered the more sophisticated phases a month or so later. Our ground crews would be taxed to the fullest and our compliment of eighteen pilots would have to be screened for suitability. We were told that should we fail to fill all of the positions from within the squadron, we could call on support from the other two operational Lightning squadrons. We treated this as an absolute last resort and determined that we would use as many of our own pilots as possible.

One of the flight commanders, F/L John Curry, had been a member of the famous Treble One Squadron Black Arrows team before its disbandment two years earlier. He was an excellent pilot and all squadron members respected his ability both as a pilot and as an officer. His previous experience was invaluable and we relied heavily on him to provide the leadership during the planning and early training phase.

John had sketched out a variety of formations all based on the simple vic, box, line abreast and line astern models. We began our work-ups using these relatively simple and familiar formations until we had reached an acceptable standard of formation aerobatics. Once this was achieved we planned to increase the numbers in the formation and felt that once we had perfected the nine aircraft loop, we could begin to experiment with the more complex formation shapes and changes.

At this preliminary stage, our squadron ground crews were also busy. They had designed a smoke system for the aircraft that allowed us to trail coloured smoke during our on-stage manoeuvres. The installation required a few days downtime for each aircraft involving the isolation of a fuel tank in the port flap and a run of piping to a nozzle positioned in the jet efflux just aft of the tail pipe of the lower engine. Smoke was activated on the command of the leader and each pilot had a press to activate switch mounted on the control column. The system worked very well and it required only diesel fuel with added colouring to provide a final dimension to the aerial presentation.

Training progressed well and I was amazed that Fighter Command had shown so little involvement in our work-ups. As we entered into the nine-plane phase, we had some trouble with the loop. The outer wingmen experienced very narrow power margins and frequently had to select afterburner to stay in formation. After several sorties dedicated to the nine-plane loop we found that we were unable to perform it with any confidence. The aircraft was just too heavy and the flight envelope too narrow to allow it to be completed reliably every time.

The nine-plane roll was a similar story. Try as we might we were unable to guarantee a clean roll of the nine aircraft in formation. The power and airspeed margins between the inner aircraft and the outer wingmen was too narrow.

The size and weight of the aircraft dictated nearly one hundred percent power on the outside of the formation, while the power settings for the inside aircraft were barely sufficient to maintain airspeed. This caused a tendency for the formation to dish badly as the roll progressed presenting a crescent-like image rather than a tight straight line. By the time we reached Paris we had perfected the manoeuvre to a degree but our mastery of it was unreliable. We used the nine aircraft roll a few times but only under ideal conditions.

Finally one day in March we received a message stating that the CinC, our old friend Air Marshal Sir Hector MacGregor, would like to come over to see how we were progressing. This was not a demand but more - let me know when it would be convenient.

The Station Commander and the WingCo Flying had been encouraging us as we went through the phases of our training. They were confident that we were ready for a review. By this stage we had discovered that of the eighteen pilots, one recognising his dislike of formation aerobatics, volunteered to do the squadron PR, a task for which he was well suited.

Another two pilots volunteered to carryout the flight-testing and ferry flight duties, a need that was beginning to occur frequently. Early spring transfers reduced our squadron strength to 16 leaving us with fourteen pilots who we continued to train. Sadly another pilot Flying Officer Mike Cook was lost to us due to a mid-air collision over the airfield during a bomb-burst. He survived the accident but unfortunately his flying career came to an abrupt end. Following the investigation our training resumed in earnest and we were removed from the ORBAT so that we might direct our full concentration to formation aerobatics.

Our squadron pilot strength had been reduced through circumstance to the minimum level we needed without reaching outside the squadron for assistance. We needed ten performers, a spare and a solo performer. Our team roster was becoming set but we began to recognise another problem. We had some very good solo aerobatic pilots on the squadron but none had much experience in low-level airshow aerobatics. The solo position was causing us some concern. We went to our sister squadron on the base at Wattisham for support.

F/L Bugs Bendal from 111 Squadron was seconded to us as the solo display pilot. He was a slender man of medium height and great intensity. Within days he had happily established himself as a solid member of the team. Bugs had honed his aerobatic skills a few years before with the internationally famous "Treble One" Squadron Black Arrows equipped with Hunter VI aircraft. With the solo in place we were gradually bringing our choreography to a level that would allow us to put on a presentable show over the airfield. Fighter Command were advised accordingly.

We began to practice over the airfield but had been limited to a minimum altitude of not lower than one thousand feet above ground.

A few days later the CinC arrived on the base in a single seat Hunter VI and asked to be included in our pre-flight briefing. He sat, still in his flying suit at the back of the briefing room listening intently and without comment. As we headed out to line to strap in, the CinC accompanied by the Station Commander proceeded to the control tower. Preparations had been made for them to watch our performance from the outer balcony of the tower.

The show was exactly twenty-five minutes from take-off to landing and we intended on reducing that to twenty or twenty-one minutes maximum. We had made the take-off part of the show. We were proud of the Lightning's performance and manoeuvrability and felt it should be showcased as part of our presentation. All twelve aircraft participated in the take-off sequence and it made an astonishing amount of noise during the take-off portion of the show.

All twelve aircraft lined up on the runway created a thunderous roar as the engines were run up to 100% power. The leader selected afterburner and sequentially at two-second intervals each aircraft began the take-off roll. All twelve aircraft were rolling down the runway two seconds apart. As each aircraft reached one hundred and seventy knots, the pilot pulled back on the stick with a force of four "Gs" into a near vertical climb. The noise itself was spectacular but the sudden vertical climb of twelve aircraft one just behind the other was an awesome sight for the spectator.

On reaching five thousand feet the leader assumed straight and level flight long enough for the formation to join into a tight nine aircraft diamond. While this was in progress, Bugs was performing a tight four "G" turn inside the perimeter of the airfield in full afterburner.

The tenth and eleventh aircraft positioned themselves off stage. Following the nine-plane opener the big formation broke into two five plane formations, the tenth aircraft filled out the number five position in the second section. The spare set up a holding pattern backstage ready to replace anyone experiencing problems.

Following our opening nine aircraft pass in plan view, we performed a level bomb-burst directly at the crowd followed by a quick rejoin in two sections of five. The two sections alternated aerobatic manoeuvres at centre stage. The smaller formations were much more manoeuvrable and as the crowd watched one section depart centre stage, the other section was positioned to enter centre stage from the same direction as the section departing. In this manner the crowd always had one section or the other over the vicinity of centre stage. The solo performer waiting in the near wings, filled the dead moments at centre stage as both formations repositioned between manoeuvres.

We had developed a series of straightforward formation changes that were accomplished at centre stage. We would build on these later as we all became more confident in ourselves and each other. For our first performance for the CinC we kept it simple.

Our recovery was also designed as part of the show and following the final nine aircraft upward bomb-burst we reformed hurriedly into a large vic formation we called the Pterodactyl. It was a cumbersome formation and it was said that had we shut down our engines the thing would have flown on it's own. After a hasty reform in full sight of the show area, the Pterodactyl was manoeuvred into the run-in position for a sequential break and landing. On the call of the leader the formation began its break to the downwind position from the outer wingmen breaking left and right working in to the centre and finally the leader who was next to last to land.

Twelve big supersonic aircraft airborne for twenty-five minutes from take-off to landing and never out of sight of the audience – it looked as though we had the makings of a show.

The CinC joined us for the debriefing and as the Squadron Commander finished his critique, Sir Hector rose and said, "I believe you have made remarkable progress, I congratulate you – you are cleared to practice down to no less than five hundred feet above ground". We were overjoyed and we honoured this limitation until a few weeks later when the CinC reduced our limits to the standard air show criteria of two hundred feet above ground.

We were now considered a fully qualified aerobatic team and the requests started to roll in from all over the UK. We began to get national publicity throughout Great Britain, and within a few days the interest broadened to the international level.

A week or so after one of our media sessions on the base I received a clipping from my father of a picture of me that had been published in the Edmonton Journal. It was accompanied by an article about a Canadian from Alberta serving on an RAF aerobatic team. Needless to say, the "Colonial" became the focus of good-natured ribbing by the rest of the team and continued for some time.

Our prime focus however remained the Paris Air Show. This would be our supreme test and we looked forward to it eagerly. Unfortunately, a few weeks before we departed for Paris, we were advised that the Russian team participation had been cancelled. This came as a disappointment to us as we were looking forward to meeting the Russians under peaceful but competitive circumstances. We consoled ourselves with the thought that perhaps they had learned of the excellence of the RAF Firebirds and found our fame intimidating.

We had reached the peak of our performance in late May and began preparations for the move to Paris for the mid-June air show. It had been arranged for us to arrive a few days early to allow our ground crews an opportunity to familiarise themselves with airdrome services and support facilities at Orly International Airport, the home of the Paris Air Show. It also allowed time for the crews to clean up any aircraft unserviceabilities before air show day.

The team spent two relaxed days enjoying the ambience of Paris before engaging in the routine of the daily airshow. The day before the show was to open was a designated practice day and allowed us to familiarise ourselves with the local area and fine tune our aerobatic sequences. We noted with some pride that we were selected as the closing event on the air show programme. The Firebirds would provide a continuous thunderous roar as twelve supersonic aircraft looped and rolled in ever-changing formations before an enthusiastic crowd. It was a powerful show and each of the performances during each of the three days was lauded with Gaullic passion in the Paris media.

On the final day we flew one of our better shows and as the programme came down to the final manoeuvres, we positioned for the upward bomb burst, the leader commented casually on the radio. "This is it chaps", he said, "tomorrow we will be home". It was all right for him to take such a light-hearted approach but for me in the line astern position or "stinger" in the front five of the pterodactyl, there was one more intricate manoeuvre to come.

I was the last to break for the bomb-burst from my position just behind the leader. The remaining ten aircraft joined on the wings forming a huge "V" or "Vic" formation. As the "smoke off" call came I was still hurtling vertically upward in after burner at high speed. I throttled back to idle and carved down toward the airfield looking desperately for the rest of the team. The leader, like an old horse heading for the barn, had tightened up his wide approach to the landing circuit considerably from what we were used to and I realised that I would have to hustle to rejoin into my position before the formation began to break for landing.

Selecting full afterburner I pulled around and headed for a cut-off point that would take me quickly into my place in the formation. Because of the tightness of the pattern others in the formation were having similar difficulties with the rejoin and I could see a cluster of aircraft ahead of me all heading at high speed to the same point in the sky. The leader was pressing his smoke button periodically to identify himself for the rest of us and it appeared that the rejoin would be completed just prior to the final break and landing sequence.

I now had all of the other aircraft in sight and was concentrating on getting into my own position as quickly as possible. I did a quick cockpit check as I began to close and found to my chagrin that my airspeed was in excess of seven hundred knots. A glance at the Mach meter indicated 1.1 Mach – I was supersonic at about six hundred feet above ground and looking straight ahead at the Eiffel Tower not more than six or seven miles away. I immediately throttled back to idle and with speed brakes out, I slid comfortably into position just seconds before the leader called for the break and landing. I had a burning vision in my mind that the path of my aircraft over the ground would be devastating as the supersonic shock wave swept across the city during the Firebirds final contribution to the 1963 Paris Air Show.

I was the last to land and wrestled with the turbulence created by those landing ahead of me. Once safely on the ground I began to imagine the repercussions from my breach of low-level airspeed limitations.

As we taxied in to the line, I noticed a black staff car waiting ominously by the hangar. Air Marshal Sir Hector MacGregor was there to meet us. As we dismounted our aircraft and somewhat hesitantly approached his staff car, he lifted the trunk with a flourish and his driver began to mix screwdrivers for the team. Not a mention was made of sonic booms and I am sure there was at least one. The Air Marshal formally toasted the 56 Squadron Firebirds and it was a fitting celebration at the end of our major air show of the year.

Later that day I carefully watched the TV coverage and other media reports of the show and there was not one mention of a sonic boom. Perhaps the noise we were making over the city drowned out the effects of the low-level Mach 1.1 phenomena.

We returned to Wattisham somewhat disappointed that the premier event of our season was now behind us. After a few days off for both pilots and ground crew, we returned to our UK air show circuit for the rest of the summer.

CHAPTER FOURTEEN
POSTING TO OTTAWA – THE TRANSITION

It was disappointing. My posting message had arrived at Canadian Joint Staff in London and Group Captain Carling-Kelly had called to tell me that I was to be transferred to Air Force Headquarters in Ottawa in the fall.

We were approaching the end of our air show season and #56 Squadron RAF, the official formation aerobatic team for 1963, was preparing to return once again to the NATO order of battle in the defence of Europe.

My last trip was to be on Battle of Britain Sunday. We were to participate in a mass fly-past consisting of scores of different types of RAF aircraft. Our route was down The Mall and over Buckingham Palace. Once past the Palace, we broke free as a smaller nine-aircraft formation and proceeded immediately to Biggin Hill, an RAF Station that was home to #56 Squadron in 1927. It was famous for fighter operations during the Battle of Britain. Here we performed an abbreviated air show sequence. Following this performance the squadron proceeded to RAF Station Brise Norton in the Midlands where the Firebirds were featured in a second Battle of Britain air show of the day.

In deference to my longevity on the squadron and my imminent departure, I was allowed to participate in the first portion of the mission. I dropped out of the formation following the Biggin Hill performance as my replacement, who had been training for several weeks, slotted in allowing me to recover on my own back at Wattisham.

It was sad and lonely return to base as I contemplated my last flight in the Lightning aircraft. It was the end of one the most delightful tours of my career. I had expected that because of my Lightning experience, I would be posted somewhere in the new CF 104 program and was disappointed that I was returning to a dreaded staff job. This important phase of my flying career had come to an end.

I took advantage of my last flight in the Lightning aircraft by performing a brief aerobatic display over the airfield before my final landing. I was treated to several pints by the squadron ground crew after I had signed in. Much to my surprise I was presented with a squadron plaque that hangs on my wall to this day. It reads "Presented to F/L T.R. Thompson by the NCOs and Airmen of #56 Squadron Wattisham September 1963". No medal or commendation could be more meaningful to me than this small gesture made by the people I had come to look upon as family.

Our last farewells both formal and the more intimate gatherings with neighbours and the close friends we had made in the three years we had been on the base were somewhat emotional. We realised that we would not likely see most of the people with whom we had become so close again. We took great pleasure in distributing freely the remains of our rather prodigious liquor stock that we had accumulated over the three years of our tour. Unfortunately, we did not know at the time that we were entitled to import the contents of our "wine cellar" on return to Canada. Unaware of this until well after our return home, I had a few quiet retrospective moments contemplating what might have been.

The C-47 flight from London to the Canadian base in Marville, France is just a blur in my memory. It was the same during our flight back to Canada aboard the Yukon aircraft of

RCAF Transport Command. I hadn't seen my country in three years.

Unlike our luxurious if somewhat rough trip across the Atlantic in 1960, there was little time for reflection. Our arrival in Trenton was under cover of darkness and we were both surprised and pleased that the children had slept the entire flight. They had proven themselves to be seasoned travellers as they were put to bed at mid-night shortly following our arrival and slept for another ten hours.

The usual frantic search for housing ensued as we arrived in Ottawa. After a week or two of house hunting and ordering the furniture out of storage that we hadn't seen in three and a half years, we settled into the suburb of Nepean on the south-western outskirts of Ottawa.

There was only a brief pause in the whirlwind of activity as I prepared to report to the Director of Air Defence and Tactical Operations and a whole new set of anxieties intervened.

I turned up in full, dress uniform for my first day in the headquarters only to be told that the Operations Branch day to wear the uniform was on Mondays. The rest of the week we were to wear civvies. There was no clothing allowance to cover this but we were expected to wear suits or slacks and sports jacket and tie. The purpose of this was never clear to me.

At one time I was told that it was to conceal the number of military personnel in Ottawa from the enemy. This may have been so but later I came to look at it as the political intent to conceal from the public the number of military personnel serving in the nation's capital. This policy was to be exploited later as the politicians began to use the military as a new means to manipulate a docile electorate.

The air force had only just instituted a junior officer staff-training course a few years earlier. As an old fighter pilot, I was deemed to be immune from this course and my training would be like all air force officers before me - on the job - hands on and devil take the hindmost.

To be fair, it was expected that the Flight Lieutenants would train the Flying Officers and the Squadron Leaders trained the Flight Lieutenants in the complexities of the staff function. That's just the way it was and had been since the birth of the RCAF in 1924.

Following the signing in procedure on my first day, I proceeded cautiously to my new directorate where I was marched into the Group Captain's office. He was a tank of man of medium height and heavy-set build. I remembered my last encounter with him several years earlier.

It was at one those Friday night beer calls at RCAF Station Bagotville in northern Quebec. Beginning sedately, the event usually degenerated into a free for all of mess games requiring great feats of strength, skill and stupidity.

The game of the day was called torpedo and the competitor was required to launch himself horizontally from a distance, assume the full standing at attention posture while airborne and hit the cushioned portion at the front of the bar headfirst at or near the end of the trajectory. To fall short disqualified the player. Underestimating the distance brought about a bone-shattering crunch into the bar. Distances were measured from the take off point and the participant that covered the longest distance was the winner.

The Station Commander at the time was Group Captain Ralph Ashman. He was the undisputed champion throughout the air force in demonstrating the finer points of his skill in estimating his airborne distance accurately. His shorter stature was no impediment to the distances he could achieve and only occasionally did he misjudge his take-off point slamming headfirst into the bar at near terminal velocity. It was said that he didn't need to wear a hardhat while flying.

Now as I renewed my acquaintance with Group Captain Ashman, he had his cigar firmly clenched between his teeth. He barely looked up as he said, "Thompson, you can either become a staff officer or you can be a coffee maker in this headquarters, it's up to you to decide". I had no idea what he was talking about and retreated to my assigned desk that had once been used by Billy Bishop or one of his colleagues.

There was a Squadron Leader and a Wing Commander between the Group Captain and me. One was recovering from a heart attack and the other seemed to spend a lot of time on temporary duty down in Omaha planning US Strategic Air Command bomber flights over Canada. My staff training was conducted by a Group Captain who didn't seem to have a lot of patience, which I attributed to too many head-on collisions with various bars throughout the air force.

My first year was a demoralising experience and I spent more nights than I care to remember at our dining room table. Long after the family had gone to bed I spent hours redrafting, revising and reworking numerous staff papers that had mysteriously become my responsibility.

I usually arrived at work with the ladies in the typing pool who were the first early morning souls to arrive. I had the feeling they dreaded the sight of me as I presented them with yet another version of my latest masterpiece of military writing excellence. Unfortunately, my self-confidence never lasted more than the first reading of the day when I would be sent back to my desk devastated that I had once again missed the mark.

Far too many times it seemed to me I heard the words, "Take that back and rework it from the start - and stop using conjunctive adverbs". What the hell was a conjunctive adverb? I had no idea and scurried off to find the latest version of Her Majesty's Manual of Service Writing.

I had become despondent. I was six months into the job and I still didn't seem to have a clue as to what was expected of me as a staff officer. I had graduated almost seamlessly from the laborious task of writing my first very simple memo to more complex conceptual military papers. Yet I was still made to feel as though I would be sent down to some lesser job pumping the gate at RCAF Station Tuktoyaktuk or some such other enchanting base that air force included in it's real estate portfolio.

It was a dreary day early in the fall of 1964 and we had just returned from lunch in the greasy spoon just across Elgin Street from the headquarters. It was a Friday and we were contemplating a few beers after work at the Gloucester Mess when the crackle from the squawk box signalled that the great man with the cigar needed some attention. "Is silver pen there" was the question emanating from the speaker.

There were three of us in the office and we looked at one another wondering which one of us deserved such praise. Finally, sensing some confusion on our end, the Group Captain snarled, "Thompson, Get your ass down here".

Well that was it, "let the last be first", the saying went and I proceeded down the hall contemplating my future at Tuktoyaktuk.

As I entered his office on this occasion the Group Captain shouted, "Mary, bring two cups of tea". A chair was indicated and I sat down wondering why two cups as tea was not one of my preferred drinks at the time. I was soon enlightened as the secretary placed two cups of black tea in front of the Group Captain and retreated to her office carefully closing the door behind her.

The Group Captain reached under his desk and produced a bottle of whiskey from which he poured a liberal dollop into each of the cups that had been filled only to the point where an ounce or two of fortification could be added. Once the pouring ritual was complete he passed me a cup across the desk and said, "Well, you've done it, congratulations you are now a staff officer". My painful year of apprenticeship was complete and I was being welcomed into a very unique fraternity of AFHQ officers who had survived the trial by fire. It was now someone else's turn to make the coffee.

My euphoria was to be very short lived as new challenges began to loom on the horizon. Had I not suffered the Ralph Ashman school of hard knocks, I would never have been prepared for what was to come.

CHAPTER FIFTEEN
THE DESK JOB

I had not paid a great deal of attention to politics prior to my arrival in Ottawa. Apart from closely following the progress of the CF 105 Arrow program a few years earlier, I had been essentially disinterested in the whole political spectrum.

It was during my apprenticeship at headquarters that my interest in politics awakened. My staff training had reached the postgraduate level and we were being bombarded with studies on the "what ifs" of forces integration. Study after study was produced showing how the medical, dental and food service systems were either integrated or nearing completion. While integration in these and perhaps a few other areas like some forms of transport and military policing made sense, most of our own studies pointed to the futility of integration of the operational branches of the services.

The anti-nuclear theme resurfacing on Parliament Hill was also becoming a subject of concern. More importantly our deteriorating relationship with our NATO allies was to my mind foolish and would only serve to reduce our influence with our NATO partners.

Earlier in my career I had little time or inclination to follow the intricacies of political philosophy or policy gyrations. Now I was in a position to witness decisions in the making that had a direct impact on the future of the military and the country. I was beginning to develop my own assessment of the significance of the political impact on the Canadian forces and the important interface between national defence and foreign affairs.

My interest in politics became fuelled by curiosity. I subscribed to Hansard and reviewed its contents daily. I attended the visitor's gallery in the House of Commons at every opportunity and watched the defence-related debates. Often I would sneak over to watch question period and I marvelled at the intensity of the rhetoric as our members of parliament debated the issues of the day.

I viewed the bobbing and weaving of the politicians with detached fascination. A new Minister of Defence named Paul Hellyer took up the reigns of the department. As his policies began to take shape he became more affectionately known around the headquarters as Paul the Prudent Pruner.

The studies escalated in number and frequency. Many a long night was spent attempting to find ways to deter the government from its unrealistic policy of integration and eventual unification of the Canadian forces. Admirals, Generals and Air Vice Marshals were either resigning or being forced into early retirement. It was a credit to the senior officers of the times that they counselled the younger junior officers who were also indicating their dissatisfaction, to remain in place. We were told that we formed the bulwark of the officer corps who would maintain the honourable traditions that had been so painfully earned by our predecessors.

We needed replacement aircraft programs. The CF 101 introduced just a few years earlier was dated as an effective operational fighter. The CF 104 employed in the tactical nuclear role in Europe was distasteful to a government seeking to relinquish the nuclear role. The strategic transport fleet was becoming obsolete, as were most other air resources. The army needed tanks and new armoured personnel carriers; the navy needed new ships and aircraft. All defence policies and roles were questioned, examined and re-examined. They were written, rewritten, revised and revised again. It seemed endless.

The government was relentless and impatient in it's intent to wear down the military structure. Our military allies in the beginning did not assign much importance to the struggles evident in all three Canadian services. As time and much agonising continued, both disbelief and a lack of understanding was becoming evident among our NATO and NORAD partners. Why three such proud, efficient and effective services were being so systematically ravaged was beyond rational understanding.

The Canadian forces on land, sea and in the air had gained the respect of the world and they were being savaged by political whim. All three services were committed to NATO and all three services supported the numerous Canadian government trade missions attracted to the rapidly growing European economy.

The Canadian military establishment in NATO provided an intermediate link between the members of the European economy aiming to market their products in Canada and the US. Meanwhile, the Canadian Air Division and Brigade Group headquarters in Europe were increasingly relied upon by Canadian trade delegations for support in their overtures to the European governments and the corporate sector.

As the Canadian government's emphasis on its NATO commitment began to wane, Canada became threatened with trade sanctions by our European allies. The hole that would open up in the western defence structure, should Canada prematurely reduce or withdraw its military support to NATO, was difficult to contemplate.

The geopolitics of the Europeans and their North American allies began to take on more importance among military planners. More attention than ever before was now being given to the inter-relationships of the burgeoning European economies. Military equipment acquisition became more complex as NATO member countries began to compete for the lucrative military dollar, pound, franc and mark.

In Ottawa, Air Force Headquarters and the naval and army counterparts were renamed Canadian Forces Headquarters. It was as if this new name would make everything right. It was joked that Defence Headquarters was in reality just another radio station, "This is CFHQ with your morning news".

Many senior officers in all three services were becoming more outspoken as government pressure for the integration of the Canadian military increased. Admiral Landymore was the more prominent of those opposed to the integration process and ensured that the politicians knew exactly where he stood. Close behind the Admiral was my old friend and mentor Group Captain Bob Braham, who let it be known in no uncertain terms that he would not serve in an integrated armed forces. He had stated clearly in a letter to Defence Minister Hellyer that he could not and would not continue to serve should integration of the forces proceed.

These and other outstanding senior military officers opposed to integration expressed their opinions vocally and in writing, at confidential meetings and in correspondence. They were not prepared to have their opposition made public and in the end used against them as examples of the insubordination of some of the senior military generals. Yet that is exactly what transpired, the government ensured that the views of the dissenting officers were made public and it was even hinted that their resistance bordered on treason.

In keeping with the sentiments that were running rife throughout the military establishment, I had quietly applied to join United Airlines. To my surprise, I was accepted within about two weeks and was now faced with the final decision. One night over a beer or two, I confided in Bob Braham that I was considering leaving the service. His reaction surprised me. "Whatchyer cock", the old expression I had heard years earlier in my career came ringing back to me. "It's OK for me", he went on, "I don't have that much time left to serve, you still have your whole career ahead of you and people like you must stay on to ensure that none of the traditions that have been created by those before you are ever lost. It is your responsibility to preserve the proud service traditions for those who follow". The next day, I called United Airlines and withdrew my application.

For the next fifteen years I worked diligently to attempt to make the integration experiment work as demanded by my government. All the while attempting to ensure that Air Force values and traditions were maintained.

The one bright spot that served to keep me sane during my early days at the headquarters was the practice flight. Actually, there were two practice flights when I arrived in Ottawa in 1963. There was a T-33 Jet Practice Flight at Uplands and for the multi-engine pilots there was a C-45 Practice Flight at Rockcliffe. Since I was qualified on both jet and multi-engine piston, I decided to register for both. I saw no reason to tell one about the other and until the C-45 Flight was disbanded a year so later, I maintained my qualifications on both.

All staff pilots were required to get a minimum of 25 hours a quarter to maintain their qualification. Clear justification was required when exceeding the minimum requirements. Flying records were carefully monitored and as the magic 25 approached it became more difficult to reserve an aircraft for practice flying. Amazingly, no one cross-checked with the flying activities at the other practice flight and I was able to maintain just over 50 hours a quarter flying time on two aircraft types.

Because practice flying was to be conducted after business hours, the few of us who maintained our flying currency spent a goodly number of our weekends in the air. Those pilots who did not maintain currency would often reserve an aircraft and then try to find somebody with an instrument rating to fly them around the country. We got to know them after a while and usually found some reason why we couldn't accommodate them. The practice flight supervisors eventually caught on to the subterfuge and those who were not current qualified pilots were not allowed to book aircraft for weekend flying.

It was a tough way to fly but at least we kept our hand in and it had the added advantage of allowing us to get out to the bases frequently and find out first hand the problems affecting the operators in the field. This was not only useful in guiding us in carrying out our jobs but it added a degree of credibility to our operational discussions in the headquarters.

I had one other flying advantage during this phase of my headquarters tour that helped me to maintain my balance. For a time I was given the responsibilities of desk officer responsible for the operation of the F-86 Sabre Transition Unit at RCAF Station Chatham NB. The venerable Sword had found one last useful niche in the air force before its retirement.

The STU was established for pilot's transitioning to the CF 104. High speed-low level navigation skills were honed to a fine art by pilots prior to proceeding to the CF 104 operational training course at Cold Lake.

Add another 25 Sabre hours a quarter to my 50 hours of practice flying and I wasn't really doing too badly despite my assignment to a staff job. This did not take up an inordinate amount of my time but when questions came up regarding this phase of CF-104 training, I was expected to have the answers.

Meanwhile, we were beginning to integrate the forces. A prospect not readily acceptable to any of us in all three services. By now I had been on the headquarters staff for a couple of years and had kept a record of all of the action contact offices (as I called them) around the complex. I knew who the doers were in the army, navy and airforce including administrative, technical operational and personnel. I had solid contacts with those who if they could not help me directly could give me a valuable lead to those who could.

I began getting calls from officers in the other services who were less seasoned than I in the workings of the headquarters. Invariably they needed advice on how best to tackle a particular staff problem that may or may not have anything to do with the airforce.

There were many occasions during this period when our superiors reached an impasse in their negotiations at higher level staff meetings and those of us at the more junior levels would gather, find a consensus and feed it up our individual chains of command for approval.

This is not to say that we were smarter than anybody else, it merely indicated that often through the very tense and pressurised evolution of the integration process, the generals often found themselves in horse trading exercises from which it was difficult to extricate themselves. Presented with a well-researched solution prepared through negotiations by their own staffs, it was much easier for them to agree in a final approval phase.

Meanwhile the organisation was changing daily. Reorganisation upon reorganisation not only confused the outsiders but it confused the players. Personal positions on the status of the forces were hardening and many good officers were seeking employment elsewhere in civilian life.

While the airline industry was furiously hiring pilots, a buoyant economy was beckoning all members of the forces at all rank levels. There were dark signs on the horizon that bespoke of trouble ahead.

Some of us regardless of service background felt that because of rampant inflation, rising defence budgets for all western democracies, the forces integration experiment could be attempted under certain controlled conditions. Some of us even said openly that we could agree to go along with the process providing the government promised that we wouldn't go to war until the integration concept had been proven one way or the other. The Canadian Forces, because of our distance from Europe and hot spots elsewhere in the world, were probably in the best position of all to attempt such a radical departure from well proven military principles.

The concept from a fiscal point of view was reasonably sound and many common functions in all three services were already integrated. To extend this concept to include the combat arms and the immediate operational support systems was sheer folly.

General Jean Victor Allard, a huge teddy bear of a man, had agreed to come out of retirement to preside as the first Chief of Defence Staff over an integrated Canadian military. He liked to tell the story of his immediate post-war experience as a Canadian Military Attaché to Moscow.

He enjoyed hockey and conscripted other members of the embassy to form a team. They practised frequently but had no competition, so Major Allard sent out an appeal to Canada for the donation of used hockey equipment for use by the less fortunate and war ravaged Russians. The response was overwhelming and soon there was enough equipment in place to outfit several teams throughout the Moscow bureaucracy. It was his boast and justifiably so, that he had introduced Canadian ice hockey to Russia.

General Allard liked to refer to himself for a time as a "FINK", a Flying Infantryman with Naval Knowledge. He wore a wing that he had earned after a few hours of instruction on a light observation fixed wing aircraft. To my knowledge he never flew as pilot in command of any other aircraft. His experience on the high seas was of passenger status. The phrase however was catchy and the PR folks thought it was wonderful while the serving military looked upon it with disdain.

Even most lowly privates knew that there was a vast difference between an infantryman and air force communications technician. The army Provost Corp's training and background had little to do with maintaining the security of a warship. The thinking was just plain muddy and no amount of logic could change the minister's bull-headed, politically biased decision to integrate. It was the beginning of the end.

General Allard was a fine soldier and had served his country well. He truly believed that integration was the way of the future for the Canadian Forces. However, he did not foresee the looming civilianization of the military headquarters nor could he have foreseen the negative impact this would have at every level of all three services.

We toiled long and hard to make military integration work. We all laboured together developing equipment acquisition programs. We provided each other with vehicle, aircraft, and equipment numbers needed to support the various operational programmes. We were not confident of success but we gave our best effort all the while attempting to preserve whatever we could of our individual service traditions.

Numerous studies were completed on the Canadian Advanced Multi-role Fighter Aircraft (CAMRA) as it was called. My former squadron commander at Comox, by now Group Captain Hal Bridges, headed up our team of specialists in developing the multiple requirements of an aircraft that could perform all of the roles that were being accomplished by three or four aircraft. The new concept called for a specifically designed aircraft to perform all of the air combat roles.

One airframe/engine combination that could be quickly reconfigured on the flight line to carry each of the various weapons suits as may be needed in any given strategic or tactical situation was the aim of the study team.

After amassing numerous computer models, detailed examination of metallurgy requirements in each role, a variety of weapons systems and finally an exhaustive cost analysis, it was determined that such an aircraft as the CAMRA was not feasible then or in the foreseeable future. The sophistication demanded by high altitude supersonic parameters was too expensive to expose to the increased survivability hazards in the low-level tactical roles. A less expensive airframe/engine combination optimised for these roles was much more cost effective

Furthermore, the superhuman pilot who could be trained and maintain a high level of proficiency in all of the roles had not at the time been cloned. Nor do we appear to be any closer to that sort of hybrid human today.

The CAMRA study had taken up the best part of a year and an atmosphere of panic entered the arena. Canada desperately needed a fighter aircraft to fill the tactical air support role recently converted from that of nuclear strike in Europe. Furthermore there was a general but unwelcome push to provide the Canadian land forces with a close air support capability. The CF-101 in the air defence role was still adequate but would need replacing in a few years. The tactical air support and air defence roles were both in support of our international commitments but, there was no military necessity to foster a dedicated air to ground support role for Canadian land forces.

The Canadian Army brigade in Europe could call upon NATO tactical air support when required and, from an airman's point of view, to create such a standing tactical air to ground force dedicated to a relatively small Canadian land force was not feasible and certainly not cost effective. We knew that Canada would not go to war alone and any involvement by the Canadian forces would be based on the mutual reliance on a muli-lateral force each contributing its specialised and complimentary forces to the whole.

Despite all of this, the Minister decided that a close support capability within the Canadian forces sufficient to support a small Canadian land force deployment was imperative.

Our aircraft requirements cell began to look at alternatives in the aircraft selection process. Initially, the McDonnell F-4 aircraft was favoured to replace all of the aircraft currently employed in Canada's fighter forces. It was a twin jet engine Mach 1.5 capable aircraft, effective in the air defence role and had reasonable tactical air capability.

This would not have been a bad choice as the F-4 was well into mass production and was being employed successfully by other allied air forces around the world. I had thought that the F-4 was to be our final choice and looked forward to planning its introduction into the air force. Unfortunately, our focus at this point spiralled downward through the A-7, the A-4 and finally, what was to become the CF-5.

The minister didn't like the position that had been taken by airforce requirement staffs. The F-4 program at $600 million for about two hundred and fifty aircraft over ten years in 1967 dollars was deemed to be too expensive. All of the other aircraft could not meet the multi-tasking requirements needed to fulfil the full range of roles from tactical air-to-ground through air superiority to the high altitude supersonic requirements in the air defence of North America. In the end the Minister handpicked his own team and because of my extensive involvement and relatively low rank (Flight Lieutenant) I was appointed to the team.

The Minister had decreed that the three aircraft he would consider were the Ling Temco Vought A-7, the Lockheed A-4E and the Northrop F-5. While the choice was supposedly open to our recommendations, the Minister went on to point out in no uncertain terms that he favoured the F-5.

This was my introduction into the backward thinking that politicians invariably impose in those areas where they have no understanding or expertise. We were being squeezed to fit our equipment acquisition plans into the budget and not to meet any lofty Canadian international foreign policy. Quite apart from the budget, there was an additional non-military requirement to build whichever aircraft we selected at a Canadian factory in Canada. A worthy goal when possible and feasible and can also have a positive impact on the Canadian aviation industry and the labour force. But as a criterion to meet the nation's military equipment needs for a strong, cost effective defence force, it has always been a prerequisite given far too much emphasis in the military equipment selection process.

Within weeks this new team had completed its study and had recommended the selection to the Minister in the following order of priority. Top of the list was the A-7, a subsonic US Navy fighter-bomber that had a range of 7000 nautical miles without a bomb load and was attractive to the army because of its close support weapons delivery capability. Both the A-7 and the A-4 were configured for carrier operations but the navy favoured the A-4 because of its air superiority capability in the role of fleet defence. The F-5 in the consensus of the team came out last in the selection process.

As an air force fighter pilot I didn't think much of any of the choices that had been selected by Hellyer. My early exposure to those who fought in WW II led me to conclude that somehow fighter pilot skills across a broad spectrum of roles had to be maintained. Pilots needed to experience the smell of cordite in the cockpit during gun firing; they needed to know how to harmonise their gun sights as well as their guns. They needed to know how to drop bombs and fire rockets or missiles. They needed to maintain an air to air combat capability. We were going to be behind in technology but at least I felt that it was imperative for us to maintain the basic skills.

In my own view, one that I shared with anyone who would listen, the F-5 was the only aircraft of the three choices that we had available to us that could satisfy a basic minimum in all of the tactical air roles. It would allow us to maintain a reasonable, broad spectrum of operational capability among our pilots.

Many of my air force colleagues had favoured the A-7, an aircraft that hadn't yet flown, and we had only seen at the factory in plywood mock-up form. It seemed that I was a minority dissenter in our final aircraft acquisition submission to the Minister.

There occurred an event that turned the tide. It was at a mess dinner at the Officer's mess at RCAF Station Rockcliffe. Following the dinner all of the attendees gathered at the bar for after-dinner drinks. I found myself standing beside the Minister. I usually try to avoid such encounters and I stared studiously ahead as the bar staff went about their business.

Finally, the Minister turned and said in a quiet voice, "Thompson, what do I have to do to convince the selection team that the F-5 is the best aircraft for us at this time". Somehow

Hellyer had heard that I had been supporting the F-5 aircraft selection.

I had naturally given this subject a lot of thought over the months I had been involved in the various programs. I knew the government was under pressure from the opposition and the media to make a decision on the new fighter aircraft selection. I was also aware that Northrop, manufacturers of the F-5 had offered to license Canadair to build the CF-5 at its plant in Cartierville PQ. As previously indicated this was of major significance to the government, as it wanted the maximum benefit of any manufacturing program to accrue to the Canadian aviation industry.

Whether he knew it or not the Minister's question to me was loaded. "At this time" sounded like a scramble bell in my mind. After a sip or two of my drink I said, "Mr. Minister, perhaps if you would assure us that the F-5 will be an interim aircraft, it is possible that the selection team might be willing to entertain a compromise". He shrugged his shoulders as if to say "so what" and turned to move about in the crowd. I was left in a thoughtful mood for the remainder of the evening.

A day or so later I prepared a draft of a letter to the Minister to be signed by the CDS and presented it to the selection team at one of our a routine meetings. The team by this time was in a stand-off position with minister's staff and not a lot of conviction was accorded my draft but it was finally approved somewhat reluctantly and after a few minor changes sent off to the CDS for signature. It merely stated that should the minister agree that the aircraft selected would be considered an interim aircraft, then the team might reconsider its recommendations. To the surprise of us all, a few days later a letter was passed to us from the CDS's office signed by the Minister.

He had agreed in very short paragraph that should the F-5 be selected, it would indeed be considered an interim fighter aircraft. Future fighter aircraft acquisition would be dependent upon the finalisation of government defence policies through a coming White Paper on Defence. This ended the impasse and the team reluctantly endorsed the government's position on aircraft selection but not without winning a major concession.

During another multi-role aircraft selection process leading to the CF-18 ten years later I was asked by the project manager, General Paul Manson, if I knew of such a letter. In the selection team office I found a bank of filing cabinets that looked familiar. They hadn't been opened in several years and no one had the combinations. The service police had to be called in to cut the locks on the cabinets. Sure enough, after a bit of rummaging among the dusty old files and probably exactly where I had filed it years before, I found the Minister's letter signed by one Paul Hellyer. My letter to Paul the Prudent Pruner had come back to support yet another successful aircraft procurement program.

In 1966 however, the confusion in the headquarters was rampant. Everyone was afraid to question policy because it might be a policy of one of the other services. Airmen were working for army Lieutenant Colonels or naval commanders who had little or no understanding of the other services. Some very irrational decisions were generating ridiculous policies that had no acceptance in any of the services.

The acquisition of what was now referred to as the CF-5 had been approved by cabinet and was ready for parliamentary debate. There was little doubt that parliament would approve of the cabinet decision but to be safe the Minister asked the Director General Air Force, Air Commodore Mike Pollard, to sit with him in the House during question period. I was dispatched in civvies with my pockets full of notes to sit in the members' gallery and have ready answers to any sticky questions that might be posed by members of the opposition. It was an entertaining hour for me and I kept one young page very busy running messages down to the general who was seated in the House next to the Minister. I never did find out how useful this exercise was but the Air Commodore delighted in telling the story for several years thereafter.

Once the decision on the CF-5 aircraft had passed parliamentary approval, I turned my focus away from the big picture involving the three services to the task of introducing the CF-5 to the air element as we were inelegantly called at the time.

A conversion-training syllabus needed to be prepared for the conversion of pilots at Cold Lake. I prepared a letter to the Chairman of the Joint Chiefs of Staff of the US military forces. It was duly signed by the Chief of Defence Staff extolling my virtues as a fighter pilot and requested that I be provided with some familiarisation training with the US F-5 conversion-training unit based at Williams Air Force Base in Arizona. Throughout the USAF the base was known simply as "Willy".

Within ten days I was making the final arrangements by phone with the Commanding Officer of the Skoshi Tiger Squadron at Willy. The Skoshi Tigers had a distinguished history that had developed from the famed Flying Tigers during World War Two in the Pacific. The commanding officer, Lieutenant Colonel "Hoppy"

Hopkins had completed one tour in Vietnam and prior to that had attended the RCAF staff college in Toronto. He had an admiration for the RCAF and told me he was looking forward to meeting me on my arrival at Willy.

It was about this time that a group of Northrop representatives were in town and on hearing of my arrangements with the USAF at Willy suggested that I come to Edwards Air Force Base for a few days. They would arrange to have me checked out on the NF-5 that was the prototype for the CF-5 production aircraft at Canadair.

Off I flew to Los Angeles where I was briefed by Northrop engineers and test personnel. I was then dispatched over the mountains to Edwards AFB in a six passenger aircraft used to ferry personnel between the factory and the Northrop test establishment at Edwards.

During this visit I flew the NF-5, the Northrop prototype of the Canadian version, in all of its possible configurations. Ferry configuration, guns/rockets and bombs. I flew the flight profiles of all of the roles that the aircraft was capable of performing and basically enjoyed the life of a test pilot for a few days at Edwards.

I was airborne on one of my "test missions" when the top secret Valkyre bomber undergoing a test sequence experienced a mid-air collision with its chase aircraft over the desert. The bomber crew and the pilot of the chase aircraft were lost in this disaster. It was a sad day at Edwards and it signalled the end of a very expensive but highly controversial bomber aircraft acquisition for the USAF.

A week or two after my return to Ottawa, I was on my way back to south-western US and Willy. Many of the instructors had just returned from operational tours in Vietnam. They were beginning work-up trials to test the F-5 in the Southeast Asian War and would be flight refuelling across the Pacific in a few weeks. I suggested to the squadron commander that if he happened to be short of pilots, I would be willing to assist. A few days later I received a telephone call from someone in the Minister's office in Ottawa stating that under no circumstances was I to go anywhere near Vietnam.

I had not been confident that the USAF would even consider my participation in the Skoshi Tiger operation and was not the least surprised that senior officials in the Minister's office had reacted the way they had. The only surprise for me was that it had gone as far as it did.

A week later I received another call from the Minister's office. I seemed to be getting rather popular at a level at which I was unaccustomed. "Just a minute, the Minister would like to speak to you", I heard as I picked up the phone. The Minister came on the line and chatted amicably for a minute or so before he came to the point.

John Gellner, a defence critic, former Wing Commander in the air force and senior member of the Canadian Defence Association was coming to LA for a visit to Northrop. He was researching an article he was writing for the Canadian Defence Quarterly on the CF-5 selection and been outwardly critical of the choice. I was to get over to Los Angeles as soon as possible, meet him on his arrival and escort him wherever he went. Following his visit to Northrop, he would be going to Willy. Evidently, the staff at Willy were being notified as we spoke and arrangements would be made to host him for the day or two he was to be there.

As soon as the Minister hung up, I phoned my boss back in Ottawa to tell him what had happened, thinking that there must be some way out of this for me. There wasn't, the Minister's office had already advised my chain of command of their intentions and I became nursemaid for a visiting wallah who I looked upon as an enemy.

The base personnel at Willy were very understanding and I was dispatched in a two-seat F-5 to the Northrop factory near LA. Once there I worked out an itinerary with the Northrop folks that included a tour of the plant and then onward by company executive flight to Edwards Air Force base for a brief visit to the Northrop test facility. We would then proceed on to Williams Air Force Base to complete Mr. Gellner's tour

I met him in LA on schedule and my concerns vanished as he and I hit it off from the start. He had flown with the RAF during the war and was familiar with fighter pilot vernacular. It turned out he was highly critical of Hellyer, which delighted me, but he was also critical of the CF-5. Over several scotches, I explained to him why I thought the F-5 was a good interim aircraft and recounted my own history in the aircraft selection process. By the end of our first evening together he had mellowed his opinion considerably.

As Mr. Gellner's visit to Willy came to an end, he had become a staunch F-5 supporter while carefully cataloguing its limitations as a front line fighter and emphasising the fact that it was an interim aircraft. This would be the first time that the fact that the F-5 was an interim aircraft would be released to the public.

I was left alone for the rest of my stay at Willy. Several pilots that were assigned as instructors to the Skoshi Tiger Squadron had just returned from tours of operations in Vietnam. Most of them had witnessed the horrors of the war and were in a state akin to shellshock or in today's terms, Post Traumatic Stress Disorder. The behaviour among a number of them was unruly and they spent their time, when not flying or sleeping, in the bar. On any other occasion I would have welcomed these parties as a happy diversion from after hour boredom a long way from home. This however, represented a behaviour that I had not experienced before. It seemed that they were trying to forget some of the things they had seen and engaged in anti-social activity in defiance of some hidden or perceived evil that lay lurking within them.

One Sunday morning, I was sitting in the officers club enjoying an excellent Sunday brunch. It was the custom on the base that wives and children were invited to join in, particularly those whose husbands and fathers were serving in Vietnam. I had finished my meal and was about to depart the club to get on with rest of my day when the door burst open and two very drunk pilots, still in flight suits from the Friday flying program, staggered into the dining room. They came to a stop, arms around each other more for mutual support than anything else and surveyed the gentry before them.

Finally after a moment of silence, one of them shouted drunkenly, "Anyone want to get laid around here"? Fortunately, there were some of their squadron mates present who hustled them out of the room in short order. But the damage had been done and the brunch broke up prematurely as wives and mothers gathered their children and hurriedly left the club wondering what had happened to two otherwise nice young American pilots.

This was my first exposure to the ravages of the Vietnam War and the effect it was having on the American serviceman. I had witnessed the thin edge of the wedge and this incident was symptomatic of similar occurrences that were being played out elsewhere. As more of these occurrences became known, the Department of Defence instituted numerous rehabilitation programmes catering to over-stressed veterans returning from the war in South East Asia.

While the bar activity was trying at times, I found the flying to be exhilarating. We flew in four-plane sections and completed the whole range of air to ground tactics. At least once a day we flew air to air combat firing live guns against a drone towed by another F-5. The air to ground sorties each consisted of three events - bombs, rockets and strafing with 20mm cannon on the range. Following a routine four-plane formation take-off we took up a heading to Gila Bend. Holding over the beacon at ten thousand feet we awaited the clearance onto the range. Once cleared in we attacked our targets as a four-plane formation with sufficient intervals between aircraft to allow for safety. The air to air firing sorties were similar but at a higher altitude and involved only the 20-mm cannon.

There were two Moroccans who had been assigned by their air force for weapons training on the F-5 during the time I was there. One was an excellent young officer who enjoyed the finer things in life including the occasional social drink. His compatriot on the other hand was a very devout Muslim and denounced all worldly pleasures. There was little love lost between them to the extent that the scheduling officers had to make special provisions for them in the flying program. They were both good pilots and it was thought prudent to separate them in the formation. I became a permanent number three in the formation with one or the other of the Moroccans on my wing so that there could be no temptation for one to shoot the other down – accidentally.

Despite the international intrigue, I flew frequently with the squadron staff. On these occasions we always each dropped five dollars in the pot before the sortie. Whoever achieved the highest score during the mission would take the pot. I didn't win many with this group but I won a few. One day I was flying number two to the Squadron commander. I was getting rather frustrated because I never seemed able to beat him in the air to air event. I soon found out why.

I came off the perch a bit early on one of the attacks and could clearly see the squadron commander not too far ahead of me. It would be close but I judged that he would be off target by the time I was in a position to fire. The squadron commander closed on the target and kept closing. As I began to move the pipper in my gun sight slowly up to the target I saw the drone disintegrate behind the tow aircraft. The Styrofoam debris engulfed the leader who emerged unscathed on the other side of the debris cloud.

On return to base I went straight into the debriefing surrendering my five dollars along with the other two pilots to the superior shot. At the conclusion of the debriefing, I lingered in the photo room to go over my own gun camera film from the previous day. While my score wasn't overwhelming, I seemed to be doing everything right and in accordance with regulations, I never flew in to less than the fifteen-degree angle off the target heading. This was to provide a margin of safety for the towing aircraft.

On a whim I asked the operator to put up the squadron commanders camera film. I watched for several seconds thinking that his approach to the target was much like my own. After watching a couple more of his attack runs I realised why he had shot off more drones than anyone else on the squadron. He was ignoring the safety limitation of no less than a fifteen-degree angle off and flying his aircraft almost into the line astern position on the drone. In this position one only had to hold the aircraft steady for a second or two, pull the trigger and wham – splash one drone.

On my last night with the Skoshi Tigers we had a bit of a party at the bar. After a few beers, I confided to the squadron commander that I had found his secret. At first he tried to deny that he had taken unfair advantage until he couldn't contain himself any longer. He burst into peals of laughter and my dinner and drinks for the remainder of the evening went on the squadron commander's mess bill.

On my return to headquarters that June of 1967, the sheer confusion and lack of direction was becoming more obvious. Senior civil servants had assumed key positions at many senior staff levels. The military influence was giving way to the political prerogative. Rules and regulations, orders and directives were all being developed with political aspirations in mind. The social engineering of Canada's armed forces had begun and there was no one in uniform that came forward to resist.

Out of the blue, I was promoted. Not to Squadron Leader which I coveted, but to the rank of major which I initially found distasteful. However, the pay was the same and it was another notch upward in my career. I have to admit however, that during my frequent visits to American bases over the years, I was becoming frustrated at having to explain my rank level to airmen and NCO's in the USAF. Squadron Leader nursing sisters made as much sense as did a female Pilot Officer dietician.

In 1968 I was selected for Staff College and joyfully departed the headquarters for a welcome respite from the pressures of the desk job. I had been there for five years and probably knew more about the headquarters operation than anyone at that time. My return a few years later was an eye opener as I encountered a whole new breed of military officer serving the country behind a desk.

My new posting to Staff College was somewhat bittersweet. I had wanted to attend Staff College and was told that I would be going to the Air Force College in Toronto. To say that I was surprised and disappointed to find myself assigned to the army Staff College would have been an understatement. I called General Bill Carr who had replaced Mike Pollard as the new Director General Air Force and asked if the posting could be changed. His advice was simple, "Get on with it Thompson, it will be good for you and for the airforce".

I had no idea how many rifles there were in a rifle platoon nor could I have cared less. The first tutorial was a total pain in the ass for me as it had little to do with tactics and concentrated on the statistics of the infantry in the field, how they got there, in what numbers and with whom. Oh I learned a bit about enfilade and defilade; I learned about erdilators, a machine that turns slough water into something semi-drinkable and I suppose I learned a little about squads, platoons, companies and battalions.

All of the hierarchies of the regimental system became clear and I even began to recognise many of the regimental march-pasts.

These things were all important to the grunt on the ground, but only of passing interest to a fighter pilot travelling at over 600 knots several hundred feet above the battlefield. Fortunately, this tutorial was only of six weeks duration and somehow I managed to endure the experience to its conclusion.

The remainder of the tutorials began with armour, then artillery, the supporting corps and joint operations. Interestingly, I found that the army students in general looked upon both the navy and the air force as nothing more than a supporting corps. The air force and the naval students on the course quickly disabused them of this misunderstanding.

Toward the end of the course, studies of combined operations were interesting and revealing.

A much better understanding of army operations was invaluable to one whose combat capability rested with technology and the skills required in maximising the manoeuvrability of an agile fighter aircraft.

The big picture was becoming bigger.

CHAPTER SIXTEEN
PEDAGOGY

To this point of my life I seemed to have spent a goodly part of my flying career in operational or quasi-operational roles. I avoided any talk of a posting to Training Command for many years and as an operational pilot and a staff officer, I always felt that I had other more important things to accomplish.

There comes a time however, when no matter what you can dream up for an excuse, it no longer counts. The career manager gets to impose his will regardless of how one might complain. The career managers always seem to win in the end regardless of how many valid reasons you can come up with as to why you should be posted elsewhere.

If they can't sweet-talk you into your next posting - they will do it by cunning, intrigue or open threat. However, they are pilots in the personnel branch filling a staff job. They try their best to do what for me would be a distasteful job. They are often unfairly maligned by their clients in the field

Thus it was that I proceeded reluctantly to Moose Jaw and the training establishment I thought I had left behind for good sixteen years earlier. The thought of mingling with instructors who had never had an operational tour did not fill me with happy thoughts as I contemplated the Flying Instructors School (FIS) then located at RCAF Station Portage La Prairie.

The saving grace of this base, that the Gods and the Chief of the Air Staff forgot, was that it had a reasonably good bar. It was showing some signs of wear from the days I had passed through on my T-33 course years before but it was otherwise an oasis on the prairie.

There was a modicum of time spent in ground school initially as I learned all about pedagogy, a science heretofore unknown to me and challenged me with an initial difficulty in learning to spell it properly.

I soon got into the swing of things and began to enjoy the flying. After a year at staff college preceded by a long tour at whatever they were calling the headquarters in Ottawa at the time, I began to enjoy the life of a line pilot once again.

The flying was really no sweat but I did have to relearn the exactitudes of the flying profession that for years I had taken for granted. The instructor's demands for perfection were a bit difficult to accept after years of concentrating on weapons systems accuracy. Basic flying was a given and as long as you delivered the aircraft and its weapons systems to the right place in space at the right time, it was mission accomplished.

I soon began to realise that my flying skills were no longer subject to my own personal satisfaction but had to be exact in order to demonstrate to my future students that the demands that I would make upon them were attainable.

I began to view well disciplined flying with the zeal of a fanatic. In my operational roles, accuracy was a priority thing. If the pipper needed to be on the target, that's where it would be, if the airspeed and desired altitude were off a few knots or a couple hundred feet well - what the hell.

So it was that I began to make demands on my own flying skills that I had paid little attention to since my own early training. I sharpened up my instrument flying. If the book called for a certain speed I flew at that speed. My tolerance for altitude control was reduced to few feet either side of the planned datum. I was amazed at how accurate one could be when not distracted by other ancillary systems that drew one's attention away from precise flying. I became what I feared the most - a numbers freak.

Now I looked forward to flying accurately by the book, something I would never have admitted as an operational pilot. I took delight in flying the aircraft precisely whether with my instructor, a fellow student instructor or solo. However, if I thought that my well-honed flying skills would impress my first student, I had obviously missed something and it caused me some concern when I began my instructional role

On arrival at Moose Jaw we concentrated on settling into our assigned PMQ, registering our kids, now numbering three boys, for school and all of the usual settling-in activity the military family faces on arrival at a new base.

My familiarisation with the training mill revealed a change that occurred from my own training days. The student pilots were all commissioned officers. The old undergraduate title of Flight Cadet had been eliminated. The student pilots were now coming to us from the military colleges and from the universities, the latter known as the Reserve Officer Training Plan. They had all graduated either from Royal military College or their universities with a degree and during their summers had been exposed to various aspects of service life.

The several weeks of familiarisation in the military environment during their summers did not seem to be too well co-ordinated and their attitudes bore the unmistakable stamp of academia. Several openly voiced the opinion that they hoped they would be posted to a transport squadron after wings graduation so that they would not have to shoot at anyone.

The moral dilemma posed by the Vietnam war had been voiced in colleges and universities across North America to the point where the graduate students were developing a pacifist approach to the world about them that naturally posed a problem to those more dedicated to a military ethic. The military colleges were not immune from this attitude. It was not our intention to discourage free and open discussion among the students and we avoided confronting any dissenting views on the subject of the war.

We did however, attempt to describe by reason and example the loyalty to one's country and the dedication and duty expected of an officer in the military. In this we were reasonably successful but inevitably there were a handful that quietly objected to the basics of warfare. Of those few that managed to conceal their disagreement with military conflict, I felt confident that their attitudes tempered by their own experience and maturity as military officers later in their careers would have a modifying effect on their youthful views.

In this atmosphere my introduction into the instructor's role began. Bolstered by my new title of "Probationary, B Category Instructor" I was assigned to one of the training flights for a brief period to earn my spurs before taking over the responsibilities of a Flight Commander. I was not entirely in agreement with this move and felt it was just another attempt by the training establishment to put me in my place in the training pecking order. However, I went along with it without comment and looked forward to my first student training flight.

There were many revelations in this early stage of my instructing career and my first student's mission, Clear-Hood One, was the first. It was intended as a basic familiarisation flight for the young student pilot. In the aircrew selection process he had been exposed to previously, the student pilot had put together enough flying time on a small piston aircraft to satisfy the minimum requirements of the selection criteria. If he managed to go solo during that phase he was lucky as no successful solo check qualification was required for him to proceed to the next level of training.

The pilot aptitude tests no more than confirmed the ability of a human being to walk, talk, chew gum and wind a watch simultaneously. I have always maintained that you can probably over time, teach a monkey how to fly an aircraft, but the trick is to make him think.

My first fledgling student came to Clearhood One unsullied by any previous exposure to jet aviation. This young pupil seemed to be terrified from the time I commenced his first very elementary briefing. The air exercise was a simple, get-to-know the aircraft sortie and to have a look at the local area from the air. The students under training had all acquired a reasonable measure of flight simulator time and so were accustomed to all of the switches and controls. My young charge easily strapped himself into the cockpit and after a brief verification that everything was in order we were off.

Vaguely remembering my first famil flight in the Harvard, I put on my best casual tone and tried to put my student at ease. He was pale and apprehensive. He had difficulty answering simple questions or responding to the observations I was making as we ran through the cockpit checks together and taxied out for take-off.

In my best old boy manner, I talked him through the engine run-up and the release of brakes. I even gave him a rousing verse of "Goin' ta dance with the dolly with a hole in her stockin'" as we accelerated down the runway and became airborne. Gear and flaps up we settled into the climb. As I finished off the last verse of my old favourite, I looked across the side by side cockpit of the Tutor to check on my student.

That's when he barfed. It didn't only fill up his mask; it started to ooze out under his eyes and across the bridge of his nose. It even began to drip out between the bottom of his mask and his chest. I was crestfallen at the thought that my hearty rendition of an old song might in some way have been the cause of this trauma in my student.

As a sharp thinking brand new instructor pilot, I switched my own oxygen system to 100% and tightened my mask to shut out the smell. I had the presence of mind to suggest that if he were to remove his mask it would make for easier breathing and he might survive his ordeal from which I'm sure he thought there was no escape.

I found a barf bag in the map case beside my seat that someone had left there from a previous trip and casually handed it to him as if it were part of the training session. With his mask free of his face, his breathing began to improve and he attempted to mop up the mess with the barf bag. In doing so he only succeeded in spreading the mess about. In a panic, I shouted, "don't touch a thing, don't move" and proceeded back into the landing pattern for quick touchdown and return to the ramp.

The ground crew had little sympathy as the canopy opened to reveal the odorous mess and as was the custom, my first student was left to shamefacedly clean up the cockpit he had defiled minutes before.

I was dejected. What had I done to terrify this nice young man to the point of extreme sickness? He would probably ask for an instructor change and I would be left to explain my actions to those senior and aloof members of the training establishment.

Still, I could not shirk the responsibility to finish off what I had started. As I was finishing my post-landing coffee, my young puke came into the flight room looking refreshed. He walked over to where I was sitting and looked at me expectantly. As he began to apologise, I became concerned that he would embarrass himself in front of his fellow students and I invited him into one of the debriefing cubicles.

I sensed immediately that he was more upset with himself than was I and we proceeded to chat amicably about flying in general. After a time I asked all of the usual questions, had he suffered any kind of motion sickness previously, was he feeling the symptoms of the flu or a cold, when had he last eaten? He was adamant in disclaiming the first two or three questions. However, the final question revealed at least part of the problem.

Thinking he would not be flying the next day he had a quaffed few beers with his course mates the night before. Nothing out of the ordinary but he had been slow to rise in the morning and had missed breakfast. He was not aware of the change in schedule that included him on the flying roster until he reached the flight line. The realisation that he would be flying with an ugly old fighter pilot had filled him with trepidation that wouldn't go away.

What was left of the previous night's dinner gave in to the stress of his first flight and had ruined his introduction to pilothood. We went on to discuss the attributes of the Tutor aircraft and flying in general and I terminated the debriefing by suggesting that he would be scheduled again the following morning and that he should be sure to have a good breakfast before heading for the flight line. I wrote up the lesson report as an aborted training mission and left it at that.

The next day my young puke turned up well fed and eager to repeat his first lesson. I figured that he had probably been briefed enough on the basics of Clear-hood One and invited him to brief me on the mission. This he accomplished easily with a flare and candour unusual in such a junior officer and I was pleased that he had at least fulfilled a small part of the flying experience. After wheels up, we would find the proof in the puddin'.

Clear-hood One was accomplished in fine style. Puke had completed the start-up procedure himself; he handled the radios with ease and ran through the checks to the letter as we taxied out to the runway. His take-off while a bit shaky, was accomplished without assistance from me and I thought I could even hear a bit of "Goin' ta dance with the dolly" as we settled into the climb.

Puke finished his flying training at the top of his class. We soon forgot his embarrassing start and maintained a friendly relationship through to his graduation. Last I heard he had become an F-18 pilot of some distinction.

There was an inordinate number of what we called pipeline instructors at the school. The "pipeliners", following their own wings graduation as newly trained pilots were posted back into the training mill as instructors.

They were good and because the Tutor was the only aircraft most of them had ever flown, they knew the aircraft and systems inside out; they flew the numbers more accurately than I was capable of doing when I first arrived at FIS. They were not much older than their students and that factor made it difficult for some of them to establish an easy instructor/student relationship. They didn't have role models and it was often difficult for them to relate to their older instructor peers who had previous operational experience. They were numbers orientated and had difficulty assessing student potential.

Formation flying was an outstanding example. Their training had provided them with the rudiments of the art but insufficient time was spent in fully developing their skills. Their course mates who had gone on to fighter aircraft developed their formation flying skills very quickly by comparison. It simply formed a major part of their advanced operational training.

The pipeline instructor pilot, with all of his fine attributes was, during his first year as an instructor, nothing more than a student level formation pilot and he was expected to impart this skill to his students. To sit in the instructor's seat and watch a student pilot wrestle with joining up in formation and then to perform effective station keeping was often more than one could expect from the green pipeline instructor. If he wasn't close to the controls, he was on them, causing his student to lose confidence in himself. Knowing when to take over control and when to let things go was paramount in teaching formation flying and one could only become proficient in this art through constant practice.

This also applied to other aspects of flying and the pipeline instructors, as good as they were, had difficulty differentiating the fine line between letting the student make the errors that facilitated the learning process and avoiding an unsafe situation before it became disastrous.

I was one of four or five old sweats that had been posted into the training system at around the same time. It wasn't long before we all recognised this situation as a problem and as we assumed our own supervisory positions at the school, we began to encourage formation flying among the instructors.

The old sweats slowly but surely led the younger pipeline pilots through increasingly difficult formation manoeuvres. Staff formation-flying practice became a regularly scheduled event. The standard of formation flying on the base became more refined and the standard of instruction improved immeasurably. The spin-off of this process to other areas of clear-hood and instrument instruction was a natural follow up.

The pipeline pilot, we soon discovered, had been treated as some sort of an elite persona who, because of his knowledge of the aircraft, its systems and his ability to fly the numbers accurately, became the young God of the training system. Some of the younger pipeline instructors resented what they thought of as our cavalier approach to flying instruction. They were supported by some of their older, more senior peers who had spent their entire careers in the training mill.

The training atmosphere had over the years become incestuous and we, the operationally experienced newcomers, were in danger of being labelled as aged, has been fighter pilots. Led by a base commander, who held little patience for prima donnas, the atmosphere began to change.

It wasn't long before the old guys took over the ground school and its syllabus. Changes were made to training systems and techniques were updated. The flight line failure rate began to diminish as the troubled student was subjected to additional check rides with his flight commander before a dreaded standards check was imposed.

Standards squadron now commanded by older pilots with a wider range of experience in all aspects of airforce operational flying let it be known that a student achieving a pass on a standards squadron cease training check would bring his instructor's qualifications under scrutiny. Flight commanders began to monitor and supervise their instructors more closely. Instructors for their part began to look at their students in a more positive light. They looked for and encouraged the good characteristics in their students. They devoted their time and energy toward assisting in correcting faults and inspiring their students to higher levels of performance.

No longer was flying by numbers a major prerequisite for the young fledgling pilot. The importance of flying accurately was still stressed but more emphasis was placed on the ability of the pilot to think his way through an in-flight exercise. Instructors began to search for the potential in their charges rather than just demand that they meet some arbitrary criteria.

As student/instructor relationships improved, so did the relationships between the old sweat and the pipeline instructor. The pipeliner began to see that he could learn from those with operational experience and the whole training atmosphere improved for everyone.

The flight commanders took on a new role, as they became the front line recruiters for the career managers when looking for junior pilots from the instructor ranks to fill operational cockpits. Lieutenant A shows an aptitude to be a good helicopter pilot, Lieutenant B displays the potential to make an exceptional transport pilot and so on. There were now people making recommendations based not only on the skills of their staff but also on their own experience and background in other operational roles. The whole armed forces pilot cadre was the better for it as the graduating pilot standards improved as well as those of the pipeline instructors.

The old sweats all had various pet sequences, manoeuvres or patterns that they would pass on to their students. I used to preach endlessly to my students and younger instructors alike that the designers had made most aircraft idiot proof. A good pilot should understand completely the capabilities and the limitations of any aircraft he flew. The aircraft could be flown safely to the edges of the flight envelope and the professional pilot would find those edges and explore them.

One of my favourite teaching manoeuvres was an upward spin. I had one young student who was very uneasy accomplishing a normal spin sequence. His entry was slow and cautious and he always tried to recover before the spin had fully developed. His other flying was all at or above an acceptable standard and so I spent a considerable amount of time practising spins with him during our clear-hood lesson plans.

We weren't making a lot of progress until one day I took control and flew along straight and level for few minutes while the student regained his composure. I was running out of the patience that I had been preaching to my instructors for some time now and decided that perhaps some drastic action was needed.

I performed a spin entry from straight and level flight allowing the airspeed to bleed off at a constant altitude. I provided a running narrative of my every move as we went through the manoeuvre.

"Throttle back to idle, maintaining altitude, airspeed decreasing, keep the back pressure on the stick, airspeed one-twenty, one ten, one hundred, stick full back into your gut, full right rudder, the nose comes up and swings to the right. Once settled into the spin the aircraft becomes stable, neutralise the control column, full opposite rudder and as the aircraft straightens out you allow the speed to build up and recover from the ensuing dive".

We did several of these entering at different altitudes and attitudes. Finally, as a last resort I explained that you could enter a spin from any attitude and as I was explaining this, I pulled the nose up so that we were climbing vertically. As I throttled back the airspeed decreased rapidly and I began my casual spin entry monologue.

The airspeed was falling through one hundred and fifteen knots when I entered the spin and after a few turns I told the student to complete the recovery. He had been introduced to another dimension of flying and had no trouble with spins from that point on.

It mattered little that my student had finally achieved a level of confidence in spins as some overly cautious wag at headquarters had decided that student solo spinning was to be prohibited. Thus another student pilot confidence builder was arbitrarily eliminated.

There had been a fatal accident near the base a few months before where an aircraft had inadvertently entered a low altitude spin and failed to recover. The student ejected successfully but the instructor was killed in the crash. There was no mechanical failure that would indicate any reason for the mishap. However, it was known that the instructor who lost his life was nervous about spins and very likely panicked during his recovery attempts.

I made a point of suggesting to the more proficient students, that if they were to enter a spin during some of their solo practices they should keep it to themselves.

If it helped a student pilot understand and experience a minor flying complexity that could enhance his future career as a pilot then it was worthwhile. I will always wonder if this young man who learned a valuable lesson from those circumstances ever taught his own students how to do an upward spin.

I had one other surprising experience flying the Tutor. During the massive restructuring of Training Command in the early 1970s, the FIS had been moved to Moose Jaw and placed under Training Standards Squadron. Since Moose Jaw had become the primary basic pilot training establishment for the forces, this made a lot of sense.

Contrary to criticism from some quarters, standards of pilot instruction did not falter but actually improved in many significant ways. Efficiency of air training operations was achieved as both students and instructor students could share the same facilities through judicious scheduling of ground school courses, simulator training and of course a combined pool of aircraft on the flight line.

I was doing a formation checkout on one of the instructor trainee's one day. We had completed our turn as the leader of the two-plane formation and took our place in a comfortable echelon starboard number two position. After several steep turns in each direction we began as agreed during the briefing to increase the level of difficulty and began to execute a series of high wing-overs.

We had successfully completed a couple of these manoeuvres and as we pulled up for the next in the series I noticed that our airspeed was a bit lower than previous entry speeds. Never mind I thought and as our angle of climb became steeper, I quietly suggested to the student instructor that he move out a "titch" in case we had a problem. With the airspeed now passing downward through ninety knots, he managed to provide a more comfortable half wing-span of space between ourselves and the leader.

Sitting out in a more relaxing position on the leader, I watched as the nose of the two aircraft reached apogee. In a few seconds we would be starting the downward shift as gravity would begin to take effect on our formation. Suddenly, the nose of our aircraft pitched violently upward, the aircraft flicked to the right and we sailed well out of the formation and out of harm's way.

My student instructor was yelling that he had lost control of the aircraft and I took control immediately. In the process I realised that we had entered an inverted spin. Now the Tutor doesn't do inverted spins. I told all that would listen that the designer wouldn't let that happen and yet here I was.

The whole silly episode was over in seconds as the aircraft performed its surprise, inverted spin through about two revolutions and then snapped upright. Normal spin recovery action was applied and we were out of it.

What had caused this stable, reliable little aircraft to spin inverted? I really don't know and I never did find out. Our airspeed was too low for the wing-over manoeuvre in formation but nothing serious. Our attitude was a tad high at the top. Nothing terribly wrong here either. I didn't have my hand on the control column so I don't know if the student instructor had put too much forward pressure on the stick while trying to maintain formation.

I think in the final analysis it was a combination of a number of factors. My student instructor was coming back to the training system from an operational tour on fighter aircraft. Neither one of us had experienced an inadvertent inverted spin in the Tutor or any other aircraft before. But it did remind us that there is no room for complacency in the cockpit. Yes, the designer can make the aircraft as idiot proof as it is within the capacity of technology to accomplish. But he can't fly the aircraft for the pilot.

This was a corner of the Tutor flight envelope that I had not previously explored and it re-enforced my contention that the successful, professional pilot should be aware of all of the edges of the flight envelope even when admiring his more straightforward manoeuvres.

The proof that you can teach an old dog new tricks is ever present in aviation and during my tour at Moose Jaw, I was to experience yet another challenge to my own preconceived ideas.

211
CHAPTER SEVENTEEN
THE SNOWBIRDS – A CANADIAN ICON

I feel very fortunate to have been associated with the early development of Canada's world famous Snowbirds, the official aerobatic team of the Canadian Forces. At the time though, the idea of supporting a full time dedicated aerobatic team provided me with an ethical dilemma. It was about mid-way through my tour at Moose Jaw that I was forced to confront a philosophical problem that had troubled me for several years.

In early 1964 I had been stationed at Air Force Headquarters in Ottawa for about six months. I was bewildered with the duties of a staff officer and unsure of what was expected of me but somehow I was maintaining a small sense of usefulness even though my confidence level was low.

It was at about this time that the policy of the Golden Hawks, the RCAF formation aerobatic team came up for review. The "Hawks" had been performing internationally for years and were favourites throughout the North American airshow circuit. There was a strong lobby around the headquarters advocating their disbandment.

As a former formation aerobatic pilot while on exchange with the RAF, my opinion was sought out and initially given some weight. In my final report as an exchange officer, I was critical of the use of a front line fighter for the purpose of performing circus shows for the public and felt that it was a very expensive way to drum up public relations for the service.

To suggest that I did not enjoy my participation in the RAF Firebirds would be an excessive distortion. I did enjoy the aerobatic flying that I would probably never have encountered elsewhere. I look on that period of my flying career as one of the best experiences that a pilot could add to his resume and I was proud of the performance of the team and the esteem with which we were held by the British public.

The military calling is a learning process and I had come to the headquarters as a single-minded fighter pilot. I had performed most fighter roles successfully to this point in my career. But now I was expected to apply my field training and experience to the complexities inherent in performing a meaningful staff function. I had in the past taken delight in referring to the officers at the headquarters as idiots and now I was one of them.

To be honest with myself and with the service, I realised that I had to confront some of the basic philosophies that I had formed in the field. Yes, my operational experience was a valuable asset in the headquarters but many of the opinions that I had formed over the years had to be put into perspective.

During my formation flying experience with the RAF we had used the Lightning Mark IA for our twelve-plane formation team on #56 Squadron and we had developed some intriguing statistics. Each of our aircraft was equipped with a recording accelerometer. These instruments, following decoding with the appropriate measuring equipment, calculated the percentage of the projected airframe life each aircraft consumed at any given time.

As we began our aerobatic work-up in the spring of 1963, the average of the theoretical life consumed by our squadron aircraft over a two-year period of operational use was just seven percent. Despite the high altitude and high Mach numbers imposed by the intercept role and despite the normal formation flying during training and during our in-flight refuelling trials, we had used only a small portion of the possible life of the aircraft. At the rate of usage in this role, our aircraft could be expected to remain in service for another ten or twelve years.

It was surprising to us all that at the end of our airshow year we had consumed over half the life of the aircraft in just a few short months of low-level formation aerobatics. Had we remained as a formation aerobatic team we would have expended the entire life projection of our aircraft by the end of another aerobatic season. In retrospect, it should not have come as a surprise since formation aerobatics are conducted at low level and under almost continuous accelerations imposed on the airframe. High G, high speed and low level is the combination that when combined tend to limit the useful life span of an aircraft.

It was with this background that I began to reassess my own support of aerobatic teams for purely public relations considerations. The cost was too high, the employment of the combat ready fighter pilot, while an excellent formation aerobatic candidate was, in my mind, a waste of valuable manpower.

It had become extremely difficult for me personally to justify the expenditure of front line operational assets in what appeared to me to be a frivolous use of resources. I had spoken out against aerobatic teams for all of these reasons and in particular, the use of an operational fighter aircraft in the PR role.

I felt it was a huge waste and I came to the conclusion that the Golden Hawks could be disbanded without any effect on air operations. But to speak out against the "Hawks" was a sacrilege in fighter pilot circles and as I had never served in an operational role on the F-86, my opinion tended to be minimised.

It might have been easy to maintain the Golden Hawks for several more years as the aircraft was being phased out of its operational role to make way for the CF-104. But the weight of opinion had gone in favour of those who opposed the use of operational aircraft for such purposes and the decision was made to disband the team.

In rationalising my Lightning formation aerobatic experience, I later came to a vitally different viewpoint.

My RAF squadron was equipped with the Mark 1A and all of the aircraft on our squadron inventory were referred to by the factory and others in the engineering world as the development batch. While we were busy performing aerobatics, other RAF squadrons were taking delivery of the newer Mark II Lightning with longer range and enhanced combat weapons systems. These squadrons were being added to the NATO ORBAT as the crews achieved combat ready status.

In retrospect, the RAF planners could see the Lightning Mark 1A with all of its speed and altitude capability was nearing the end of its useful life and would soon be retired.

As described previously in this memoir, there were rumours that a Russian aerobatic team equipped with the Mig 21; a supersonic fighter was preparing for a Paris Air Show entry in 1963. This offered the RAF a unique opportunity to use the aircraft as a propaganda weapon in the on-going battle of the Cold War. The Lightning IA would be retired in a couple of years due to technical obsolescence in any event and it provided an opportunity to exploit its final days. All of these factors had conspired to justify the formation of a Mach 2 capable aerobatic team for display at the 1963 Paris Air Show.

The excellent public relations achieved by the RAF that year were quite extraordinary. As the Paris Air Show neared, the exploits of the Firebirds had become well known in the UK and a few weeks before the show we heard that the Russian team had withdrawn their entry. We became the only high performance entry to the Paris Air Show 1963.

Now, during the first year of my posting to Moose Jaw I was to be confronted once again with the same self-struggle I thought I had put behind me during my earlier tour in Ottawa.

I had observed, almost from the time of my arrival at Moose Jaw, that the level of formation flying proficiency among the junior instructors on the flight line was very low. While meeting the basic standards in the training environment, they were clearly below an operational combat ready standard. These observations were reinforced in discussions with other senior pilots and we set out to raise the bar among our instructors.

We had considerable help in this undertaking, as there was an infusion of operational pilots who were returning to the training system following operational tours elsewhere. They were not necessarily happy about their transfers into the instructor role. But when they saw the emphasis that the senior line instructors were placing on an enhanced more practical model of instruction, they became more comfortable in the role and began to contribute positively.

The Tutor aircraft, designed and manufactured by Canadair in Montreal, had proven itself to be ideal pilot trainer. It had a small but robust jet engine that produced around 2700 pounds of thrust and allowed the aircraft to fly at altitudes up to forty thousand feet at Mach .75. It was designed as a sub-sonic trainer with strong durable airframe ideally suited to the low to the medium altitude pilot training role.

The side-by-side seating afforded the instructor the ability to observe the performance of his student often enabling him to avoid errors before they became critical. Of primary importance, the Tutor was easy to service and maintain compared to all other similar aircraft on inventory.

Our efforts to improve the level of formation flying proficiency began slowly at first by initiating more four-plane formation flying than most of the more junior pipeline instructors had ever experienced. In the spring each year, requests came in from all parts of the prairies and the Northwest US requesting fly-pasts at airshows, sports days, exhibitions and other community events large and small. They were all given due consideration and if they could be accommodated, we would oblige by sending a four-plane formation for a fly-past.

At no time was our formation flying allowed to interfere with the student-training program. The instructors practised in the evenings and on weekends after fulfilling the requirements of their primary assignments.

There were several of the former Golden Centennaire aircraft on the base inventory. They had been painted with a protective white coating after their golden livery had been stripped clean. The white lacquer was applied to prevent metal corrosion after the gold paint had been removed. They were unique aircraft and could be seen clearly from a distance. Their distinctive white colour was pleasing to the eye and the demand for their participation in air-show events around the country began to increase. In due course the paint scheme would be refined to the familiar livery that later came to be immediately recognisable throughout North America.

Most of the line instructors had now become eager volunteers, gladly giving up their summer weekends to participate in some fete, show or exhibition anywhere from Winnipeg to Vancouver, the northern states and occasionally North of Sixty. Often Moose Jaw would provide two or three separate four-plane formations to satisfy the multiple requests coming from across the continental Northwest.

In my first year at Moose Jaw there was little mention of an aerobatic team. Formation aerobatics were against flying regulations other than for officially sanctioned teams and therefore our manoeuvres were generally restricted to high wing-overs and formation low passes.

The second year saw a maturing of the formation proficiency that we had begun to build on the year before. Community requests increased significantly and we began to practice mild formation aerobatics out in the practice area. The level of expertise increased dramatically and while there were no select or identifiable formation aerobatic team members, the pool of qualified, willing pilots began to stabilise at larger numbers than we would need to form a team.

So it was that in 1970 Colonel "OB" Philp announced to his senior staff that it was his intention to form a national aerobatic team using the Tutor aircraft. He went on to inform us that he was seeking and expected approval by Training Command and NDHQ.

Up to this point I had been justifying the emphasis we had been placing on formation flying with the belief that we had improved the capabilities of our instructor pilots in advanced formation flying in a major way. We had established a basis that ensured a better quality of airforce pilot. The young instructor would be provided with a higher level of self-confidence when transferred into an operational role.

The Tutor basic flying training aircraft had proven itself to be highly capable of performing economically in the airshow role during Canada's centennial year. It was inexpensive, easy to maintain away from home base and took up much less airspace on the air show stage than the F-86. It was said that the aircraft was a mini-F-86 since many of its cockpit controls were the same as those to be found in the older aircraft and the key speeds for most manoeuvres were just better than half those of the former Golden Hawks aircraft. Aerodynamic stresses on the airframe did not significantly threaten the life of the aircraft to the same extent it posed for a high performance fighter aircraft.

Furthermore, the Tutor had one other distinct advantage. It had two seats. Team members flew solo during practices and performances, but there was a seat available during transit to and from air show venues. The team could carry its own supporting ground crew and the selection of these very important members of the team became a serious issue. Ground crew candidates were expected to be professional jacks of all trades. They had to be cross-trained and qualified in two or more trades before their applications were given consideration by the selection board.

Many of the same attributes that applied to the pilot selection criteria also applied to the ground crew. Self-discipline, flexibility, knowledge and aptitude in several trades were all prime prerequisites. Innovative ability, good character and the capacity to perform assigned duties in a manner that would bring credit to the service were critical measures in the selection process. This process had a positive impact on the recruitment of ground crew and brought another dimension to the justification for a specialised aerobatic team.

Any concerns that I still harboured about wasted resources evaporated when we were presented with an analysis on the cost of advertising during the years where we had an official aerobatic team compared to those without. While the cost figures were nearly identical, the public awareness of the military tended to tail off seriously in the years where no official aerobatic team performed. Recruiting figures decreased and attendance at air force day and other military events declined.

After a lot of soul searching over the course of the previous six or seven years, I had finally come to the conclusion that an official formation aerobatic team provided an opportunity for the air force to demonstrate its capabilities. But more than that, I began to look at it as a basic PR requirement. A means to keep the Canadian military front and centre before the public at a relatively modest cost. The use of a small, low cost trainer aircraft flown by former operational pilots was a primary consideration.

All of these factors were discussed between Colonel Philp and our group of three majors who were motivated to participate. Major's Glen Younghusband, Bing Peart and myself formed the initial training cadre. We were joined a month or two later by Lieutenant Colonel Tommy Reid, our newly appointed Base Operations Officer. It would be his task to perform the duties of team manager providing administrative and logistic support.

During the winter of 1970/71, Colonel Philp intensified his lobby of both Training Command and National Defence Headquarters for the formation of a Tutor team. In early 1971 approval was received to form a formation display team with certain limitations. Formation rolls and loops were prohibited but a high wingover was acceptable. Of course formation changes on stage were always crowd pleasers and were allowed.

We enthusiastically entered a new formation year. Bing Peart had been transferred and it left Tom Reid, Glen Younghusband and myself to begin screening our instructor pilots for selection to the team. After several weeks of intensive formation flying, we had identified a number of pilots who we felt were suitable for team participation.

Restricted as we were from performing full aerobatic manoeuvres we had to carefully craft our advanced formation training syllabus. We developed sequences that included loops and roles performed in the practice area so that our pilots would experience the variables encountered during formation aerobatics. Our initial pilot selection proved to be insightful and we even managed to bring along a couple of spares that could quickly replace those that for whatever reason might drop out of the early training.

It was another of the events of my flying career that I had enjoyed immensely. Perhaps as much as actually being on the airshow circuit. Monitoring a good formation pilot who had not flown formation aerobatics before was both challenging and enlightening. All pilots, particularly fighter pilots, have their own notion of what cockpit management is all about. They all do things in much the same way and even though their flying proficiency meets the same high standard, the manner in which they go about their business in the cockpit varies from pilot to pilot.

Some of the techniques I had developed in the training of student pilots had to be put aside as I became a coach for an experienced pilot who wanted to take his skills to another level. Instead of demonstrating and then talking the student pilot through each manoeuvre, it became my task to brief clearly and describe the sequence or manoeuvre beforehand and then watch as the pilot completed the task in the air. Rarely did I have to take control or offer advice during a manoeuvre and I basically provided a debriefing consisting of constructive criticism and advice as required. When errors became evident most pilots would ask for my assessment of what had gone wrong and how best to correct it.

The formation aerobatic pilot must be smooth to accommodate the wingman that may be close to the edge of his flight envelope on the outer positions in the formation. He cannot afford to manoeuvre his aircraft roughly without endangering others. And he cannot devote his full attention one aircraft in the formation. He must continually appraise the motion in the rest of the formation, anticipate and recognise relative situations as they are developing. It is too late for analysis after an event has occurred.

Formation aerobatics is the supreme test of a fighter pilot's skills. He must be able to read where the formation is and where it is going. He has to be prepared for the aerodynamic changes that affect the pressure on his controls as speeds and altitudes change. Above all he must be very much aware of those that are flying on his wing and behind him. One unexpected move can throw a wingman out of the formation, sometimes with dire consequences. All of this a pilot must do while flying his aircraft at speeds of between one hundred and four hundred knots maintaining his position a few feet away from other aircraft in the formation.

These were all observations that I could make from the perspective of an ageing formation pilot. Like an older hockey player, I could do the job and do it in spades but the fire was beginning to flicker and it was time to pass the glory to others.

I thoroughly enjoyed the team work-up phase and assisting in the training of replacements as members of the team were posted on to other duties. This was a procedure we had established at the start. There would be a planned turnover of fifty percent of the team members each year. Once established this allowed each of the pilots a two year tour with the team and ensured a continuous infusion of new blood each year.

In February 1971 Major Glen Younghusband was selected as the leader of the demonstration team and final selection trials from among the instructor staff commenced. I had known Glen for several years as we had served together at National Defence Headquarters in Ottawa during the early days of integration. We had attended Staff College together and had both been posted to Moose Jaw on graduation.

Glen hailed from Summerland, BC and had extensive experience on the F-86 and CF 104 aircraft earlier in his career. He was a smooth pilot with a steady hand. He had a very responsible approach to flying operations in general and formation aerobatic flying in particular. Blessed with a broad yet subtle sense of humour, he was an ideal leader to begin the process of forming a Canadian air force aerobatic team second to none.

The official approval had been granted for the formation of a demonstration team. Our foot was in the door. It would be up to us to prove that we had a team not only capable of performing before the public but one that would be a credit to the armed forces and an inspiration to Canadians everywhere.

Once the team members had been selected, there began an even more intense training period where, with final adjustments to the choreography, we were getting very close to a professional twenty-minute presentation before the public. In the first year, many of the high wing-overs looked very much a like a loop and a "nudge-nudge, wink-wink" attitude was taken if during a public performance Glen managed to take his wing-over too close to the vertical.

By the early spring the team members had been selected and intensive practice of what had become a full time display team was well underway. Saskatchewan folk living in close proximity to Mossbank in the Southwest of the province can justifiably claim ownership of the team. They suffered through the initial work-ups over the old abandoned airfield at Mossbank. They watched as the team perfected their manoeuvres and tried out new sequences. Farmers on their tractors, in their hay fields and tending their stock were treated to a daily display of the Moose Jaw formation aerobatic team as it blossomed into a team with the potential for World-Class status.

By the late spring of 1971 it was time to move the show to centre stage. The team practised at Mossbank during the day and in the evening after normal day time pilot training operations ceased, they performed over the base before the critical eye of their peers and their wives and sweethearts. At this stage, my role was relegated to observing the performance from the ground and offering constructive criticism as required.

Occasionally, I would be called upon to check-ride a pilot who was experiencing difficulty. Even this role became obsolete as the team quickly matured and began to set and maintain its own very high standards.

The Moose Jaw Air Display Team was ready but – it needed a name. It was the leader, Glen Younghusband, who suggested that the search for a suitable name be assigned to the school children on the base.

Principals and teachers alike enthusiastically embraced the task. Rules were developed and a full-scale contest among the school students commenced. There was a deluge of entries and the task of judging had been assigned to a committee composed of school teachers, one or two of the team pilots and other base personnel. The base commander reserved the position of chairman and final arbiter for himself.

The annual spring migration northward of the snow geese was still vivid in everyone's mind. Local radio and television stations had been featuring Anne Murray's wonderful version of "Snowbird" for several weeks and it was at the top of the charts.

Strangely, only one entry of Snowbirds was submitted. Twelve-year old Douglas Farmer, the Base Chaplain's son, proposed the winning selection and "The Snowbirds" became a household name. On the thirtieth anniversary of the formation of the Snowbirds, Doug was rewarded with a trip with the famed team. In his words, "An event I will never forget".

In 1972 however, the Snowbirds were beginning to find their foothold on the national stage. During one of the early shows at CFB

Trenton in Ontario, the team suffered its first fatality.

A co-ordinated routine had been developed for the two soloists. Their sequence was fairly simple but involved the two aircraft approaching one another head-on, passing each other at stage centre. It was a breathtaking sight for the crowd and was, when performed properly, a very safe manoeuvre.

One of the soloists was designated as the lead aircraft for the pass and flew a steady course down the air-show centre line. The second aircraft, approaching from the opposite direction, judged the passing distance and provided a spacing of several wingspans between himself and the lead aircraft. The profile of the two aircraft passing each other head-on at high speed was a crowd thriller, as the aircraft always appeared much closer together than they were in reality.

On this day however, altitude, aircraft speed and an adverse wind were all variables that the pilot of the second aircraft had to take into consideration as the two aircraft approached centre stage at a closing speed of up to eight hundred miles per hour.

Unfortunately, the strong unpredicted crosswind provided the second soloist with a situation that would have been difficult for any pilot to judge and the two aircraft came into contact head-on, wing-tip to wing-tip. One aircraft survived the collision and returned for a safe landing, but Flying Officer Lloyd Waterer, age twenty-six, lost his life as his crippled aircraft impacted the ground.

This marked the first Snowbird fatality for the team. Because it was in their first year, it was natural that those opposed to formation aerobatics attempted to use this sad event as justification for discontinuing the team.

Following a great deal of debate throughout various military echelons, it was decided to allow the team to continue. The cause factor influencing the accident was human error in that the pilot had misjudged the wind velocity of the crosswind and allowed his aircraft too little room for the successful completion of the manoeuvre.

Fatalities are always a calamitous and sombre event in any dynamic profession but flying accidents during air displays are among the most spectacular. It is well known that a significant number of people attending air shows do so with the morbid expectation that they might witness a sensational crash.

Yet the pilots themselves do not harbour fear while performing. The fear for them exists in the unknown. Their training is intense, their pre-mission briefings are detailed, their self-confidence is well developed during their training and their confidence in each other is honed through practice. There is little left to chance.

But no matter how well prepared one might be getting into a car - no matter how closely the rules of the road are followed, it cannot be said with all certainty that an accident will not occur on the way to the supermarket. The potential can be minimised but never eliminated.

Regardless of advances in technology and the adoption of strict safety standards, the unpredictable will challenge man in all of his undertakings. A fraction of a millisecond can mean several hundred feet at very high speeds and occasionally all of the negative factors combine to cause grief.

It doesn't mean that you no longer drive your car to the store following an accident no more than it means that flying stops because an accident has occurred. For most pilots, an accident means a search for the cause. Once the cause is identified, then steps are taken to minimise a recurrence of a similar accident. I don't know of any career pilots who have hung up their spurs because of a flying accident.

The Snowbirds finished off the air show season that year without further incident and they had established themselves as the premier Canadian formation aerobatic team with an international stature.

Prior to their 1972 season, the Snowbirds were given approval to fly a fully aerobatic air show. They were no longer a demonstration team, they were a recognised Canadian formation aerobatic team already renowned throughout Canada and parts of the USA even at this early stage of their existence.

As they matured as a seasoned team they began to express their self-confidence in many different ways. They adopted the same civilian dress patterns, they attended social functions together and for all intents and purposes they acted as one.

This is not unusual in formation aerobatic teams and sometimes it can be taken to extremes.

An example of how another North American aerobatic team got carried away with themselves was exemplified toward the end of the second season for the Snowbirds. The "Birds" were sharing the stage with a US Air Force team of some renown. This team decided to take formation manoeuvring to extremes by doing everything simultaneously. This included the taxi out, which was common for all teams. Simultaneous start-up and when ready to taxi all aircraft in the formation lowered their canopies and left the line as one and with a simultaneous turn onto the taxi way they proceeded out to the runway in close line astern.

This US team however, took the procedure further and had developed a formation entry back into the flight line following their performance. They returned to their parking area in a close formation and simultaneously turned into their parking spots together. They then shut down on command from the leader; opened their canopies also on command and dismounted their aircraft as one. In unison they marched out twenty paces or so in front of their aircraft, snapped to attention and saluted their leader as he took the compliment some distance out in front of the whole performance.

Not only was this phase of their performance lost on the general public, it became a focus of good-natured but pointed humour among the other performers and technicians who had to witness this spectacle after each air show.

On the final day of the Abbottsford Air Show 1973 the Snowbirds performed an act of one-up-man ship that endeared them to their fellow airmen. As they taxied in from one of their better performances of the season, they duplicated the shut down and dismounting procedure adopted by their US counterparts.

Following their dismount and the march twenty paces out in front of their aircraft, each team member stood smartly at attention as the Leader, Major Glen Younghusband marched briskly down the line. He stopped in front of each of his pilots and exchanged crisp salutes. The leader then planted of a kiss on each cheek of his pilots in turn. This formal exchange complete they were dismissed with military precision.

Needless to say, leaders of teams performing in air shows in Canada and elsewhere in North America from that time onward took a more temperate approach to their flight line discipline.

In the years following their 1971 debut, the Snowbirds have been featured in either the opening or closing roles for air shows throughout North America. They have joined a very exclusive and elite group of international air show performers that are at the pinnacle of their profession. The fellowship and camaraderie that they share with their opposite numbers in other air forces is a testament to their success in the highly competitive air show circuit of today.

The Snowbirds have become a Canadian icon. They owe their hallowed place in aviation history to the skill and dedication of several generations of Canadian pilots who have performed so effectively and publicly for their country.

CHAPTER EIGHTEEN
THE DESK JOB REVISITED

During the years spent in my last desk job between 1963 and 1968, I had always felt that I was in an interlude between flying tours. Now in the spring of 1974 as I re-read my posting message, I realised that my flying career was nearing an end.

I had been considered for a tour on the CF 101 aircraft on one or another of the eastern squadrons but in the end, my revised posting message read NDHQ - Directorate of Flight Safety. I had never been a qualified flight safety officer and I wondered why I was being thrust into this new world.

As it turned out, I had been placed in a holding pattern. My promotion to lieutenant colonel was on the horizon and the personnel folks were waiting to make it official. Unfortunately, I was by-passed on the first round as the promotion board reached well below me on the promotion list to satisfy their francophone quota and hence the holding pattern.

Naturally, I was disappointed and somewhat frustrated by the delay but in true air force fashion, I accepted things as they were. I happily took the flight safety officer's course in Trenton and returned to Ottawa ready to take on the world of flight safety. I had known Colonel Joe Shultz for some years and was pleased to be working for him in his directorate. He wasn't too sure what to do with me but had agreed to take me on board temporarily as the career managers did their thing.

The flight safety world is a very closed organisation within the headquarters. It has everything to do with flying operations and little to do with military strategies or tactics. If there was an aircraft involved, flight safety was involved. It quite rightly, maintained a lofty distance from vehicle or ship safety and industrial safety was only considered in an aviation context. I found that as a generalist, I had little to contribute and Joe Shultz tried his best to keep me gainfully employed by dispatching me on tours to military flying installations around the country doing various studies and surveys.

Eventually, I was posted to Fort Fumble by the Rideau, a name I had christened National Defence Headquarters well before my departure to staff college in 1968. At that time NDHQ consisted of three very large "H" shaped temporary buildings that had been constructed in the late 1930s as war loomed on the eastern horizon. They were located on the corner of Elgin and Laurier otherwise known as Cartier Square. Apart from the occasional coat of paint, the buildings had remained unchanged until they were torn down in the seventies.

In the mid 1970s the Department of National Defence began casting about for replacement quarters for the old temporary building complex. There were other branches in the department that were scattered around the city from Rockcliffe to Tunney's Pasture and multiple locations in between.

DND planners had determined that it would be most cost effective to locate all of the branches, divisions and directorates along with all of the other associated defence agencies under one roof. Following the usual number of extensive studies it was determined that the ideal location would be at the existing base at Rockcliffe.

Coincidentally, construction had just been completed on the new Ministry of Transport building at 101 Colonel By Drive. Even before construction was complete it became obvious that the bureaucracy in that department had outgrown the available space.

Since governments like to be seen to be modest with the use of tax payers money it wouldn't do to have the spanking new building sitting in the middle of downtown Ottawa with no one to occupy it. The government felt that the military should be visible in a nation's capital after all and since the move would only entail a move just across the canal, it made eminent sense to the bureaucratic mind that DND should slide into the vacancy. The new building was a modern, imposing looking building centrally located and it remained within marching distance to Parliament Hill.

It didn't seem to matter that the building would only house about thirty percent of the national defence headquarters establishment. Notably, the personnel branch for the military were re-located to another new building on the corner of Gloucester and O'Connor Streets. I often wondered if it was coincidental that the RCAF mess was just a two-minute walk away from the centre of career planning activities.

The new building at 101 Colonel By Drive was not built to defence specifications. It occupied a very vulnerable downtown location and in most ways was unsuitable as a military headquarters. The government said jump and the military said how high?

At this point it is worth a pause to examine what had occurred since I had last served in the headquarters in 1969. The integration of the three services within NDHQ was more or less complete as I departed for staff college. Much of this was unrecognisable in the field, as the new green suits had not yet proliferated the service units outside Ottawa.

The field formations routinely dealt with their opposite numbers in the headquarters and were not often exposed to the complexities of integration. However, on the surface, uniformed officers still made the day to day operational decisions in the headquarters. Their civilian counterparts were only consulted on technical or procedural matters that were mostly administrative in nature.

The thin edge of the wedge was becoming visible at the Assistant Deputy Minister level as civilian bureaucrats began assuming appointments as ADM Finance and ADM Logistics and Supply. Control over the money, the budget and all of the resources had been achieved in one set of appointments. The usurping of senior military positions below the ADM level had only just begun.

Seasoned military staff officers who had become efficient in their previous jobs found themselves working in a civilianized atmosphere that was foreign to their background and training. The civilians had easy access up the chain of command that provided them with an insight that was not available to their uniformed colleagues. Many of the civilian officers were on a first name basis with their seniors two or three levels above them.

Significantly, the civilian bureaucrat had experienced the majority of his career in the shadow of the Peace Tower. He had an intimate knowledge of the inner workings of the bureaucracy and had established a network of like-minded civil servants with many a mentor at the senior levels. Most senior military officers were quick to recognise the expedient of politics in the bureaucracy. This was the beginning of the politicisation of the military officer in NDHQ.

Initially, most officers exercised bureaucratic politicking cautiously with the good of the service foremost in their minds. As they became more adept at manipulation some of them began to recognise the potential to further their own careers based on their contacts and new relationships with the senior mandarins with whom they were in daily contact. The opening was there; it was to be a matter of time until it would become routine for many career-minded officers to use their contacts for personal gain.

Until my departure for Staff College in 1968 most good staff officers had become adept at avoiding the bureaucracy or at least circumventing it. They were able to identify the best routes through the staff maze to follow and those to be avoided. Meanwhile, the military officer's civilian counterpart who was much more skilful in the manipulation of the institution, could often recognise an end run and would move to counter it. This before a developing military policy that was not politically sanitised could proceed too far up the chain of command. This was the activity that was beginning to surface as I departed the headquarters in 1968.

Now as I assumed my new role in NDHQ in 1974, I quickly discovered that not only had the civilian influence on the military increased, it had reached rather remarkable proportions. The civil servant comes to the bureaucracy out of university and has little experience either professionally or in life management. He has limited interpersonal competence and develops only those people skills that are necessary to allow him to function reasonably well within his tiny corner of the bureaucracy. The budding bureaucrat begins his tenure at a junior level and after a period of apprenticeship is routinely moved into more responsible positions. After few years of being moved around in a department or even between departments, he learns how the system works and the bureaucratic process consumes him.

As in any other profession, the bureaucrat works his way up the organisation structure that is government in all of its aspects. He advances based on his own capabilities but unlike his military peer, he lacks an understanding of the military ethic. Leadership of men in the field means little to the bureaucrat.

To make matters worse, I discovered a new breed of military officer in the headquarters who had blatantly cast military loyalty aside to further their own careers. They were easily identifiable and had to be treated cautiously. Through personal observation they learned first hand from their new-found civilian counterparts. They began to manipulate the system in a manner that would best enhance their own career progression. Such manipulations were not always in the best interest of the service and worse still they often betrayed the loyalty of those serving under them.

It was about this time that General Ramsey Withers was appointed as Chief of the Defence staff. One of the first challenges he issued to his general officers was to bring accountability back into the military culture. Prior to the integration of the forces, accountability was assumed. An officer who was given responsibility and authority for an action also assumed the accountability for his actions. It was an attribute of a military officer to welcome additional responsibility and all that went with it.

The difficulty posed to the more junior officers serving in the headquarters beginning in the early 1970's was complicated. Firstly, from the early stages of a junior officer's career, accountability was a given, it was rarely discussed and was accepted as part of the process. A junior officer was assigned a task that his immediate commander had assessed him as capable of performing. If he failed for any reason, he accepted the consequences without hesitation.

In his early years, the junior officer's neck was frequently on the line and he occasionally failed but his early risks were low and the consequences of his errors were relatively minor.

He learned from his mistakes and was a better officer for it. However, as his career progresses up the chain of command his responsibilities grow more onerous and the consequence of error becomes more severe. Prior to integration, the headquarters staff officer was selected based on his ability to assume more important responsibilities and to accept accountability for his actions.

The new bureaucratic environment into which the eminently field qualified military officer was thrust was a vast departure from all that he had learned in subordinate headquarters or formations. As civilian integration became entrenched, even more senior officers with solid experience in the field found themselves thrust into this foreign environment where authority, responsibility and accountability had become a blurred grouping of ill defined characteristics.

It became possible to cherry-pick any one of these characteristics by a senior manager and withhold one or more of the others to suit a whim. Unclear direction given with strings attached had the effect of handcuffing those assigned a task.

Management had usurped the solid principles of leadership. It was forgotten that a good leader had to be a good manager. To place management ability above leadership was a bureaucratic trap that allowed those with responsibility to duck the consequences of bad decisions or inappropriate actions.

Ramsey-Withers did not fail in his attempts to correct this situation; he was simply overwhelmed by the sheer momentum that the integration of the civilian into the executive levels of the military had attained.

It was still possible for some officers to operate effectively under such circumstances and they stood out at all rank levels. They were the ones who were decisive at meetings and who were prepared to draft orders in a manner that left no doubt to the field commanders as to what was required of them. These individuals found themselves interceding on behalf of field officers who had been given ambiguous or inappropriate direction from other NDHQ branches. Some orders and directives emanated from the headquarters without being properly staffed by the office of prime interest and the nickname "Fort Fumble" became entrenched as a more meaningful metaphor.

It was within this atmosphere that I was promoted to lieutenant colonel. My role at NDHQ changed from the single purpose duties of a flight safety staff officer to the role of Management Engineer. My new posting was in the Directorate of Management Engineering under Colonel Ron Button who I had met some years before. Ron had been an AI Navigator and a good one. He was very much management orientated but he also displayed the fine leadership qualities that had shaped his own career progression. It seemed strange that two airmen with no formal background in management engineering were posted into the same directorate at the almost the same time.

As I reported into my new office, I asked Colonel Button if he was aware that I had little formal academic training in the management-engineering field. He acknowledged this and asked if I had read "Chester Hull". As I replied in the affirmative, he advised me that it was all I needed to know. He had wanted a more practical approach to management engineering and that was the end of any discussion about my qualifications.

Many headquarters staff officers at the time held Air Vice Marshall Chester Hull as synonymous with sound management principles. Prior to his retirement he had written a book entitled "Management by Objectives (MBO)". It was on all of the military reading lists and most officers could quote a passage or two by heart. It was in danger of becoming a bible.

As I assumed my duties, I soon became immersed in the many other, flavour of the day, theoretical approaches to management. Performance Based Management, Performance Measurement Systems and Management by Results and many others all read with one eye on the Peter Principle became the tools of the manager at the headquarters. It was in this directorate that I was to examine the principles of management in more depth than ever before. I began to form principles and a style of my own.

One of my early assignments was to determine the compatibility of the various computer systems that were suddenly appearing throughout the Department of National Defence. Management Engineering Services came under the Assistant Deputy

Minister Finance who was responsible for all of the financial systems within the department. The ADM, a civilian, had become concerned when it was reported to him that requisitions for payment of bills or disbursements were amassed monthly in Ottawa and then shipped to Camp Borden in western Ontario.

Here they were processed and then dispatched by truck back to Hull where Supply Services would cut the cheques for payment. The DND computers could not communicate with others outside the department nor in most cases could the systems in operation in each of the branches within the department talk to one another.

I was a bit unsure of just where to tackle the problem and decided that it would be best to start with the experts. Accordingly, I called a meeting with the administrative heads of each of the branches in NDHQ. The meeting was arranged in a convenient conference room in the South Tower at 101 Colonel By Drive. On the day that had been agreed upon for the meeting we had a preliminary slide briefing at the ready outlining how we perceived the problem. The conflict became apparent before the meeting had even commenced.

We had ordered coffee and cookies to be set up on a side table in the conference room and my small staff and I waited expectantly for the attendees to arrive. They came one by one and to my surprise none of them knew each other. As they came in and were directed to the refreshments, I introduced them to my staff and then to each other before the meeting began. By the time we sat down at the conference table, we were all very much aware of the root causes of the NDHQ computer incompatibility problem.

In the mid 1970s computers were in their infancy in terms of the administrative support they provided. Most military staffs understood the advantages of data manipulation, storage and retrieval but few could comprehend the mechanics of how this was achieved. Not many knew the difference between hardware and software.

Furthermore, the comprehension of advantages and disadvantages of a central database versus a stand alone system was minimal. The personnel branch, as an example, had opted for a centralised data base that had the advantage of being maintained by a server company allowing the staffs within the branch the ability to input and retrieve information without concerning themselves with systems management or maintenance.

Unfortunately the centralised system had one very serious shortfall. It was designed to store remotely all of the personal records of military personnel in the service provider's computer banks. No one had given much thought to the fact that the system was not secure. The confidential information contained in the system was not necessarily open to other users but it could be manipulated by those not authorised to do so. The system was very quickly modified to prevent access to unauthorised persons or organisations. Eventually it became a dedicated system with outside access to all unauthorised persons denied.

The computer compatibility problem was typical of any large organisation undergoing the growing pains of adapting to new technology. Often common horse sense was set aside in favour of high tech hyperbole that confused even those close to the subject.

This was one of my early ventures into the world of management engineering and I was told a few years later that regular monthly meetings between NDHQ branch administrators had been established and within a year or so a degree of commonality had been achieved. I had done little to help it along other than arrange for coffee and cookies on a slack day.

I discovered that I enjoyed the new role I found myself performing and took all my responsibilities very seriously. I had attained a level of expertise in management engineering techniques where I was confident in conducting my assignments and was anxious to take on more complex projects.

In defence of senior managers, it should be noted that frequently under the NDHQ staff structure, they might have little control over the operation of the organisation into which they have been appointed. Previous policies developed to support a certain management style may not work for someone else. One can always find any number of reasons for organisation structures to go bad but it is the mark of a good leader to recognise that he has a problem, identify it and then proceed with determination to correct it.

There can be no excuse for those who refuse to admit that they have a management dilemma or indeed that they may be part of it. A stubborn approach to change and the tenacity with which some managers tend to cling to entrenched and unworkable management systems contributes to a rapid breakdown in the effectiveness of any organisation.

The two years that I served as a management engineer was an incredible learning experience for me. Apart from the hands-on studies that I participated in, I was exposed to several public service senior management courses that provided me with the theoretical and technical knowledge to expand my understanding of management systems and philosophies.

Toward the end of my tour I was invited on several occasions to preside at the final review board for the military middle management course being taught at St Jean PQ.

Frequently, I was asked by graduating students for my opinion on one or the other of the various management systems that were in vogue at the time. The faculty was never very impressed with my responses as I cautioned the students that a good manager should know and understand all of the management systems but he should not slavishly follow them.

All of the different management theories were designed to fit an organisational situation presided over by a manager whose style the theory best suited. I suggested that each manager should treat each of the systems as no more than a useful tool in his manager's toolbox. The system or the appropriate elements of a system had to be tailored to fit the circumstances and the manager's personal management style.

Unfortunately, this approach was not acceptable by an academe that wanted to standardise all managers and their systems truly believing that this was the right approach. While they treated my remarks as challenging and thought provoking for their students, they were clinging to entrenched systems that did not necessarily suit the ever-changing times. I felt that to be blind to change was a hazard that the capable manager had to avoid. Management problems should be confronted head on, unrestricted by the narrow thinking imposed by rigid management philosophies.

I had found a new basis upon which to develop my own management technique and entered a period where I was able to confidently assess most organisations within the headquarters with clarity and the resolve to recommend improvements to the areas that I found wanting.

Sadly, it was at about this time that Joan and I agreed to separate for a period that would last until well after my retirement several years later. These things are always difficult to explain. When two busy people grow apart over time, instant repair is frequently out of the question. Fortunately our three boys then in their teens were of an age to accept the situation. None of us liked the arrangement, but we all took it in stride. I moved, along with my manly possessions packed in our second car, a small economy sized vehicle in its declining years, into the Officer's Quarters at Rockcliffe.

My transfer into the office of the Director General Military Plans and Operations was both a relief and a challenge. The Canadian military was changing as were the practices and ethics of senior leadership. The good officers were fewer in number but easier to recognise. They were the dynamic staff officers who were task oriented and who single-mindedly pursued their duties to perfection. In a sense they alarmed other officers who looked upon glad-handing and networking at all senior levels both military and civilian as a means to achieving their aims.

The networkers could be seen studiously involved in longwinded telephone conversations with officers sometimes several rank levels above them. They developed tight communications webs and worked those networks until they could discern a consensus before implementing whatever decision was left for them to make. They were rarely wrong because they usually satisfied a majority. But the process was cumbersome and often delayed decision making for longer periods than necessary. Frequently, events overtook the process and the necessity to make the decision had evaporated. By popular definition, "the easy way out" was found without endangering one's career.

Meanwhile, time and events did not stand still and many man-hours and frequently, man-days were lost waiting for the simplest decisions to be made that would satisfy the network. Accountability under these circumstances was difficult to assign and many an indecisive officer was promoted far beyond his Peter Principle level simply because he had good connections and a good telephone manner.

I had been in the management engineering field for two years and had been able to witness at arms length the changes in the headquarters. The civilian influence was everywhere and the military were becoming second class citizens in their own domain.

With this over-view of the NDHQ staff function. I assumed my new duties as a section head in the Directorate of Military Operations Co-ordination and found myself for the fourth time in another whole new world.

CHAPTER NINETEEN
THE DIRECTORATE OF OPERATIONAL TRAINING CO-ORDINATION
DMOC

In March of 1976 I assumed my new duties at NDHQ in the Directorate of Operational Training and Co-ordination (DMOC). The directorate was a tasking cell in the operations branch and all military operations were tasked directly through the staff action of this small cell. My immediate superior, the director, was a naval captain reporting to the Director General Military Plans and Operations, an army brigadier general.

We were an eclectic mix of army, navy and air force. Under the circumstances we could easily have been fighting continuously among ourselves each striving to put his own service first. However, the opposite prevailed. Once we got to know each other we developed strong working relationships and in the process many of us became friends. We became "Green", husbanding the resources of the department against all demands without favour to one service or the other.

My new director, Captain Hal Tilley was a quiet unassuming naval officer with a keen insight. He was an accomplished staff officer and I found to my delight that we saw eye to eye on most military subjects.

Next up the ladder, Brigadier General Monty Wiseman, Director General of Military Plans and Operations, had a more outgoing personality. He was a gung ho, boisterous armoured corps officer who had distinguished himself in the field and displayed fine leadership qualities. He had a habit of intimidating his subordinate officers and those that avoided him as a result of it were of no concern to him. He liked a good argument and respected those who voiced their opinion clearly and with conviction. When he learned that I had been through the Army Staff College at Kingston he wasted little time in trying me on for size.

Fortunately, I had been warned in advance and responded offhandedly toward his initial attempts to intimidate me, one of the few airmen on his staff. After several failures to elicit a reaction from me, he finally advised me very soberly and in a confidential tone that he disliked airmen. I was ready with my response and retorted, "that's OK with me General, because I don't have much use for armoured corps officers".

This was met with a stony silence and a steely-eyed glare. For a time I thought that perhaps I had misread the general and had over done my reaction to his insulting remark. It wasn't very long before I came to realise that I had passed the general's little test and we got on famously from that point on.

The infantry is known as the Queen of battlefield. They are the first to engage the enemy and are usually the last to disengage. Whether on the attack or in strategic retreat, they are supported by artillery and armour. The Queen of the battlefield has little interest in battles at sea or in the struggle for air superiority but she does have an intense interest in support from any source.

Of the many air force roles during wartime is the relatively small (by air force standards) close air support role. This support is of major importance to the infantry almost to the exclusion of all other air force activities. It is an understandable mind-set when you consider that it is the infantry, the Queen of battle, in warfare or any other skirmish that is always up close and personal with the enemy. Monty as an old tank commander understood these principles clearly and those of his officers who didn't, were of no consequence to him.

As I looked around at the officers with whom I was to be associated in DGMPO, I realised that I was indeed in the presence of honourable military men. With very few exceptions, the army, navy and airforce officers that had been selected for duty in the division were of a very high calibre. They were field officers first and foremost and drafted the plans and operational orders from a field officer's view point.

I had some overlap with my predecessor who was a naval aviator and considered a streamer. He was young, well educated and displayed good staff officer qualities. He had done a good job in the position and was being posted back to a flying tour on helicopters. He had just come back from a cruise between Toronto and Montreal on HMS Britannia otherwise known as the Royal Yacht. The Queen had completed an extensive tour of Canada a few months earlier and he was invited along on the final leg of Her Majesties tour before returning to the UK. After listening to the humorous tales of his experience, I felt as though I had somehow come to the job too late for a prize perk that was unlikely be repeated.

I immersed myself in getting to know my staff, half of whom were also new to their jobs. I spent several days examining how the DMOC directorate and the section that I was to manage, contributed to the mandate of the operations branch. How it inter-related with other directorates in the department was also an important factor that needed to be explored.

I soon discovered that anything in the Canadian armed forces that moved had to be tasked from this division. A specialised message identifier alerted the recipient that the tasking was bona fide and had been subjected to the necessary staff co-ordination at the headquarters level. DGMPO was developing a reputation for issuing well staffed tasking orders dealing with everything from operational commitments, movement orders and exercises, including DND support to other government departments and agencies.

As I studied the task ahead of me, I began to realise that this was to be one of the more challenging stages of my career. I would be required to deal directly with all three services and senior elements of the civil service. There seemed to be a tremendous amount of responsibility in the position but I had difficulty determining the degree of authority I would have in conducting my routine duties. It was said that staff officers did not exercise any authority except through their chain of command.

The Deputy Chief of the Defence Staff or the CDS himself represented the authority, the staff officer was responsible for clarifying what had to be done, how it was to be done, with what resources and so on. Once all this activity was complete, the staff officer prepared the appropriate tasking order and submitted it up the chain of command, each level approving before passing it on to the next. Some authority for routine or emergency tasks was delegated down to the DGMPO level and the General designated certain officers on his staff to act on his behalf under very clearly defined circumstances.

On the surface the tasking process worked well. The difficulty often arose in the implementation. No matter how well an activity was planned and care taken in ensuring it's completeness, it was occasionally difficult to foresee the changing circumstances between the planning and the final implementation of a tasking activity.

Tasking dealing with uniformed military personnel and military resources worked exceptionally well. The problems arose when civilian and military elements were combined in support of an activity. Bringing disparate elements together in the field was difficult and it was often impossible to agree on a single purpose. Civil servants were accustomed to working with people they knew and were suspicious of and often reluctant in taking direction from military personnel.

There was no way to get around it, military orders and regulations were difficult to apply to civilian personnel and military field commanders were frequently frustrated by a civilian intransigence and reluctance to co-operate. To be fair to the civilian, he had never been subjected to military training and discipline. He viewed himself as a representative of his ministry and was quick in attempting to assume control in the field. Little did it matter that he may not have either the responsibility or the authority to take charge of a given activity.

While I hadn't personally encountered these problems first hand, I had been made aware of them by my colleagues and began looking for ways to streamline procedures and clarify line and staff functions in future tasking operations. In my examination, I discovered that often the department was authorising the use of military resources for purposes that were not within departmental policies. There were also numerous examples of worthy requests for military assistance or support that were summarily dismissed with little more than a cursory attempt to substantiate the request.

As I became more familiar with the job, I frequently encountered cases where authority was often usurped by senior civilian staff. In one instance in particular, a request had come into the headquarters at the Assistant Deputy Minister level from one of Canada's floundering charter airlines. One of its aircraft was grounded somewhere in the British Isles with an engine out. The departmental tasking system was by-passed as an air force military transport was hastily dispatched with replacement engine and a repair crew.

There was no justification for this support and there was no contractual arrangement or paper trail put in place to facilitate DND cost recovery for this expensive mission. The system had simply been short circuited at the highest level and once again the military found itself expending resources that were earmarked for other activities. No wonder the field commanders were frustrated over the activities at Fort Fumble. Activities that challenged their control over the resources assigned to them.

This rather significant support to a private enterprise had little or no relationship to the defence of Canada. It lingered in my mind as an example of blatant unethical use of DND resources. At the opposite end of tasking process was an arbitrary decision that was made not to support a request from the Boy Scouts of Canada for the loan of some tentage for a jamboree. The military of the times was certainly not short of tents and this request could have been easily supported to a very worthy cause. I was determined to eliminate or at the very least, document the improper or loose tasking procedures over which I had no control.

Each request for support no matter how trivial was examined in detail by the staff. Decisions to recommend or deny support to a vast number of requests were made as a result of these reviews. Each request would be prioritised, rated for its worthiness and the ability of the military to support it. Each request was subjected to a cost examination and recommendations were made with respect to cost recovery from the requesting agency.

One other civilian request for DND support comes to mind that was unique but represented one point on the spectrum of the range of requests that came through DOTC for approval. There was an organisation of Canadian chefs who were trying to get themselves to the World Culinary Olympics that were being held in Germany in 1977.

The request was well put together and came down the chain from the Minister's office without comment. I gave it a cursory read and passed it to one of my desk officers with the direction to verify the request, determine the category for which such support could be substantiated and to provide cost estimates of the provision of the support.

A day or two later we discussed the project among ourselves and came to the consensus that this request did not qualify for DND support. To be safe I asked the officer handling the file to try to find out if the requesting organisation had any political affiliation. To my way of thinking, this knowledge would be of assistance in defending a decision not to support it. As it turned out the request came into DND through a very strong Liberal riding in southern Ontario.

Discussions with the organisers revealed that they had sufficient funding to get their competitors over to Germany but wanted DND to ferry their pots, pans and other personal cooking utensils to the site of their Olympics. When advised verbally that should their request be approved, DND intended to recover its costs estimated to be on the order of $2500. They curtly responded that they would have cost recovery waived through their Member of Parliament. I drafted a strongly worded memo that would be attached to the denial of the request as it progressed up the chain to the Minister's office.

My accompanying memo weighed the pros and cons of providing such support and on balance ended with several reasons why this request should not be approved. There was also the fact that a precedent would be set that once in place would make it difficult to refuse other requests for support of this nature. Fortunately, the position we had taken made eminent sense to my immediate superiors and they each in turn signed off on the file and passed it up the chain. I never saw the file again and a few days later I received my copy signed by the minister.

I heard later that the request for culinary assistance had bounced back and forth between two very senior desks for a day or two before it finally went to the minister for final approval. I don't know if the roadblock was civilian or military but Monty Weisman won and my respect for him went up another notch or two.

During my first year in the job I began to analyse not only the position itself but also the dynamics of my predecessors. When the central tasking concept was first developed at DND the incumbent DOTC 2, now my position, was an old air force friend - Lieutenant Colonel Herb Graves.

Herb was a fine officer and got along well with all of those with whom he came into contact. He was a doer, innovative and direct.

He had boundless energy and performed as an architect for the new tasking function assigned to the directorate. Herb was not afraid of change and was a meticulous planner. The policies he helped to establish had undergone the tests of trial, error and time and for the most part were still intact.

I found that those who had filled the position in the five or six years since its inception were more or less caretakers and had not really massaged the division policies for more efficiency. I had no intention of upsetting anyone's apple cart but I wanted to ensure that I was able to do my job without inappropriate interference. In the late fall a red file arrived on my desk that allowed me the opportunity to make many of the changes that I determined would make the workings of the tasking organisation more effective.

Within the file was a letter from the Secretary of State to the Minister of National Defence. Written in the usual collegial terms, it basically requested DND support for a forthcoming Royal Visit to western Canada by His Royal Highness, The Prince of Wales. I decided that this request would be my breakthrough. It was the first of the requests for DND support for the year ahead and I was aware that there would be many others.

Among the responsibilities that the directorate was assigned was the tasking of military support to other government departments and agencies. This had often been abused as noted previously and there were no clear guidelines once such support had been approved as to how it would be managed and monitored. The cost was established early on in the staffing process but there were no checks or controls over the magnitude that the support might eventually demand.

Operations people in the field often found the demands made on them were well beyond those agreed upon and reluctantly responded to on-scene requests for additional military support without any regard for the additional costs that might accrue.

The Prince of Wales tour was to centre on Calgary and HRH would participate in the one hundredth anniversary re-enactment of the signing of the Seven Nations Treaty by his uncle, a former Prince of Wales. Prince Charles would also be the Grand Marshal of the Calgary Stampede parade for the year 1977. While I knew a lot about my home town Calgary and the Calgary Stampede, I knew very little about royalty and found myself on a crash course on the Royal Family, royal protocol and the support services within Buckingham Palace. In addition, I familiarised myself with the historical factors leading to the signing of the Seven Nation Treaty.

In preparing the response for the minister's signature to the Secretary of State, I carefully appointed myself as the DND officer responsible. It read in part:

> *"The Department of National Defence is pleased to accept the honour of providing the support requested at Reference A. For your information, Lieutenant Colonel T.R. Thompson of the Directorate of Military Operations Co-ordination has been appointed as the departmental representative and will be responsible for the provision, co-ordination and financial control over the resources that will be identified to support your request".*

I thought after I had written the first draft that I might be a little presumptive and decided that before I finalised the letter I would pass it by my director. Hal Tilley read it over cautiously and asked me how I intended to carry out this rather prodigious task. I stated that I didn't think overseeing such an operation was that onerous but if it was approved I would develop the guidelines necessary to ensure an effective degree of departmental support while controlling costs. In other words I didn't know, but I was sure willing to give it a try.

The letter was prepared in final and sent up the line, both Hal and I thinking that such a response would be called into question. Perhaps it was treated as a matter of curiosity as it passed through the hands of the senior officers up the chain. Each level wondering how such a task could be accomplished. Or perhaps it was a lack of understanding and a resigned approval by each level just to get it on its way.

A few days later I received a call from the Deputy Minister's executive assistant. "Terry, can you come up, the Deputy would like to see you". The Deputy Minister, Buzz Nixon, was a former navy lieutenant commander who had pursued a successful second career in the civil service.

As I appeared in his office, I thought that perhaps my letter would be treated as an affront and so I was ready for the talk about departmental protocol and to be told to do my job and mind my own business. Instead, he asked me if I was aware that if approved this letter would give me full financial control over expenditures and the use of DND resources in support of the Royal Visit. I advised him that I was aware of this and that I felt that if the department was to provide the support effectively, both flexibility of action and a strong measure of control needed to be exercised.

He then asked what would be my next step following approval. I informed him that as we spoke the DOTC staff were busily preparing a budget that would be tailored to meet the detailed requirements of the Secretary of State and would be submitted through the appropriate channels in NDHQ for approval. Once approved by DND, if the scope of the support was to change in any way it would have to re-negotiated through the appropriate offices in NDHQ. The DM seemed to be the only one who fully understood this concept and once he had satisfied himself that I hadn't lost my mind, he passed the letter on to the Minister for his signature.

I returned triumphantly to the twelfth floor and reviewed the gist of my conversation with Hal Tilley. He was pleased as it re-enforced the directorate's reputation as a thorough tasking organisation. A degree of increased respect for the division throughout the headquarters soon became evident and I was able to get on with the job at hand with very little interference from outside offices.

Within a week I had completed a series of meetings with the staff in the offices of the Secretary of State. My prime contact was a gentleman by the name of Eric Cochran. He had been a major in the army some years before and had done very well in his second career as a civil servant. He could have written the book on government protocol. He knew it inside and out both from a political standpoint and he had a firm handle on diplomatic and state conventions.

Eric had sketched out a program for the visit that was to last for six or seven days and invited me over to discuss it in detail. The RAF

Queen's Flight was to deliver the Prince of Wales to Calgary and this was the opening item with which I took exception. It seems to me; I pointed out, that while in Canada, members of the House of Windsor should be the viewed as the Canadian Royal Family and that we as Canadians had the responsibility to transport members of our Royal family while conducting Canadian business in Canada. This concept met with enthusiastic approval of the Secretary of State staffs.

Unfortunately on this occasion, military Air Transport Command were in the middle of their conversion to Boeing 707 and it was inappropriate to assign such a task at this early stage of their conversion. A letter from the Secretary of State was quickly dispatched to Air Canada and within a few days I had a call from Andre Gauthier or "Goach" as I came to know him.

Goach was very familiar with the RCAF as it turned out. It seems he had been Air Canada's representative in Paris immediately following the war and Air Canada and the RCAF had shared an office building just off the Champs Elysse during the early days of NATO. Not only had they shared office space, they shared living accommodations at a hotel nearby and essentially lived as family until dedicated facilities were provided for their respective organisations.

At that time Air Canada was a government-owned airline and while its employees were considered to be civil servants, their behaviour belied the fact. Air Canada was the Canadian national flag carrier. It had a strong corporate stature and behaved competitively on Trans-Atlantic routes. However, as part of its national mandate it was required to provide service to remote areas of the country regardless of the profitability or lack thereof. It accomplished all of its tasks effectively and had a reputation as one of the world's best airlines. Senior management often attempted to distance itself from government interference but it was never an easy task.

My relationship with Andre Gauthier was cemented from the start and during our first meeting we had established the ground rules under which we would operate. I would make initial contact with the Captain of the Queen's Flight in England and henceforth act as the transportation co-ordinator for the Royal Visit. Within a few weeks the pieces were all in place and the details were under negotiation.

The Captain of the Queen's Flight was a gentleman by the name of Air Commodore Archie Winskill. My initial telephone contact with the Air Commodore was quite formal as I wasn't too sure of his position in the scheme of things. He was a retired air force officer of some distinction. He had been a fighter pilot with the RAF during the war and been appointed to the Queen's Flight position following his retirement. It was his task to provide the planning and co-ordination of all of the Royal tours that involved the use of aviation.

During our conversation he acknowledged that the use of Canadian air resources in support of a Canadian tour was a good idea and that while the use of the new RCAF Boeing for this tour might be premature, an Air Canada alternative was workable. He advised me that he would be shipping a package of everything I would need for the aviation portion of the visit.

The package arrived a few days later and contained all of the usual safety tips, Royal cabin protocol and a list of food items that His Royal Highness was allergic to or downright disliked. Most of this I was already familiar with but the one item that had slipped my mind completely was the Royal Pennant to be flown as the aircraft taxied to the ramp after landing. The Air Commodore had included two or three of these pennants, as they would be needed on other aircraft assigned royal duties.

Unfortunately, the Air Canada 747 on which the Royal Party arrived was not equipped with a holder for the pennant. I was delighted to watch the Royal arrival in Calgary months later as one of the stewardesses propped up by others inside, held the pennant high and proud through the upper hatch just back of the cockpit as the aircraft majestically taxied in to the ramp. The young lady's slender arm was all that could be seen as a "Flagstaff" and its doubtful that most of those present for the arrival were aware that anything was out of place.

The media picked it up though and it made a good front page picture the next day. The Air Canada public relations people were ecstatic.

Meanwhile, Eric had refined the draft program while I had been making the air travel arrangements and we were now ready for a more detailed meeting.

Representatives from the Department of Transport, Communications Division were to provide secure communications for the duration of the visit. Bob Carrol, was the principal representative for the department and prepared his plan to compliment the master plan as it developed. An inspector from the RCMP was appointed to co-ordinate the security requirements for the visit. Vic Chapman had been contracted as the Canadian Press Officer to the Prince of Wales Canadian Staff and began to develop his media program in parallel with the Secretary of State's master plan.

Vic Chapman, otherwise known as "Vic The Kick", had played football for the BC Lions, the Edmonton Eskimos and the Hamilton Tiger Cats. He liked to tell the story of one of the few games he played for the Tiger Cats.

Apparently during a late season game, things had been going badly for the Cats and at a crucial point in the game their quarterback was injured and Vic was called in as a temporary replacement. They were at about centre field and his directions from the coach were quite clear. "Vic, work that ball down to field goal range and then kick it into the end zone". "Well" said Vic, "I passed once for ten yards and made the first down. It looked pretty good so I tried it again and made another first down. My third first down in a row took us down to the ten-yard line. I called for the field goal and put that ball right through the uprights. We won but nobody talked to me for the rest of the game and it took the coach a few days to forgive me".

Vic had worked as a bagman for Pierre Trudeau during his march to the office of the Prime Minister of Canada and for several years after he took office. He knew government senior inner circles and had a good number of valuable corporate contacts. Every one liked Vic and he had a vast number of friends and acquaintances all of whom he could remember by both first and last name without hesitation.

The Prince of Wales visit was the first of many Royal and State visits where Vic and I would participate together over the next five years. He and I developed a close friendship but it was not without some discord during our early encounters. Vic was very "un" military and had little respect for military discipline or principles. Following our first meeting I realised that we had some differences of opinion that would eventually have to be rationalised.

During one of our early planning meetings I suggested that the City of Calgary should be used as our base of operations with a small ops room set up in one of the suites of the hotel. We could utilise helicopters to transport the Prince of Wales and the accompanying officials to each of the Seven Nations involved in the treaty celebrations. This would eliminate the necessity for the arrangement for over-night accommodations in the smaller communities throughout southern Alberta.

This suggestion was met with enthusiasm and when I quietly mentioned more to myself than those present, that I planned to head out west in the next month or so to do a reconnaissance of the Native Band locations and other staging points for the helicopters. I was immediately overpowered with requests to come along.

Following the meeting I returned to my office with a long list of to-do's. We needed a transportation officer, a dedicated medical officer and a Canadian Equerry to the Prince of Wales to form the preliminary planning team. Other members would be attached to the team as the visit neared. We had rough numbers of people travelling immediately with the Royal party and we had numbers of support staff that were to be moved about as required.

Transport costs had to be worked out including helicopter and vehicle support requirements. Accommodation costs for the military personnel assigned to the Royal Visit were to be identified both for the visit itself and for the advance excursions needed in the planning process. The cost of my reconnaissance would be included. And finally, warning orders had to be issued to the field formations that would be providing the support.

Within a few weeks we had pulled a rough budget together. We had completed preliminary interviews with the key military staff that had been selected and had Secretary of State approvals of our draft budget. The budget was finalised and submitted up the chain of command in DND. It came back down in reverse order approved without comment and the final phase of planning commenced.

My low-key, unobtrusive recce that I had planned for my own edification had turned into a mini-rehearsal for the Royal Visit. Secretary of State officials made all of our commercial travel arrangements to Calgary including accommodations at the Four Seasons Hotel on 9th Avenue. Our team from Ottawa numbered five or six and we were met by our opposite numbers representing the Province of Alberta. The Provincial Chief of Protocol, Major (Ret'd) John Walley, headed up the Alberta team. Our first evening together was essentially a meet and greet. We found that for the most part we were all reading from the same page and it appeared that we would be a compatible team.

John Walley had been out of uniform for many years but he liked to be called Major Walley. Most of his staff referred to him as such. I had developed a first name relationship with the Sec State staff and other personnel on the Ottawa team and wanted to maintain a semblance of goodwill at the start knowing full well that there would be conflicts to resolve sooner or later. John Walley fell in with the rest of us as a co-conspirator and our first gathering as a group seemed to bode well..

We met early the next morning at the CFB Currie Barracks helicopter pad as planned and immediately Major Walley began giving directions to the helicopter pilots. There were twelve of us including both the Ottawa and the provincial staffs and I had tasked two Huey helicopters to support our recce tour.

Each helicopter crew consisted of two pilots and a loadmaster whose job it was to ensure passenger safety. The crews displayed a look of dismay at this barrage of orders coming from a civilian who they didn't know and whose title "Chief of Protocol" meant little to them. Finally, I had to step in and remind Major Walley that I was in charge of the military support and that the helicopters would move when and how I directed them. He didn't like this situation too much but went along with it reluctantly as we got underway.

We visited each of the seven reservations that day with stops only long enough to meet each of the chiefs and senior members of their councils. We would look at the details of their ceremonial programs later. Programs that would involve extremely intricate negotiations related to native politics and government interrelationships with the native bands.

My second challenge came at the end of the day as we arrived back at Currie Barracks. We sat down with base officials and went over the details of the plan for the Prince of Wales to conduct a formal inspection of the PPCLI. The Regimental Sergeant Major had laid out his plan of the parade square on a blackboard showing the location of Guard of Honour to be inspected, the location of the band, the media enclosure, the spectators and the routes the royal party would follow both by motorcade and on foot. It was a well-laid out plan and the Sergeant Major was justifiably proud of his presentation. I too thought it was good and said so.

Mr. Chapman however, had other ideas and proceeded to rearrange troops, bands, media and spectator locations according to some preconceived idea that I found difficult to understand. As our discussion warmed up I found that at the root of Vic's concern was that we had penned the media into an enclosure that didn't allow for their free movement during the ceremony.

At this point I took my stand and suggested that the great unwashed media had no business slouching at will about the parade-square while a solemn ceremony was in progress. The meeting drew to a close and I quietly advised the Sergeant Major that the problem would be sorted out that night and that I would advise his boss of the outcome the next day.

Once back in the hotel I had two serious tasks to perform before we went any further. We were to have a joint planning session the next morning and I didn't want to end the day without resolving the discord with two important members of the combined federal and provincial team.

We milled about briefly in the lobby agreeing to meet for drinks and dinner at 7:00 PM. I quietly walked over to where John Walley was standing and invited him up my room for a drink. I was pleased that he accepted and we proceeded up the elevator without further discussion. As we entered my room the jackets came off, sleeves were rolled up and it was obvious to both of us that we had issues to sort out.

Once I had mixed a couple of good stiff scotches we sat and chatted idly about weather and any number of neutral topics. It turned out that John had been born somewhere in the east but had made his home in Alberta after he left the army years before. His children were grown up and had left home. When I mentioned that although I had been born in Edmonton I called Calgary home. He asked me if I had been to Calgary lately, I answered that I hadn't been to the city in six months or more. He suggested that I take a tour around town the next day, " because", he pointed out, "they are still unpacking it". He then laughed heartily as we toasted one another and then began to discuss the forthcoming Royal visit.

Following our second scotch we came to the conclusion that we both wanted the visit to go well for the City of Calgary, for the province and for the federal government. John I had decided, was an army major and an army major he would always be. He was accustomed to ordering his people around and they accepted it without question. From this point forward in our relationship John agreed to come to me with any changes he thought should be made to the military programme configuration. As I was to find out later, he ran a very smooth protocol office for the Premier and was respected by his staff and most government officials.

Our meeting of minds ended cordially without mention of our disagreement earlier in the day. Over dinner that night John proposed a toast to the Canadian Forces and the team relaxed realising that one inter-relationship problem had been solved. For me it was one down and one to go.

As dinner ended, I suggested to Vic that perhaps we should have a night-cap together. He was agreeable and we repaired to the bar in the lobby. Perched on barstools we discussed the day's activities and as we talked I began to realise that Vic had little understanding of military culture. He thought that if he wanted something done on a military base, all he had to do was confront the nearest soldier in uniform and demand anything he wanted and it would be provided.

He had little comprehension of the chain of command or the need for it and the solution to my problem with Vic became obvious. All I had to do was educate him in things military. This of course was no simple task and would take me a month or two but after a bottle of 12 year old scotch we discovered that we had a lot in common and at the very least I had gained his ear.

We sat down the next morning and discussed the media plan for the parade ceremony. I soon began to understand Vic's interest in ensuring the media had clear sight line access to the Royal party. In addition he raised a problem that had not previously occurred to me – the photographers would be shooting into the sun from the locations that had been sketched out for them. I was concerned that the media with their long boom mikes would intimidate any exchanges between HRH and the soldiers during the inspection. He agreed to keep the boom mikes away and I agreed to loosen up some of the restrictions we had put upon the media.

Vic, once he understood the solemnity with which the military took such ceremonies, agreed that he would allow no movement of media during the national anthems. He understood that I expected reporters, scribblers, photographers and cameramen to stand quietly until the shoulder arms at the end of the anthems and the Royal Salute. Filming and shooting the ceremony was OK but the cameramen had to remain in static positions during the anthems. In return Vic's media liaison people would be allowed to escort camera crews one at a time from one pre-agreed position to another during the ceremonies. That was the beginning of an understanding between us that was to last for several years.

By the end of the following day a team spirit has developed between all of the players. Secretary of State, provincial and military staffs all came together with a more detailed understanding of the draft program and we returned to Ottawa feeling that we accomplished a major milestone in the planning for the Royal Visit four months hence.

The reconnaissance or advance as it was now being called by the civil servants was a success. It was just the beginning of the detailed planning that was necessary to support this very colourful and historic Royal Visit to my home province of Alberta.

As the plans developed it became necessary to provide additional helicopters in support of media operations. Not only did I have to ensure that His Royal Highness was transported from point to point in fitting style but the media were demanding coverage of both the departure from Currie Barracks and the arrival at the next point of call. In some cases we could dispatch a small group of media ahead. But often circumstances dictated that most members of the media wanted to individually cover both departure and arrival events.

I had a bit of a problem with this initially because I had very little experience with the media and like most service officers accepted them as a necessary evil that had to be tolerated but not pampered. As our negotiations continued I began to realise that half of the media would be British and professional Royal watchers. Every move, speech, handshake or comment was relayed to the news agencies back home. The coverage had to be provided and I began to look at ways to provide more positive support to media operations.

I found that co-locating all support helicopters, including those dedicated to the media with those assigned to the Royal Party, not only simplified the logistics problem but movement and timings could be better controlled. As we developed our venue schedules for the series of visits we included additional time to allow the helicopters carrying the Royal Party to depart first. We intentionally planned a slightly longer route for them. The media, following the coverage of the departure of the Royal Party, would make a mad run for their waiting helicopters and fly a direct route to the next venue so that they could be on the ground and ready to cover the arrival of the Royal Party.

We ensured that during Vic's media briefings a detailed briefing by the helicopter detachment commander was also presented. By ensuring everyone understood the details of each move, they were better equipped to participate.

We briefed our media group on flight safety regulations and all of the aspects of what they could and couldn't do in and around helicopters. As it turned out, members of the media liked being part of the operation and co-operated with pilots and crews to the fullest. A friendly camaraderie developed between them and a team spirit was cultivated between two very dissimilar groups.

I was now about three months into the planning phase for the visit and had yet to brief my superiors on our progress. My budget was undergoing finishing touches under the ADM Finance staffs but I had draft figures at hand for my presentation to Hal Tilley and General Wiseman.

The general was aghast when he saw the make-up of my helicopter armada. Four Hueys, two Voyageurs and a Kiowa. He asked if I was planning an invasion of Alberta and if so, I would need troops on the ground. I assured him that the ground transportation support consisted of a pool of some twenty staff cars, a couple of vans and about sixty drivers, dispatchers and baggage handlers. This did not include military medical personnel and others who would be on call as required. Somehow he absorbed all of this without further comment.

The security requirements for the visit were somewhat vague and I had difficulty getting a handle on what was needed. The RCMP were responsible for developing the threat assessment and as my relationship with their representatives became closer, they began to include me in their threat assessment briefings.

This was important because the military always had a company sized force at the ready to insert into national security situations on short notice. With our military obligation to provide aid to the civil power, I needed to know the threat probabilities and had to develop a mechanism with which I could activate the appropriate NDHQ offices to respond to any increases to the threat to the Royal Party. Fortunately for this visit, the threat assessment was low and while there was a provision in the operations plan, little weight other than a potential cost was attached to it.

The support requirements far exceeded the expectations of the NDHQ hierarchy and yet when the demands of the schedule were examined, it was being accomplished efficiently with a minimum of resources. The advantages far outweighed any imposition on other non-operational activities. The general public in the west were proud to be entertaining the Royal

Party and the visit was intended to be a very public series of events. The military would be front and centre throughout the visit and the public relations spin-off was priceless.

The briefing ended on a high note and everyone was pleased that a detailed budget for this support had been prepared and had received approval in principle from the department of the Secretary of State. DND would be fully reimbursed for the cost of its personnel and resources.

The remaining two advances were carried out without incident. We presented a solid front and the only problems we encountered were with the Indian Bands whose individual programs at each venue had to be finalised. Timing at each venue was critical and if the band organisers allowed their time to run late it would lead to an imposition on all of those that followed on the schedule. This presented the native leaders with some difficulty, as they had never been exposed to such critical timings before. Eventually, they saw the necessity and while they didn't necessarily agree, they all managed to co-operate in the end.

These scheduling problems were resolved on the second advance. On the third, roughly thirty days before the event, we had a dress rehearsal complete with the Prince of Wales private secretary. He was accompanied by a royal press officer and His Royal Highness' personal policeman and last but by no means least, the Captain of the Queen's Flight.

I was a bit nervous as I met Air Commodore Winskill. Retired or not, I was aware that he exercised a lot of authority when it came to assessing the safety of the Royal Family. David Checketts, the Personal Secretary to the Prince of Wales, had mentioned in passing that HRH might like to fly the Huey himself. This was a source of concern for me as I was aware that HRH while a qualified pilot, was not qualified on the Huey helicopter type and it would breach regulations for him to fly the aircraft with passengers on board.

Within a few minutes of meeting the Captain of the Queen's flight, I found that everyone else on the team was calling him Archie. He noticed my hesitation and commented that if we were to get along, we should also be on a first name basis. His very first question to me was, had I been under any pressure to let The Prince of Wales fly?

I took him aside as I considered this to be a private matter among pilots. I explained to him that the Captain of the assigned Royal helicopter was a qualified instructor and while he was directed not to let HRH fly the aircraft with passengers on board, a separate flight without passengers could be arranged. It would give HRH the opportunity to get some stick time in on the Huey if he wished to do so.

Archie was ecstatic and indicated that he would brief The Prince of Wales accordingly. This took the pressure off the Captain of the Royal helicopter and a solution was found that was acceptable to all. In the end, The Prince of Wales, due to the pressures of his schedule, never exercised this option. But its existence prevented any embarrassment during the tour.

It was during this last advance before the Royal Visit proper that an amusing incident occurred. The Royal Staff were concerned that during the demands that would be experienced during the visit, they would have little opportunity to purchase the western apparel that would be the order of dress for most of the Royal tour.

Accordingly, one quiet afternoon before their return to England, a shopping tour was arranged for them. They were accompanied by Superintendent Frank Fedor; the RCMP officer who had been assigned the responsibility for security for the visit. The group entered a western dress establishment on the Stephen Avenue Mall and were quietly browsing the clothing racks when a ruckus occurred near the front of the store.

Little attention was paid to the commotion at first until "King" of the Royal Mounted sprang into action. Frank Fedor had witnessed the struggle between one of the clerks and a customer. There was tug of war in progress as he entered the fray. The "customer" had concealed a pair of expensive cowboy boots in the sleeves of his rather loose fitting jacket and he was attempting to exit the store when spotted by an alert sales clerk.

The RCMP Superintendent and the Scotland Yard Inspector apprehended the culprit and tied him to a chair with his own jacket. There he sat in the middle of the store awaiting the arrival of the "Cities Finest" to dispense the long arm of justice.

Needless to say the very surprised store employees and some of the members of the royal staff were impressed with swift western justice demonstrated so effectively. I suspect that one very startled thief came to the conclusion that it was not his day.

In the end the visit was a resounding success. The federal and provincial governments were pleased, the public was pleased, Stampede officials were overjoyed and of course the natives were honoured to have hosted, however briefly, such an esteemed guest.

There was an unfortunate spin-off however that came back to haunt me several months later. It had been agreed that the Blood Indian Band at Standoff in southern Alberta would present the Prince of Wales with a Palomino gelding as a gift in recognition of his visit. The horse had not been broken during the second advance earlier in the spring but the Bloods advised us that there would be no problem and the horse would be parade broken by Stampede time.

Indeed the horse was very well behaved during the parade. It was beautiful horse, tall with an aristocratic bearing. He moved as if he knew he was in the presence of royalty. Following the Stampede, he was transported back to Standoff and was more or less forgotten. The intricate hand-tooled saddle also presented to HRH by Chief Shot Both Sides was collected together with all of the other gifts that had been received and were shipped off to Buckingham Palace. The horse however, remained at Standoff.

In due course I received a panic call from Eric Cochran in Sec State. The Bloods had called him and asked when the Prince of Wales was going to assume ownership of his horse. They had been feeding him all winter and were tiring of it. Something had to done.

None of our military transport aircraft were configured to carry livestock and so once again the call went out to Air Canada. Yes, they had the equipment to carry livestock but the cost would be in the neighbourhood of $3000 to air transport a horse to the UK.

Eric was not amused and said that the cost was exorbitant and something else would have to be done. I had heard that the RCMP Musical Ride would be touring the UK that summer so I placed a call to their commander at Rockcliffe and explained the problem to him. He was very sympathetic but pointed out that a blond Palomino horse among their black purebreds would not a happy family make.

I was getting desperate as I called my friend, Lieutenant Colonel Ian McNab who was the Commanding Officer of the Lord Strathcona Horse (RC) regiment in Calgary. Ian had worked for me the year before and had been promoted and transferred to his new command. He understood the problems that could be encountered in our directorate all too well. He was non-committal on the phone and said he would call back the next day and I waited somewhat impatiently for his return call.

I needn't have worried as he called on schedule to say that he had been in the process of re-establishing the regimental horse guard that had been allowed to languish over the past several years and he needed horses. He would go down to Standoff that afternoon and check out HRH's horse. It proved to be a perfect fit. The Prince of Wales was the Colonel in Chief of the LDSH(RC) and what better home for his horse than in his very own regiment.

Arrangements were completed within days and the Blood Band were happy, the regiment was happy and most of all Secretary of State staffs were off the hook from what might have turned in to an embarrassing if not expensive situation.

His Royal Highness The Prince of Wales visit to Alberta 5-9 July 1977, as the official program reads, was successful in many ways. Its primary success was the fact that it was used as a model for all Royal visits to Canada from that time forward.

For the most part, the federal team that had come together to support the Alberta visit were seasoned for the coming Royal Visits to Newfoundland, Nova Scotia, Ottawa, Toronto, Saskatchewan, Alberta, British Columbia and the Northwest Territories. The planning that had gone into the Alberta visit in 1977 was refined for each Royal Visit and the provision of support became second nature to our team of experienced Royal Visit organisers.

Many of the lessons learned in providing support to royal visits were applicable in numerous state and heads of government visits that we were called upon to support over the next several years. Presidents, Prime Ministers, Kings, Queens, Princes and Princesses were toured with dispatch and the military maintained a high level of visibility before the general public through their participation.

CHAPTER TWENTY
ROYAL SERVICE CONTINUES

While State and Royal Visits seemed to dominate the first year in my new position, the whole responsibility for DND support to other government departments and agencies took up the smallest percentage of the effort of the entire DOMC staff.

The department was being swamped with requests for support for everything from air transportation to school presentations. Much of the tasking that was bubbling up to the headquarters included a myriad of requests for support to local community events. Commanders in the field were reluctant to turn down requests from their communities and forwarded them to NDHQ for decision.

It was difficult for us to approve many of these requests because in most cases the cost of providing the support had to be borne by the local commander's discretionary budget and we were reluctant to approve activities over which we had no financial control. It wasn't long before the commanders in the field began to see the advantages of keeping local support in-house. While this sort of tasking request began to decline appreciably, local commanders were finding ways to provide community support within their own budgets and to position themselves as solid corporate partners in the local community.

Once we had reduced the number of smaller local requests requiring ministerial approval, we were able to devote our full attention to the military taskings that were more appropriately in support of the defence of Canada.

Annual exercises in North Norway on Nato's northern flank, Standing Naval Force

Atlantic exercises in defence of NATO's North Atlantic sea-lanes, deployment of support to peace keeping operations around the world and innumerable other support functions were all part of the schedule of activity. Add to this the list of bi-lateral or multilateral military agreements between Canada and our allies and the critical mass of our working schedule comes into focus.

Support to other government departments and agencies and aid to the civil power now began to account for less than ten percent of the overall military tasking assignments.

The tasking cell began to employ more personnel with operational experience as we rotated a percentage of our staff each year. Army officers by nature of their early training in staff duties in the field were superb headquarters staff officers and were thorough in examining and validating the most minor details. We improved the quality of our tasking orders ensuring that they were well researched and clear to the officers executing the orders in the field.

Tasking of military personnel and resources was our raison detre. We moved brigades, wings, squadrons, units and supporting assets. We excelled at establishing priorities and ensuring that the most important military related taskings received the full support the assignment dictated.

Aside from the purely military operational tasking, there was a still a need to provide military support to other government departments and agencies. While this only represented a very small portion of our responsibility, there were some that we looked upon as perks of the job.

More of the routine daily tasking requirements were shuffled off to the NDHQ Ops Centre. This allowed us to concentrate exclusively on taskings requiring more detailed analysis prior to seeking approval higher up in the chain of command. Annual military exercises preoccupied most of our planning and co-ordination. Whether a land force exercise in North Norway, a North Atlantic naval exercise or a massive NORAD/SAC systems test, we were involved in them all.

For all of our meticulous planning, we still had to maintain sufficient flexibility to respond to unforeseen situations. It was about mid-winter 1977 or 78, as I recall, that a Soviet satellite inadvertently wandered from its orbit and entered Canadian airspace in the vicinity of Yellowknife in the Northwest Territories.

This was treated as a national emergency and the full focus of military search and rescue supported massively by other military personnel and resources were brought to bear. An elliptical debris field twenty or thirty miles wide at its centre and several hundred miles long encompassing most of Great Slave Lake was identified and subjected to a thorough air and ground search over a three week period. Personal protection gear was issued to those on the ground since without direct communication with Soviet space officials, we were unsure of the level of nuclear or other contamination that might be encountered. Bits and pieces were sorted, catalogued and then passed on to the Soviets for their forensic study and the Northwest Territories was once again declared safe for human activity.

Support for royal and state visits had been looked upon somewhat reservedly and seemed to be treated more as a nuisance to be avoided by the staffs. My experience with the

Prince of Wales visit to Calgary led me to believe that once a standard had been established, the whole planning and execution process could be a rather enjoyable experience. I tried to look at it as a compensation for the long hours and hard work in performing the primary function of the tasking organisation.

There were more Royal Visits as the Queen visited Canada during Her jubilee year and in 1978 the Province of Alberta hosted the Commonwealth Games in Edmonton. Practically the whole House of Windsor was on the move throughout Canada during the period of the games.

Her Majesty the Queen had been invited to open the Edmonton Games. It was an extensive visit that began with the arrival in St. John's Newfoundland of the air force Boeing 707 we had tasked to pick up the Royal Family in the UK. The special VIP configuration had been installed in the aircraft for the comfort of the Royal passengers. The captain and his crew had been screened by the Captain of the Queen's Flight and were briefed on the appropriate comportment in the presence of Royalty. A pennant holder had been installed forward of the hatch just behind the cockpit.

The Queen, Prince Philip, Princes Andrew and Edward were on board. The Prince of Wales was absent. As the heir to the throne, he was not allowed to accompany the Queen in the air and was instead conducting the Queen's business elsewhere. Princess Anne who was to visit Canada the following year was the only other absent member of the immediate Royal Family.

I was in the control tower at the St John's, Newfoundland airport an hour or so before the scheduled arrival. As I listened to the radio traffic, I heard Air Commodore Archie

Winskill passing Her Majesty's best wishes to a crew attempting to cross the Atlantic in a hot air balloon. They had launched from Signal Hill earlier that day. Unfortunately, several hours after receiving the Queen's message the balloon went down in the Atlantic. While the crew were rescued without incident, the attempt was over and to my knowledge was not undertaken again by the same crew.

The Royal Flight arrived on schedule and the pomp and ceremonial activities attendant at Royal arrivals was in place and functioned perfectly throughout the formalities of the event. His Royal Highness, Prince Andrew remained on board the aircraft after arrival and would be transported to Trenton. He proceeded from there on to Lakefield School near Peterborough, his former college. Following a brief visit to the school, he joined a group of young adventurers in the Northwest Territories for a trip by canoe down the Mackenzie River. He rejoined the Royal Family later in the schedule at the Commonwealth Games in Edmonton.

This visit was one of the more demanding in terms of logistics support. Guards of Honour, bands and all of the other participants in the Royal ceremonies were a small part of the whole operation. Canadian staffs that came to be called the Canadian Household worked in lockstep with the Buckingham Palace staff. The two "Households" provided the co-ordinating function for all of the visit activities.

The itinerary for the visit began in St John's followed by stops in Corner Brook, Regina, Moose Jaw and Saskatoon prior to proceeding to the opening of the Commonwealth Games in Edmonton. Part way through the games the Duke of Edinburgh completed a side visit to Vancouver. Air transport for the Royal

Party, the accompanying staffs and the media posed a major support commitment.

Support at each of the venues throughout the visit was prearranged and in place at precise timings. Exact schedules from landings to departures for the next destination had to be co-ordinated and the complimenting ground transportation schedules were timed to the minute. This demanded a high degree of discipline and co-operation between the Canadian and Buckingham palace staffs to ensure that the itinerary of the Royal visitors maintained its schedule.

It was during the advance preparations for this visit that I met Peter Fleming. Peter was a quiet unassuming gentleman and a good friend of Vic Chapman's. Vic had recruited him to assist with the media ground transportation plan and its execution. They had spent several of their early years together on the Ottawa scene and had cultivated many mutual friends and acquaintances. Peter was an Ottawa boy, born and bred. He loved the city and had become fascinated with the centre of power.

Following his graduation from high school where he had learned to play the vibes after school and weekends, he went on tour with a local band. As Peter suggests, his father was not at all happy with his young son touring with a band and it was the cause of some discord for a time between them.

As he became better known in the music industry, Peter progressed through better gigs and found himself on tour with the band supporting the famous Liberace. It was during one of these tours that he noticed that while he would labour away hauling his vibes from the bus to the stage, setting up and tuning his instrument, the piano player merely lounged about flexing his fingers until show time. This became progressively more perplexing for Peter as the tour progressed. As the gig came to an end. Peter immediately returned to Ottawa, rented himself an apartment in a downtown high rise and had a grand piano and a bed installed. He lived there for a year surviving on take-out burgers and teaching himself how to play the piano.

At the end of his self-enforced exile he emerged as an accomplished jazz pianist and was immediately sought after by several bands in the region. It was during this period that he met his wife Liz, who also enjoyed jazz.

Peter at one point decided to go into the night club business and became the proprietor of one of the popular Ottawa lounges. His new wife Liz was none too happy about the hours that Peter was required to work as a jazz musician and the night-club life did nothing to improve his working hours. He soon began looking for another line of work. Vic by this time had been working as an advance man for the Prime Minister and he contracted Peter to assist him in the transportation arrangements for the PM while on tour.

As Vic moved from the PM's advanceman to his appointment as the Canadian Royal Press Secretary he took Peter with him. The jazz business was set aside and the two joined forces to provide support to media operations during a variety of state and Royal visits.. They understood each other and worked well together.

As Vic became more involved in visits, he absorbed Peter into his plans. They were both well connected with senior levels of the civil service and at the political level. Peter's qualities as a catalyst came to the fore. He had an uncanny sense for people's needs. He could identify a problem and while he might not be able to solve it himself, he always knew who could. Unobtrusively, he arranged for the right people to meet, seemingly by accident and under informal circumstances. Once contact was established, Peter would quietly exit the scene to allow the players to work it out.

In short order a problem was resolved and usually no one remembered that it was Peter who brought like minds together.

During the Royal and state visit travels of our team, Peter presided after hours at any bar that had a good band. He frequently filled in for the piano player, the vibes or the base guitar. When things got dull, Peter crooned the popular jazz songs of the forties to the delight of the audiences who thought he was part of the band. All of this he accomplished while suffering from diabetes. For this he was on an insulin programme not well known to others on the support team.

At an early point in the Edmonton visit, I was approached by the senior RCMP officer on the team. It had been reported to him that a number of syringes had been found by housekeeping. Some had been used and some were stored unopened in the small, refrigerated hospitality bar in Peter's room.

"Was Peter Fleming on drugs?" I was solemnly asked. I set the policeman's mind at ease and the rest of the team were quietly briefed. When Peter called on the radios to say that he was getting hungry, immediate steps were taken by the Ops centre to ensure that Peter got at least a ham sandwich to tide him over.

Peter and I became fast friends and we spent many an evening hour cruising the Rideau Canal in his Chriscraft cruiser he had named simply "The Punkin". The boat was often used to bring people together who needed to talk whether they knew it or not. Somehow, Peter always knew. The Punkin also served as a haven for relaxation after a busy day and many a hot summer's eve was spent motoring along the canal sipping cool, adult beverages.

During the Royal visit to the games in Edmonton there were many humorous and some near calamitous incidents. One of the more humorous is worthy of mention.

My military transportation officer had arranged for an exquisitely appointed VIP bus to transport members of the senior staff about Edmonton during the games. During our planning sessions it had become apparent that large motorcades would be unwieldy in the heavy traffic that was expected.

Accordingly it was decided that we would reduce the number of vehicles in the motorcade by moving everyone by bus except Her Majesty and the Duke of Edinburg who would travel by limousine. Pierre Lemay, a young lieutenant who I had recruited out of Uplands as transportation officer was given the task of making the arrangements for the number of buses required. DND didn't have any VIP buses but Pierre found a charter bus company in town that had such a vehicle and he quickly made the arrangements necessary to include it in his motorcade inventory.

The Royal Party seemed to enjoy the idea of the household staff riding by bus, which they knew to be beautifully outfitted. Unfortunately the Queen's private secretary, Sir Philip Moore, was not impressed and complained bitterly. At the first evening briefing on arrival in Edmonton he demanded a car to himself whereupon the Duke of Edinburgh poked a bit of good-natured fun at him and suggested that he should just sit back and enjoy the luxury bus.

That evening over a few beers a plot was hatched. Pierre Lemay had acquired a bicycle on loan from one of the members of the hotel staff. He had taken someone from the hotel marketing department into his confidence and had a small but official looking sign prepared that he then hung on the crossbar of the bicycle. It read: "Personal Motorcade Vehicle for Sir Philip Moore".

The whole prank was intended as an innocent inside joke at the expense one of our fellow staff members. The Royal Party was to depart the hotel the following morning and no media coverage of the departure was expected. The motorcade had been pre-positioned a few steps from the door of the hotel and therefore a view of the bicycle would be out of general view from all but a few who were in on the prank. Pierre and his bike complete with identifying sign occupied a prominent place just behind the Royal limo.

Somehow, a few members of the media got wind that something was up and suddenly appeared just as the Royal Party emerged from the hotel. To our astonishment, the Duke of Edinburgh had obviously been made privy to the prank and alerted the Queen as they exited the hotel. She cast a knowing smile in the direction of a very red-faced transportation officer as Prince Philip delayed boarding the royal limousine in order to see the reaction of the Queen's secretary.

Sir Philip Moore, who was in the small group immediately following the Royal principals, cast only a quick glance at Pierre and his bicycle and hurriedly boarded the bus. It was only a split second but the message had been delivered in spades. The newspapers and TV clips featured the two-wheeled motorcade conveyance prominently in the evening news.

Pierre was mortified and spent the next few hours worrying about his career and his potential for a future in the service beyond the Royal Visit. He needn't have as the incident helped to dissipate any nervous tensions that existed among the staffs for the remainder of the Royal Tour. It had also prompted a much-needed royal chuckle. It was suspected that Duke of Edinburg himself was responsible for the leak to the media.

One other incident provides a brief insight into the character of Prince Philip. It had come to the attention of the Queen's secretary, Sir Philip, that a female member of the Duke of Edinburgh's staff and a military member of the Canadian support staff were involved in something more than just a friendly relationship. Sir Philip raised this as a serious issue at one of the morning meetings and suggested that the lady in question be returned immediately to the UK.

The Duke of Edinburgh took all of this revelation in as it was discussed and finally turned to the Queen's secretary and said, " I say Sir Philip, get with the times". The incident was never discussed again and to my knowledge the affair that precipitated the discussion continued discretely for the remainder of the visit.

A few days prior to the Royal departure, Prince Andrew returning from his kayaking trip in the north rejoined the Royal Party. He had no official status and so a separate program was arranged for him. There was some concern that he might be bored with the proceedings and a disco night out was arranged. The Queen had agreed but had issued instructions that he was to be carefully chaperoned and kept out of trouble. Peter was sent out on a scouting mission and found the latest hot spot in Edmonton. A new disco bar in the new Four

Seasons Hotel filled the bill. It was just a block away from where we were all staying at the Edmonton Plaza.

Arrangements were made with the management to set aside an alcove for about six of us including HRH, his personal policeman, his Canadian Equerry, a young pilot from one of the operational squadrons, Vic, Peter, Wilf Fielding and myself. Wilf was a CBC producer who had known both Peter and Vic for some time and while he was representing the CBC on the visit he was sworn to secrecy on HRH's private disco visit.

Prince Andrew arrived shortly after we had staked out our alcove and he created the expected stir as he entered with his equerry and policeman. The group of three joined us. The other patrons having recovered from their surprise got on with their drinking and dancing.

By coincidence, Wilt the Stilt Chamberlain, the basketball player of some fame, was also present at the disco. He approached the Royal alcove and was invited to join us for a drink. We now had the celebrity market cornered in the club and the younger feminine set began strolling close to the lightly cordoned area that marked our territory. HRH was delighted of course and began to dance with the young women who caught his fancy.

Those of us who now formed the close bodyguard had to resort to grabbing anyone of the opposite sex who was close and who wanted to dance. There was never any problem in this regard as most of the young women wanted to be on the floor with His Royal Highness. It didn't seem to matter that he was dancing with someone else.

Once on the dance floor with a suitable partner we, the bodyguard, ran interference to the vulture-like traffic on the floor. Even Wilt the Stilt took a turn or two with a young damsel as he danced between HRH and those who just wanted to get close to Royalty. After a couple of hours the activity began to get a bit more frenetic and the security officer initiated the exit. It was then up to the rest of us to run a rear guard action allowing Prince Andrew and his bodyguard to escape on foot back to the hotel. We all had several well-deserved nightcaps when we got back to the safety of the Plaza.

The Queen asked at the morning meeting the next day how the visit to the disco had gone. "Routine", was the stock answer and the meeting continued with other more pressing business of the day.

The Royal visit to Canada and the opening of the Commonwealth Games in Edmonton was a huge success and I found it fascinating to watch as all of the members of both the Royal and the Canadian teams worked as one. The Royal household had done an excellent job of familiarising the Canadian team with all aspects of a Royal Visit. The Canadians on the other hand provided a clear insight into Canadian ways and traditions. The Royal Party accepted the fact that we were a relaxed group and responded accordingly. By the end of this tour we had become a team of experts on the conduct of major Royal Visits that would be difficult to duplicate.

Prince Charles became a regular visitor often twice a year between 1977 and 1980. The Queen Mother and HRH the Princess Margaret had also become regular visitors.

On one particular visit we encountered our first major security problem. The Prince of Wales visited the Pearson College of the Pacific for which he was a patron. Following the initial stop in Victoria he proceeded to Yellowknife to open a new Territorial museum and then on the Winnipeg for an overnight visit to one of his regiments.

The Royal Flight was an RAF VIP aircraft from the Queen's Flight in the UK and the small Royal party had been visiting in the Far East. They arrived in Victoria following their Trans-Pacific flight and a small team of us flew out to meet them and to provide the federal support for the brief tour. Following the visit to the college, the next stop on the tour was Yellowknife in the Northwest Territories and then on to Winnipeg and Ottawa.

The visit to Pearson College was more or less a private visit and no ceremonial support was required. His Royal Highness stayed at Government House in Victoria with a small personal staff that included his private secretary, his valet and the Scotland Yard and RCMP bodyguards. The rest of us, perhaps a half dozen or so were made to rough it at the Empress Hotel in downtown Victoria.

The visit to the college lasted one day, which included an evening program. The next day we were off in the RAF Royal Aircraft to Yellowknife where the Prince of Wales was to open a new museum that had been built on the shores of Great Slave Lake. We were met on arrival with the usual guard of honour mounted by Northern Region Headquarters and then we were all transported into town.

The Explorer Hotel had been reserved for our overnight accommodation. It was a beautiful April day when we departed Victoria and we were met with sub-zero temperatures in Yellowknife. The program included an official opening ceremony for a new native art gallery. A dinner affair later that evening at the Explorer Inn and the Royal Visit to Yellowknife was completed without hitch.

We boarded our aircraft the following day in the hangar where it had been kept under guard and out of the over-night ice and snow. Once aboard we were towed out to the line and waved farewell through the windows to our hosts who were bundled in parkas and quite unperturbed by the elements.

For the first couple of hours out of Yellowknife the flight was uneventful. We had enjoyed a good meal and were relaxing prior to our arrival in Winnipeg and what was expected to be a late night.

That evening, The Prince of Wales was to inspect the Royal Winnipeg Regiment for whom he was Colonel in Chief. I was quietly admiring the scenery as we went along when the valet came forward to our compartment to ask my advice on the positioning of the shoulder flashes on Prince Charles' green uniform. It would be the first time the Prince of Wales would wear the "green" of the Canadian Forces.

We discovered that for some reason the tunic provided for him was slightly marked and it wouldn't do for Prince Charles to inspect his troops in a flawed uniform.

Well, what was a good military Royal Visit Co-ordinator to do? I surrendered my freshly dry cleaned tunic for the cause. We were about the same size, the same rank and wore the same wing so there was little effort required in preparing my uniform for the event.

Meanwhile I moved about wearing a slightly flawed tunic owned by the Prince of Wales.

We had solved all of these minor problems when the captain of the aircraft summoned me to the cockpit. He had just been advised that the airport at Winnipeg had received a telephone call a few minutes before announcing that there was a bomb on board the Royal Flight.

That was all - just that there was a bomb on board and nothing else. The Captain indicated that he had a brief discussion with the flight engineer and that nothing appeared to be amiss. I advised the captain to continue on and I would discuss it with the household.

I interviewed the flight engineer myself who I found to be a very efficient RAF sergeant. He advised me that one of the crewmen had been present by the aircraft all night and that the hangar had been locked and guarded. He had checked it himself before retiring.

There was no possibility that any unauthorised person or persons had been near the Royal Aircraft. Furthermore, he was quite indignant that some one would suggest that there was anything on the aircraft that shouldn't be there. With this information in hand I felt better equipped to brief the private secretary.

Squadron Leader David Checketts (Ret'd) was an old fighter pilot and had become adept at analysing such situations. He quickly asked me what I thought.

Referring to the comments of the flight engineer, I said that I felt that we should ignore the threat. He was of the same opinion and together we entered the royal compartment to brief Prince Charles. He listened to us each in turn without comment and when we had finished he said, "I agree but let's be sure we are not going into a blood and thunder situation". We nodded and I left to brief the captain of the aircraft.

By this time we were in direct contact with Winnipeg approach control. The officials on the ground were in a mild state of panic and were advising us that the base had requested that we taxi to a remote area of the airfield for disembarking. We advised them that we were confident that any suggestion of a bomb on board was a hoax and we would ignore it. Furthermore, we would taxi to our predetermined parking position where there awaited the guard of honour and a large crowd that had gathered to witness the Royal arrival.

As we taxied in following an uneventful landing, I decided that for safety's sake I would make a minor adjustment in the Royal protocol. Ordinarily the protocol rule of thumb was that the royal principal was always the last to board the aircraft and the first to disembark.

The Base Commander was somewhat shocked when the door opened and I emerged in a somewhat less than the standard order of military dress. I had asked the crew to give me two minutes before they opened the door for HRH. In that time interval I was able to satisfy the Base Commander that the aircraft was not going to blow up and that all of the appropriate security precautions had been taken before we left the ground at Yellowknife. A minute or so later the door opened once again and the Prince of Wales emerged to the warm response from the large crowd of Royalty watchers.

We didn't get an opportunity to chat until later that night when the Base Commander advised me that the threatening call had come in to one of the local radio stations who had relayed it to the base. Naturally, the base responded in accordance with the procedures established to deal with such emergencies. They were unprepared however for the adamant denial of the presence of anything even mildly dangerous on board the Royal Flight. I think the base Commander was disappointed that he couldn't exercise his base disaster plan in full view of the international media.

Today there are very strict and inflexible rules and regulations governing such situations. Highly necessary in the post 9/11 atmosphere but at the time the procedures were more guidelines than they were mandatory regulations.

Following the departure of the Prince of Wales after his very brief visit to Canada, I returned to my more military responsibilities at the headquarters.

Between NATO conferences in Belgium and Lahr Germany, exercises in North Norway and defence of North America and conferences with various military agencies in the US, my schedule was full and challenging. Royal and state visits that came along were to me a holiday and I enjoyed both the planning and the execution.

I felt however that I should really start training others to do the job I had been doing for almost three years. I involved two officers on my staff in the detailed planning phases for one or perhaps two visits and finally gave up the part I enjoyed most - the execution.

The earlier training that I had experienced in management engineering and in particular the work I had done in analysing the financial management structure in the NDHQ Financial Branch had provided me with a sound understanding of financial procedures and other instruments of financial management.

The staff became adept in the development of accurate budgets to support various taskings ranging from Royal and State Visits to Russian satellite recovery operations on Great Slave Lake.

By early 1979 I had been a "tasker" for about three years and was beginning to contemplate where I might be posted next. I had indicated to the personnel branch that unless they had a flying job for me, I would just as soon stay where I was. It was a bit of wishful thinking on my part because I was now forty-seven years old. It meant that they left me alone and I didn't have to fight off endless offers of other jobs elsewhere in the headquarters.

In the meantime, I was living a full and challenging life. I seemed to be involved in everything "military" that was going on in Ottawa. My association with Royal visits brought me into contact with officials from Government House and I became more involved in the planning sessions for the Governor General's travel schedules. This association led to invitations to various social events at Government House. Skating parties at the outdoor rink on the grounds and a whole range of other social functions began to appear on my social calendar.

All of this of course did nothing special in the advancement of my career and I shunned any inclination to take advantage of the situation in which I found myself. However, through these associations I became involved with the media both professionally and socially more than at any time in my career.

It was foreign to me at first because for years I had been told that everything we did in the military was classified. The lowest security classification was "Restricted". That meant not for general release and we took this to mean particularly the media. Therefore as my association with the media grew closer I was somewhat amazed to discover that most of my media friends knew almost as much about classified information as I did and were quite capable of withholding it from release to the public if necessary.

Of course this did not apply to all media and it was necessary to be selective as to who in the profession one could relax with without fear of being misquoted or otherwise ambushed in the morning papers. I soon discovered that I was privy to secrets on Parliament Hill that could be damaging to national security but were quantum leaps away from having anything to do with the military.

As my acceptance into the "Hill Set" progressed, I found that the yardsticks I had begun to apply to the media in terms of those I could trust, could also apply equally to the politicians. There were those with whom I could spend a pleasant evening and not be the least concerned that I might reveal information provided me by others in trust. On the other hand there were those with whom I discovered that I had to be very careful in what I said and how I said it.

Without realising it, I was becoming centrist in my views. If it didn't happen within the sound of the Peace Tower bells, it didn't happen.

It wasn't long until I became aware of the western lament that they voted for their MPs and sent them to Ottawa to represent them and they came home some time later representing Ottawa to their constituents.

My interest in politics was expanding considerably and I was beginning to examine my attitudes with respect to the relationship between government and the military. I became interested in many of the policies emerging that a few years earlier would have been of little interest to me.

CHAPTER TWENTY-ONE
EVACUATION OF CANADIAN NATIONALS
FROM IRAN

Naval Captain Mike Barrow replaced Hal Tilley as my immediate superior. Mike was a bit younger than Hal and shared many of the same values.

Hal and I had become good friends and I was concerned that I would have to accustom myself to a new style of management but this was not to be the case. Mike and I clicked from the start. He took up where Hal had left off and there was little disruption to the systems and other activities that were proven over time to work for those of us in the directorate.

Another close friendship that I had developed while assigned to DMOC was Colonel Bentley MacLeod. Bentley was the Director of International Plans Co-ordination. He had assembled a fine staff of operational officers who concentrated their planning skills on the operation of Canadian ground troops in the field for both exercise purposes and those assigned to operational roles in the international community. Bentley had been in Korea with the Van Duexs in the early fifties. As a unilingual junior officer, he had excelled in the field despite his limited facility in the French language. He was living proof that the language of war was universal and while he supported official bilingualism, he was not happy with the manner in which it was being imposed on the military. Following his Korean experience, he "re-badged" to the Black Watch and served with that esteemed regiment until his retirement.

Many of us were not in agreement with the blatant emphasis on a bilingual capability frequently nudging aside the merit principle as a prerequisite for promotion. It was very obviously creating chaos in all of the promotion boards and was the source of a significant level of dissatisfaction at all rank levels.

An old fighter pilot and an old infantryman had discovered that we had more in common in our approach to military matters than we had disagreement.

Both Bentley and Mike Barrow enjoyed the occasional beer and we would often discuss difficult operational problems in a quiet corner of the Bytown Mess on Lisgar Street. Navy, army and airforce could under most circumstances come together amicably to achieve an aim. One of the problems we were facing was with a project that required our participation on an External Affairs team monitoring the growing upheaval in Iran.

During the latter part of 1979, the Ayattolah Khamenei who was at the time exiled in Paris, issued a warning to foreign nationals in the country indicating that he could not guarantee their safety in the event of a revolt.

The External Affairs count of foreigners working in Iran was quite high and most countries that had people working there were becoming uneasy. It was estimated that there were approximately six hundred and eighty Canadians as part of a much larger group of foreign nationals in Iran. Other than the diplomatic and consular staffs most of them were involved in the petroleum industry.

The team headed by External Affairs officials met regularly in the operations centre at the Lester B. Pearson building on Sussex Drive. It was here that up to date intelligence briefings were provided on the situation as it developed.

External Affairs had dispatched a team of communicators to Ankara and Tehran with orders to install secure two-way communications between the two Canadian embassies in each of those cities. The team of communicators, as it turned out were two of the same MOT officers that had provided for the communications support to Royal Visits. Thus good interpersonal relationships fell into place and I felt that should the military be called upon to assist in anyway they would be useful contacts.

I had spent several hours in the External Ops centre on an unseasonably cold day toward the end of November 1979 and it past noon as I arrived back to my own headquarters. Mike was waiting for me as I entered the office and suggested that we debrief at the bar.

We made our way on foot over to the Bytown Mess where we enlisted Bentley. Once out of earshot of others, I brought them up to date on the situation in Iran.

I explained that travel within country was dangerous and the Canadian Embassy had advised all Canadian Nationals to stay close to home. The embassy had set up an alert system based on the pyramid principle. A dozen or so calls to key people located in areas where high concentrations of Canadians worked began the chain. Those receiving the initial call would in turn call their own assigned list of people and so on. The system had been exercised and should evacuation be necessary, every Canadian citizen working in country could be notified to move on very short notice.

The problem was that there were no evacuation plans in place and diplomatic relations such as they were, had reached high tension levels which made for difficult negotiations with the Iranian government. Evacuation arrangements should they become necessary were developed without direct consultation with the Iranian authorities. While some diplomatic overtures had been made, the Iranian government essentially viewed queries from foreign governments with suspicion and were reluctant to enter into any kind of information exchange.

We were becoming somewhat desperate to come up with a plan that would provide for safe passage of aircraft conducting air evacuation operations in the country. We needed safe air corridors and designated airfields that could be used for evacuation and assurances that the road networks leading to those airfields would be open to Canadian nationals. Unfortunately by early December we were still at an impasse and the situation in Iran was worsening daily.

One Friday I was involved in a negotiation for DND support to some other cause and it was decided that Mike would attend the morning briefing at the External Ops centre in my place. It was after twelve o'clock noon when I returned to the office where my secretary advised me that Captain Barrow had asked her to tell me to get down to the medical inspection centre as soon as I returned. She added that I was to meet him in the Naval Mess when I was finished with the medical folks.

I had no idea what was going on and dutifully reported to medical centre thinking that they wanted some information concerning tasking of medical operations or whatever. To my surprise, I was ushered straight into the clinic to be met by two nurses armed with needles for everything from sniffles to cholera. I asked what it was all for and they suggested that by the kind of needles I was getting it would be either the Middle East or North Africa.

Extensively inoculated against almost any kind of disease known to man, I proceeded to the Naval Mess feeling like a pincushion but otherwise none the worse for wear. I was met by loud guffaws as I entered the bar from the only two officers who knew what was going on. Equipped with a beer, I was escorted into a private room where Mike and Bentley advised me that I would be leaving on Sunday for Iran.

I had a quick lunch and we all got back to the office to prepare as best we could some kind of plan that would allow me to operate flexibly in the area. It was decided that I would fly to Ankara and attempt to get into Iran from there. All diplomatic channels with Iran were now closed and I would work with the two Canadian embassies in Tehran and Ankara. I was issued with a diplomatic passport and enough US dollars to pay off the mortgage on my house.

Whether the Iranians knew it or not the evacuation of Canadians from their country had begun. Transport Command had six Hercules aircraft on the move from bases in Canada and Germany. Ankara had been selected as a safe haven and the international airport there would be the terminus from which Canadians evacuated out of Iran would find onward transport to Canada or elsewhere as directed by their employers.

Airline tickets to Ankara were provided to me in a few hours and I had only to prepare myself and my kit for a period of temporary duty that was open ended. External Affairs were against me wearing a uniform and I packed a couple of three piece suits that I hoped had a diplomatic look about them. But I cautiously included a uniform in my bag just in case.

On Saturday afternoon I was finalising my travel plans when I had a call from the Commanding Officer of 412 Transport Squadron in Trenton. He advised me that he was departing Trenton that night for Lahr and then on to Ankara. He had been chosen as the Commander of the air contingent of Boeing 707s and Hercules aircraft assigned to the evacuation. He asked me if I would prefer to fly over on his Boeing 707 instead of travelling commercial. A quick check of my travel schedule indicated that by travelling on the air force 707, I would arrive in Ankara a good day earlier than if I were to travel the commercial alternative.

The Squadron Commander was an acquaintance and I was pleased that there would be someone involved that I knew. I was contemplating how I would get myself to Trenton when he cut me off. "Don't worry about it," he said, "I'll stop in Ottawa and pick you upon our way over, We'll be there at eight PM sharp tomorrow night".

The plan went like clockwork. The tasking that had been initiated in our office was clear and concise. One Boeing, six Hercules aircraft, support staff sufficient to sustain flying operations for a month and a communications group complete with secure communication equipment. The Hercs departed early on the Saturday and being somewhat slower would likely arrive about the same time as the Boeing on Sunday evening.

I reported in my best three-piece suit to the passenger desk at the Air Movements Unit at Uplands to be advised by a startled looking sergeant that, "no sir, the AMU is closed for the night and there are no aircraft movements". I stood my ground and said that I would just wait a few minutes. It was about seven forty-five. Fifteen minutes to go before my personal transport was to arrive and it was snowing heavily.

At five minutes to eight my friend taxied his Boeing into the lights on the tarmac. A stairs truck appeared and a diplomatic looking gentleman in a three-piece suit scurried up and into the aircraft baggage in hand. The stairs were removed, the door closed and the aircraft turned on the tarmac disappeared into the night. I have often wondered since what that sergeant must have thought as he went to bed that night reviewing in his mind the unusual spectacle he had witnessed earlier on the flight line.

A brief stop in Lahr was required to refuel and re-provision the aircraft. We were also carrying a team of about twenty communicators and their equipment and so there were mouths to feed on both legs of the flight. We arrived in Ankara late in the evening on Sunday night having lost eight hours due to the time change.

The Canadian Ambassador to Turkey welcomed us at the airport. He seemed relieved to have me aboard and we departed immediately for downtown Ankara. The Commanding Officer of the air contingent was left to look after his aircraft and crews. I discussed the local situation with the ambassador over a bottle of scotch that someone had thoughtfully placed in my room and then, bidding the Ambassador bon soire, retired for the night.

My hotel was a brief walk from the Canadian embassy, an attractive high rise building located in the centre of Ankara.

I was to discover later that the Ambassador's residence had been designed by a Canadian architect. It was really a very remarkable edifice surround by lush gardens that included trees that were indigenous to every part of Canada. I have no idea how much this beautiful bit of Canadiana cost and I didn't have the nerve to ask at the time or in the years since.

The next morning I was up with the sun and enjoyed the short walk that helped to clear my head for what was to come. I noted with interest that the roof of the embassy was festooned with communications antennae and found it hard to believe that the communicators we had sent over a few weeks earlier had been able to perform such a complex installation in such a short time.

I soon found out that it was the same communications group that accompanied me from Ottawa the night before. On reaching the hotel they had changed their cloths and had gone right to work with the installation. We would be able to communicate with all of the participants assigned to the mission and would only activate the system when the evacuation began.

Meanwhile the Turkish General staff took an intense interest in the sudden activity in the otherwise docile Canadian Embassy and the antennae bristling from the roof had become a cause for alarm. The Canadian Military Attaché at the Embassy was an army colonel and was bending over backwards to be of assistance. I remember only his first name - Sid. He advised them that our concerns were for our own people in Iran and that there was no war-like intent on our part to threaten the peace of Turkey. The country at the time was under military rule and while friendly relations had been established with NATO, the Turkish military were suspicious of our every move.

I began getting calls from the airport from our Air Commander demanding that I do something to allow his men to get back onto the airfield. They didn't have proper clearances and the Turkish army guards were blocking the access to their aircraft. I barged in to Sid's office at the embassy and suggested that we had better damn well do something and fast. Fortunately, the attaché had a good contact in the Turkish General staff and he was able to arrange a meeting for us right after lunch. Meanwhile our crews had to return to the hotel to await further instructions.

We met with several Turkish generals who I quickly discovered were sympathetic to our plight and after a cordial half-hour of sipping tea and discussing the problem, they became receptive to all of our requests and issued orders accordingly. I immediately took the car and driver assigned to me by the embassy and headed for the airport some twenty miles away. The change had occurred while I was enroute. Our crews, who had all returned to the airport in anticipation of a successful meeting, had been issued with passes and were becoming friendly with the guards.

The Canadian military man has a penchant for making friends quickly and it pays off handsomely when getting difficult things accomplished. Smooth, cordial interpersonal relations in any language make life easier for everyone and when accomplished at the working level they are invaluable. The Canadian NCO and his men are specialists in this technique.

There was still an issue about the use of parking space on the airfield and also the use of one of the two hangars that our people had identified as most suitable for our maintenance needs. It turned out that the airport manager was the brother-in-law of some senior government official and had recently been appointed to his position despite the fact that he knew little of aircraft or airport operations. A quick phone call to one of my new found army friends on the Turkish general staff quickly rectified the situation and from that point on the airfield belonged to Canada.

It had taken not quite two days for us to assume an operational posture in a country far from home. We had taken over the hotel in which I was staying in Ankara and it was rapidly becoming Canadianized. The hotel staff looked after our every need. Since our arrival there had been no flying and the ground crews attended their aircraft for a few short hours daily to ensure that they would be ready when called upon. They spent most of their idle hours in around the hotel enjoying the special treatment.

I had a standing reservation on Turkish Airlines to fly into Tehran every morning departing at eight o'clock. Each morning I called Canadian Ambassador, Ken Taylor in Iran on our secure link only to be told that it was not safe for the embassy staff to travel out to the airport to meet me. Furthermore, it would be unsafe for me to try to get into town on my own. I thought perhaps they may have had a vision of John Wayne in a green beret riding a tank into Tehran with bayonet drawn. However, even after I assured them that I would travel in my civilian attire, they continued to insist that it would not be safe for me to come.

I was getting desperate as I had no contact with my superiors in Ottawa and was acting pretty much on my own. After about the third day of inactivity, I decided that I would use a military approach. After all it worked on the Turks, why not the Iranians? I had met several Iranian officers previously at various training establishments in the States and found them to be intelligent, friendly and often helpful.

Once again I took Sid aside and asked him to make contact with Iranian Military Attaches office in Ankara. I asked that he advise them that it was our intention to try to come up with an evacuation plan for Canadian nationals currently residing in Iran and that we needed to discuss such a plan with the appropriate Iranian military authorities.

The meeting was arranged at the Iranian embassy for after lunch that day. To my surprise Sid was dressed in full uniform while I had not yet taken my uniform off the hanger in the hotel. We were welcomed to the embassy by the senior attaché, a Commodore in the Iranian navy.

We were ushered into a well-appointed room and introduced to an airforce colonel, an army colonel and a couple of officers of lieutenant colonel and major rank. The meeting began cordially and we were served with a very sweet Iranian tea in small sherry sized glasses that were inserted into a basket-like copper holder. As we sipped, we discussed everything from the weather to the education system in the United States. The Iranian officers were quite familiar with the US system as most of them had either attended university in the states or their children were attending there.

Each time I tried to explain my purpose in requesting the meeting, the subject would be turned to something else of little importance to me. I must admit to being a little astonished at my own patience as ordinarily I didn't have that much time for such obfuscation. I tried two or three times to get down to the subject at hand and each time my overture would be turned to other mundane issues.

Finally, I said to Sid in the politest of terms that perhaps we should be getting back to our own embassy and we all rose and headed for the door. Sid retrieved his hat and began shaking hands as we reached the door. I went to follow the same ritual when the Commodore took my arm and suggested that perhaps I would like to stay behind. I was overjoyed and while I didn't know what to expect, I felt that any conversation that might take place was better than what we had been able to achieve so far. Sid suggested that I call our embassy when I was finished and they would send a car to pick me up. This was met with a statement by the Iranian commodore that the Iranian embassy would see me safely back. With that we turned and re-entered the room where we had just sipped tea.

Once we were all inside the door was closed and buzzers were pushed summoning two or three junior staff officers equipped with maps and charts. These were all laid out on the table and one of the bookcases that had stood innocently along the wall beside the conference table miraculously turned into a bar. A bottle of Johnny Walker Black Label was uncorked, an ice bucket appeared, jackets came off and sleeves were rolled up as the business of planning evacuation routes began.

I found out later that most military attaches receive some level of training in information gathering and observation. When on posting abroad military attaches treat each other as spies and therefore avoid all possible discussion of significant military matters. They had decided as a result of all of the idle conversation leading up to my aborted departure that I was "safe", meaning ignorant in intelligence matters. With Sid prudently out of the way it would be safe to proceed in the planning process with the non-spy from Canada.

Several hours passed as we co-ordinated routes, timings, radio and navigation frequencies. We had selected several airfields that I was assured could handle both the Hercs and the Boeing including the ground support equipment, fuel and most other needs for the operation. Notably, the army colonel advised that they would ensure safe passage routes for Canadians travelling to the selected airfields during an evacuation operation. Several scotches were consumed along with the gourmet food had been brought in on trays to keep us going.

It was close to mid-night as I bade my new friends farewell. Loaded with scotch and an armful of planning documents duly approved through an exchange of telex's between the embassy in Turkey and the Iranian government in Tehran, I departed in the Iranian ambassador's chauffeur driven car to return to the Canadian embassy.

Both the Canadian ambassador and Sid had been waiting for me since about five o'clock that afternoon and had consoled themselves at the embassy bar while waiting. Their discussion centred on whether or not they were to have a diplomatic incident on their hands perpetrated by a mad old air force fighter pilot.

With a fresh scotch in hand, I briefed them on the basics of the plan and assured them that the appropriate co-ordination with the Iranian government had been completed by telephone and telex. All that remained was to agree to a launch time for the evacuation to take place.

The next morning I called Ambassador Ken Taylor in Tehran to advise him that I wouldn't need to go into Iran as I had completed the plans the night before at the Iranian embassy in Ankara. He seemed pleased although not with the enthusiasm I had expected. He signed off once again by asking me to relay to External Affairs in Ottawa that his houseguests were still OK. This did not come as a surprise since a month earlier we had tasked nine military policemen from Canada as temporary guards for the Canadian embassy in Tehran. It was this group to which I initially thought he was referring and began to wonder why he or External Affairs should be so concerned for their well being.

After a week of inactivity I was getting worried that I would have some one hundred crew and support staff stranded in Ankara for Christmas. We had been treated well by the embassy staff and were invited to many of the diplomatic Christmas functions hosted by the different embassies in town. But I couldn't seem to get a decision as to what was to be done over Christmas. I wanted to pull the whole air group back to Lahr where if we had to spend Christmas away from home at least it would be on a Canadian base and only five hours flying time by Herc to Ankara.

By December 22nd we still had no feed back from Ottawa on what they expected us to do. I knew that my old friend Colonel Bentley MacLeod was monitoring our situation closely and was confident that he would do everything in his power to generate some positive activity one way or another. About mid-day our orders finally came. We were to withdraw to Lahr with our Hercules fleet the next day. A Boeing would be waiting for us at Lahr for those returning to Canada for Christmas. The Boeing that had taken us to Ankara had been recalled earlier to perform other priority tasks.

I was told to bring all of the plans that had been developed with the Iranians and would be debriefed on my arrival at Lahr. We were out of Ankara as quickly as we had arrived and battled headwinds on our westward flight across the Mediterranean. We were forced into a refuelling stop at Brindizi on the south coast of

Italy and since we did not have diplomatic clearance to land in country, we were held in a marshalling area under guard and some distance from the main terminal.

The area was unlit and the refuelling had to be carried out in darkness. While we were allowed to disembark onto the infield near the aircraft, we were not allowed to leave the immediate area and a trip to the airport restaurant was out of the question. We broke open the survival rations in the kits on the aircraft and munched on cold crackers, soups and other disagreeable forms of digestive assault.

It was around eight in the evening when we finally arrived at Lahr and the Boeing was waiting for us as promised. I was met by a senior Canadian diplomat on arrival and briefed him in detail on the plan that had been developed with the Iranian military authorities. He accepted my plans and was to present them to a consortium of countries in Stuttgart the next day. There were several countries that had citizens working in Iran. The British, Germans, Belgians and the Japanese were interested in getting their people safely out of the country before the Ayatollah moved out of his exile in France.

I asked if there was any need for me to go to Stuttgart and was told no, that wouldn't be necessary and I could proceed home to Canada.

As it turned out my teenage son, Stephen was visiting friends in Lahr and was scheduled to return to Ottawa on the flight that I was about to take. The flight seemed to be fully booked and Stephen was bumped to make way for me. Since I had to be back in NDHQ the next morning, I told him that I would take the flight that night and we would get him home for Christmas by commercial airlines the next day.

Naturally, he was disappointed and as he escorted me to the departure desk, I chided the sergeant supervising boarding that he had an empty seat on the aircraft. It was getting late in the day and the sergeant had been harried for most of it. Without blinking an eye he did a quick recount and sure enough there was an empty seat. Coincidentally, it was next to the one I had been assigned. Father and son returned home for Christmas thankful for small mercies.

The next day I briefed the senior staff on my activities while in Turkey thus ending my direct involvement in the Iranian evacuation.

The Department of National Defence hosts an annual New Years Day levy at the headquarters building at 101 Colonel By Drive. It was in full swing at twelve noon on January 1st, 1980 when I was called to General Wiesman's office for an emergency meeting.

The launch of the evacuation had been ordered and the fleet of aircraft would be departing Trenton later that day. I was disappointed not to be going but as it turned out the wheels of diplomacy had been churning over the holiday season. The meeting in Stuttgart on Christmas Eve had combined my draft evacuation plan with those of other countries. Agreement was reached that while Canada would bear a major share of the airlift, foreign national personnel would be evacuated using the resources of all participating countries. All evacuees would be moved to safe havens by the most expeditious means whether by land, sea or air.

I returned to the Levy feeling somewhat left out but comforted with the fact that my planning session with the Iranian Military

Attaché staff had contributed in some way to ensuring that innocent Canadians working abroad and their families were being safely removed from harms way.

Back to work after the New Years day celebrations there was little left to do with respect to the evacuation other than to monitor its progress from a distance. The Ayatollah arrived triumphantly into Iran several days after the evacuation was complete and most if not all foreign nationals other than a small number of diplomatic staffs had found safety.

In one of our morning intelligence briefings we were told that the house guests to whom the ambassador had been referring in the messages I had passed to Ottawa were actually eight American citizens who had been unable to escape earlier. Ken Taylor, the Canadian Ambassador had given them safe haven in the Canadian Embassy in Tehran.

In the House of Commons, the opposition had been battering the government for days demanding to know when the Canadian embassy in Tehran would be abandoned and the embassy staffs sent home.

During one heated exchange, the Honourable Flora Macdonald, then Minister for External Affairs nearly let it slip when she retorted in response to an insistent Member of Parliament, "if you only knew what we know". At that moment the great deception almost faltered and as unintentional as it might have been, a handful of American and Canadian lives where put to greater risk.

Canadian passports were hastily prepared for the American "House Guests" and they were spirited out of the country and to safety before they could be too carefully scrutinised. The remaining embassy staff closely followed them and a page in Canadian diplomacy in Iran was closed for a time.

CHAPTER TWENTY-TWO
EVACUATION OF SOUTHEAST ASIAN REFUGEES

Early in 1980 yet another red file appeared on my desk. It was from the Minister of Immigration requesting DND support in the evacuation of refugees from South East Asia. A relatively simple task I thought to myself as I headed out to what I assumed would be a preliminary planning meeting.

As I was preparing to depart my office General Monty Wiesman came by and casually suggested that I not give away the farm. I was well aware that we had been severely overtasking our air transport resources. Air Transport Command were experiencing difficulty in fulfilling all of the requirements imposed on our small fleet of four Boeing aircraft. We had made a decision to arrest the rate of tasking on the Boeing fleet until we could catch up the backlog of our airlift requirements.

With Monty's instructions on my mind, I made my way over to Hull and the Department of Employment and Immigration. As the meeting got underway I was asked to explain how many aircraft we were prepared to provide in support of the evacuation. I pointed out that for the next several months our transport fleet was fully tasked and unless we were directed to change our priorities we could do little to help. I added however that I was prepared to open negotiations with various commercial airlines that might be interested in providing charter services for such an operation.

To my astonishment, I was told that the Minister of National Defence had given his support to the operation and that the evacuation of Southeast Asian refugees to Canada would be the number one priority.

Having no formal indication that this was a priority DND were aware of, I remained silent. For the rest of the meeting I took notes for future reference on the various preliminary planning aspects of evacuation planning.

On return to my office, I debriefed the senior staff and we contemplated our priority tasking list with view to identifying those air transport taskings that could be set aside to make way for a fairly formidable evacuation operation. Immigration had indicated that up to fifty thousand refugees would be brought to Canada and the department was counting on DND to provide the airlift.

A few preliminary calculations indicated that it would take half of our Boeing 707 fleet committed full time for at least eight months to complete the task. If the government were to insist that we carry out the evacuation, we would have to charter most of our Trans Atlantic scheduled flights with commercial carriers.

The availability of charter service on such short notice was questionable and we were facing the possibility that we would be unable to support all of our other existing commitments. I was sent off to put pressure on my Ministry of Immigration counterparts to charter commercial air directly. In the meantime General Wiesman briefed his superiors on the implications posed to DND should we provide full airlift support to the South East Asian evacuation operations.

The next day I met with the officials from the Department of Immigration. They had been designated as the lead department for the operation and most of the political negotiations had already taken place. The mandarins had assumed that DND once ordered would participate enthusiastically. There was some surprise therefore when I advised them that they shouldn't take DND support for granted. I repeated that we were already heavily committed to other government-approved tasks and that our participation would be entirely dependent on the availability of our resources for that purpose.

We set the airlift problem aside and proceeded to identify the ground support that would be required at the refugee camps in South East Asia and at the reception centres in Canada. Singapore, Kuala Lumpur and Bangkok had been selected as the locations for the screening camps that would be manned by immigration and health and welfare personnel.

Medical authorities would be responsible for all of the necessary preliminary medical screening while immigration would ensure that all refugee documentation conformed to Canadian government policy.

Little was required of the Department of National Defence in-theatre but we agreed that we would provide a small contingent of military doctors and nurses to augment the Health and Welfare mandate if needed. Military medical facilities in Canada would be tasked to the fullest at the reception camps that would be established to support such a mass influx of refugees.

We tasked CFB Namao near Edmonton as the western reception centre. At the time it had an excess of single living accommodation on the base and could easily support up to about five hundred people for short periods of time. CFB Long Point, a former air force supply depot near Montreal was designated as the eastern terminus for the refugees.

Sponsoring agencies composed of church groups and other community organisations across Canada had applied to sponsor the settlement of the refugees in their communities. With the two reception camps operating also as distribution centres the dispatch of refugees either to a community of their choice or as selected by the sponsoring agency simplified the logistics problems. Every effort was made to ensure that their transition to Canada would as smooth as possible within a welcoming environment.

All of these plans were developed smoothly and with little conflict. There were now three government departments working on the operation and for the most part our relationships were becoming harmonious. The problem of airlift however, still hadn't been resolved and I was being told to hold firm by my DND superiors while my colleagues in immigration were maintaining constant pressure on me to resolve the situation.

Earlier I had suggested that the Department of Immigration contact the Canadian commercial air operators to determine the interest and availability in the industry to provide a charter service. Air Canada, Canadian, Wardair and Quebecair all claimed that they were over-committed and could not possibly participate in the operation. Furthermore, they had little desire to participate in what they assessed as a mundane role for a commercial air operation.

This came as a bit of a surprise to me because during the Royal Visits that I had supported over the past few years, I had come into personal contact with Max Ward on several occasions. During one of our many conversations, mostly involving the transport of the Queen on his Dash 7 aircraft to remote venues in Northern Alberta, he had mentioned that he thought his fleet of 747 aircraft were under tasked. He demonstrated through rapid manipulation of his ever-present calculator that with astute scheduling, a significant number of additional productive flying hours could be achieved. This had impressed me at the time and it now returned to my mind as an interesting possibility.

Immigration had exhausted their search for a commercial carrier and were beginning to increase their demands on me to break the impasse they perceived at DND. I took a copy of the list of airlines they had contacted and also the names of the officials at each airline they had spoken to. The next day I called the commercial carriers once again. The larger airlines either didn't have the right equipment to participate or were fully committed to other operations.

As I picked up the phone to call Wardair one last time, I recognised the name of the official that had been contacted by the immigration department. He was a scheduling officer in the Ward Air ops centre at the Toronto airport, a good man but not a decision-maker. I quickly checked the credentials of the other contact persons on the list and discovered that in all cases they were schedulers who had no authority to make decisions on flying programme priorities..

I spent the rest of the day contacting airline officials several levels higher than the ops centre level only to find that Air Canada, Canadian Pacific and Quebec Air really were not able or perhaps in some cases unwilling to participate. Quebec Air did not have the right aircraft for such a long-range evacuation and other smaller airlines had similar problems. Finally I called Max Ward in Edmonton where he was headquartered at the time.

When he came on the phone, I good-naturedly chided him for turning down business. He knew that I had few shares in his company and he would tell me from time to time how rich I would be one day. After a few pleasantries I asked him if he was aware that we were looking for chartered airlift for South East Asian refugees. He hadn't heard of it and I provided him with a quick thumbnail sketch of our situation. With little further discussion he advised me that he would have a negotiator in Ottawa by noon our time the following day.

I met Brian Robertson at the airport at about 11:00 AM the next day. We proceeded straight to a meeting with the intergovernmental co-ordinating group and I briefed him in the car on the way.

Brian and I had worked together on the Queen's visit to the Commonwealth Games in Edmonton and through that association we had become good friends. He was a senior planner and logistician of the highest calibre and was used by Max Ward as a point man for all of the airline's major projects. He had done his homework well and had been up most of the previous night calculating costs for the charter service and the ability of the airline to meet the demands of the operation.

On reaching the Department of Immigration offices in Hull we completed the introductions without delay. Brian and I sat together and listened to the briefing, taking notes from time to time but not saying very much as the briefer went over the ability of the combined Southeast Asian and Canadian screening and distribution centres to absorb the refugee load.

As the briefing ended there was a pause while Brian confirmed some calculations in his notes and then suggested that Wardair could probably mount two flights a week for a few weeks but could not sustain that frequency of operation for a much longer period. He advised that Wardair could probably average one 747 flight of just under five hundred refugees a week for the duration of the operation.

This brought a sigh of relief from all concerned. One flight a week from Southeast Asia to alternating destinations between Edmonton and Long Point was about the maximum that both the screening centres in Southeast Asia and the reception centres in Canada could handle. The price per seat of about $850 per refugee was quickly negotiated, a cost that would be covered by the immigration department and would be recovered from the refugees after they became settled in their chosen communities. The plan was in place as I drove Brian to the airport at around five o'clock that afternoon. He would be home in time for supper and I would spend the evening contemplating the increased value of my shares.

While all of this preliminary planning had been going on, our Boeing 707s had not been idle. We had flown two flights of refugees of about 200 persons each to Canada.

The first flight was a disaster as we had received some faulty dietary advice in terms of the provision of in-flight meals for the refugees. Relying on North American standards, some dietician decided that heavy emphasis on dairy products would be suitable for hungry people and children in particular. While well intentioned, the fact that a large number of Asians suffer from lactose intolerance was overlooked. The condition tends to induce a violent digestive response not welcome in most forms of travel.

The first flight began normally and everything was going well until the meal was served. The meal itself was healthy enough but unfortunately milk was featured prominently among the beverage options. The reaction was delayed but only for about a half an hour when the run on the washrooms began and was continuous for the remainder of the flight. Many were violently sick to their stomachs but most experienced a diarrhoea-like affliction that kept them busy and far from the effects of in-flight boredom.

The aircraft effluent holding tanks were on overload and the situation was becoming desperate just as the aircraft came to a merciful stop at the Namao military air terminal in Edmonton.

Apart from the near disaster of the first flight, everything else had gone according to plan and all of the logistic support worked as intended. Coke replaced milk for subsequent flights and the problem was rectified.

On the second flight another first was logged for the operation. One of the air force flight attendants exercised her training to the fullest as she delivered a Vietnamese mother of a new Canadian as they crossed the International Date Line. There was some difficulty in ascertaining the date and time of birth. In the end they selected the local time in Namao. There is now a grown person somewhere in Canada who experienced a very unusual birthday and was born several hours or perhaps even a day before reaching his place of birth.

Two more air force Boeing refugee flights were flown before Ward Air took over to complete the evacuation and Max Ward asked if he could see one of our Boeing aircraft after delivering its load of passengers to Edmonton. I was conducting a visit to the Namao facility and it was convenient to arrange a visit for him the next day. Despite the protests of Customs and Immigration officials, we boarded the aircraft immediately after all of the passengers had disembarked. Max did a quick tour of the passenger cabin and on exit turned to me and said, "the cabin is in better shape than some of our Sun Flights from Hawaii". It would seem that "Sun Flight" travel wasn't all glamour.

Over lunch he explained that frequently on the Middle-eastern flights, some Arabs would often try to cook in the isles with their oil fired cooking pots and after most pilgrimages were complete, carpets and upholstery would have to be replaced before they could be returned to normal service. Various oils and sand in particular could not be cleaned out of cabin carpets and upholstery and had to be replaced. There was also a problem with cabin crew, as the many an Arab would not take direction from a woman. Cabin crew scheduling went through a major upheaval to ensure that there was always a male steward on each of the Arabian charters.

It was on this last of the Boeing flights inspected by Max Ward that one of the refugees ran into some difficulty. He had disembarked earlier that day and it was discovered that members of his family and his sponsoring agency were in Mississauga Ontario. He could not speak English and became confused about what was happening to him. The immigration authorities had booked him out that afternoon on a direct commercial flight to Toronto.

In the meantime he had taken a shine to one of the staff car drivers that had moved him around the base and entrusted him with a box wrapped in brown paper. The young corporal who was trying to be helpful, thought little about it and threw it in the trunk of the staff car. Distracted by other duties he promptly forgot about it.

The refugee was whisked off to the air terminal protesting loudly but without much sympathy.

The following Monday morning the corporal returned to work from his weekend off and was promptly assigned the same staff car that he had driven a few days before. To his surprise, there in the trunk was the same box that he had left there in safe keeping for his refugee friend. The package was to have been returned to the refugee over the weekend but had been overlooked. He turned the package in to his sergeant who advised him that the refugee in question had been sent to Toronto days earlier but that the parcel would be forwarded to him.

At some point someone decided that they would subject the package to a careful inspection and the box was opened. To everyone's astonishment, the box contained ten pounds of solid gold. This refugee had liquidated all of his savings into a commodity that could be easily converted to his advantage in his new home. He was overjoyed of course when he received the news in Toronto and was deeply impressed with the honesty of those who had been charged with his welfare during the ordeal of his evacuation.

The operation ran smoothly all summer and Max Ward had been coaxing me to take one of the dead-head flights over to South East Asia to see for myself the operation at that end. I had been trying to fit it in throughout the summer but everything was going well with the evacuation and because of the pressures of other tasks I had trouble finding an appropriate time to do it.

Finally in late September I was advised that if I was ever going to do it, this would be my last chance. The final flight was due back in

Canada at the end of October and if I was going to go at all it had better be soon.

I approached my new boss who was an air force colonel. He decided that he couldn't authorise temporary duty for me so I announced that I would be taking some leave in October and would go anyway. He wasn't very happy but went along with it in the end. Once again I was issued a diplomatic passport which facilitated my movement about Southeast Asia.

I boarded a Wardair 747 at Malton in Toronto on October 12th and experienced an enjoyable flight to the Nisku terminal near Edmonton. This was the location of the main Wardair maintenance facility. The aircraft was refuelled, re-crewed and provisioned within a couple of hours of landing and then we were off, bound for Singapore with a refuelling stop at Narita Japan. There was an extra cabin crew on board that would be relieving another crew operating a Wardair charter in the Middle East. The annual Arab pilgrimage to Mecca was in progress and the airline had been charted for service between several Muslim countries.

There was lot of speculation among the crews as they had been told they would have a passenger on board but were not sure who it was to be. While I had packed a uniform, I was travelling in civvies and some explanations were required as to the purpose of my presence. Once satisfied that I was not some sort of company or government inspector, everyone relaxed and we all enjoyed the flight for the remainder of the way.

The aircraft had been stocked in the usual Wardair fashion and between the galley and the bar it was impossible to contemplate a diet of any sort. Halfway across the Pacific, I went below to the big empty cabin and jogged twenty lengths in my stocking feet. I was told by the flight deck crew later that I had jogged my way across the international dateline. Some sort of record, perhaps.

My stay in Singapore only lasted for three days and I was unable to get close to the refugee screening centre there. I spent my time enjoying my leave and behaved very much like a tourist. The head of cabin services for the airline was inspecting Wardair operations in the theatre and since she had little to do in Singapore, we toured the city together. We crossed part of the large and well-protected harbour in a cable car that resembled a ski-gondola at any North American or European ski resort. We visited one of the biggest and best-kept zoos in the whole of Southeast Asia and enjoyed numerous other tourist attractions in Singapore.

MaryAnn was married to an RCMP officer stationed in Edmonton so we had a paramilitary relationship in common. Through this association I began to learn more about the inner workings of Wardair and concluded that the employee/management inter-dependence was much like family. There was a great deal of respect both ways and it was reflected in the performance of the employees. During the three-week close relationship I had developed with many members of the company, not once did I detect a sour note toward management. Max Ward himself was referred to by first name and with esteem as were the vice presidents and other senior managers in the company.

The flight that had taken us to Singapore had proceeded further west to participate in ferrying the pilgrims to Mecca. We boarded Thai Air for the flight to Bangkok. Brian and Cun Tula, a local Thai who had been hired as a consultant to Wardair for their in-theatre operations had arrived in Singapore from Kuala Lumpur a few hours before our departure and joined us for the trip north. Tula was a sociable sort of fellow who enjoyed people and we quickly established a friendly business relationship. The Cun I found out later is a form of formal greeting. It is not gender specific and is used in reference to either a lady or a gentleman.

We arrived at Bangkok at around midnight just after a squall had passed through. It was hot and muggy as we disembarked to be met by Cun Bong, Tula's right hand man. We were spirited through local customs and immigration without pause and into a couple of cars that been arranged by Bong to deliver us to the hotel downtown. The Montien Hotel more or less in the centre of this large and sprawling city was an imposing multiple storied hotel boasting over 400 guest rooms. The floors throughout the public areas, including the large stairways were made of marble, while trim throughout was of gold plate. It was an impressive hotel with large comfortable rooms each fitted with an honour bar for the convenience of the guests.

Bangkok has a wealth of variety to offer the tourist. We visited temples, parks and shopping malls. One temple in particular attracted our interest. It had been constructed around a huge Buddha that the Thai's had rescued from the jungle following one of the many wars with neighbouring Burma. Evidently, the Thai's threatened by an imminent attack by the Burmese several centuries ago hauled the giant Budda deep into the jungle. We were told it weighed over ten tonnes and it was said to be made of solid gold. It took a herd of 100 elephants to move it to its jungle hideaway and as many to move it back to its present resting-place a few centuries later.

While in the jungle, the Buddha was covered in a thick mudpack that hardened over the years concealing the gold beneath and for several centuries it was not given much attention. Finally a group of Thai officials examined the jungle Budda in some detail and discovered the golden secret that had been lost in the mists of time. It was returned triumphantly to its original home in Bangkok and to the approximate site that ancient records indicated as its origin. A huge temple was built around it and it has become a major centre for worship and a tourist attraction of international renown. Fact or myth the story of the golden Budda was fascinating and has stayed with me for years.

As we toured through the temple we observed several monks entranced in prayer. Some leaning at seemingly impossible angles in their kneeling positions. Our guide informed us that it was not uncommon and some of them had been in that position for several days.

One of my big disappointments in Bangkok was the bridge over the River Kwai. The image of Alec Guinness leading his troops out of the prisoner of war camp to construct a magnificent bridge over the River Kwai was indelibly engraved on my mind. However, reality disappoints and I would have preferred to retain my memories of the movie intact.

The magnificent structure was destroyed and the remnants of a rickety foot-bridge marked the place of its passing. My military background however told me that in the minds of those that built it, it was indeed a magnificent structure constructed under the most arduous circumstances of human misery. The Colonel, a leader to the end influenced his men by setting a goal that would take their minds away from their appalling conditions.

They established an aim and set about achieving it. Viewed from this perspective it was, in my mind, truly the eighth wonder of the world.

After a day or two touring around Bangkok, I decided that I would pay a visit to the Canadian Embassy. It was within easy walking distance from the hotel and I made my way through the teeming crowds that never seemed to diminish regardless of the hour of the day or night. I went fairly early in the morning before the heat of the day seized hold and was pleased to be ushered directly into the Ambassador's office on my arrival. I was introduced to the Ambassador who was about half way through his tour at the embassy. I was amazed to find that he knew only the general aspects of the Canadian evacuation operation in Southeast Asia and I spent some time briefing him on the project.

He seemed surprised to learn that Wardair had been conducting such extensive operations and in particular the two or three flights a month out of Bangkok carrying refugees to Canada.

By this stage of my career I had become very conscious of publicity and I had asked Brian earlier if there had been much media coverage of the Canadian refugee operation. He was not aware of any publicity whatsoever and I had determined that public relations would be high on my priority list in any discussion that I had with Canadian embassy officials. As I briefed the ambassador I became acutely aware that he was also uncomfortable at the oversight of a major on-going event that would provide good publicity for Canada and also for Wardair.

We chatted for an hour attempting to determine how we could best remedy the situation, given that the aircraft on which I would be returning a week or so later would be the last of the Southeast Asia evacuation flights. The ambassador was open to suggestions and we discussed several options. We eventually settled on a combination luncheon/press conference where we would make a presentation to the local media explaining our humanitarian operation. I would turn out the whole Wardair crew to assist in hosting the lunch and to be available for questions following the meeting. The ambassador agreed and only then summoned his press secretary who he introduced and left it to us to work out the detail.

I departed the embassy just before lunch with several cases of duty free liquor of the forty ounce variety and a couple of shipping cartons full of duty free cigarettes for the crew. Brian was excited to hear about the arrangements for the next day and assembled all of the Wardair personnel and briefed them on the event. The Canadian press secretary spent the rest of the day contacting all of those on a long list of media who we agreed should at least be aware of the proceedings.

That evening all those associated with the evacuation gathered for the cocktail hour in my spacious hotel room. This evening however was different from previous such events where I entertained from the honour bar in my room. Following inventory checks each morning, the resulting financial devastation would be added to my ever-increasing hotel bill.

We now had duty free booze at a very much-reduced cost and the most expensive part of the hour was the tray of finger food someone (one of the cabin crew I suspect) ordered from room service. For an hour or so we talked informally about the Wardair project and the senior Wardair pilot had been in contact with his headquarters in Edmonton to ensure a party line. The press secretary would host the meeting the next day and I would make the introductions and represent the Canadian military.

Pilots, cabin crews, ground representatives and contractors were all informally briefed by the senior Wardair pilot to tell it how they saw it and to be honest in answering any questions posed by the media. There was a lot of excitement among the crew about the exposure their airline would achieve in Southeast Asia. I relayed to the group the information provided by the Canadian press secretary indicating that at least one of the Bangkok newspapers had a circulation of ten million. On this upbeat note, the cocktail hour was adjourned and we all headed out in smaller groups to enjoy the gourmet delights of Bangkok.

The event the next day was quite straightforward. The media numbering around twenty journalists representing both the press and the electronic media arrived exactly at the appointed time and following a short period we had allowed to meet and mingle we all sat down to an excellent lunch hosted by the Canadian embassy. We provided a short brief on the reasons for the press luncheon and opened the proceedings to questions from the media. There were many and the question period continued for over an hour after the luncheon tables had been cleared. I had noticed that the media were enjoying a particular brand of local white wine and as the supply at the table diminished, I ordered more.

This, much to the chagrin of the press secretary who informed me that his annual entertainment budget would be decimated by this one event. This did not cause me any concern as I felt that the excellent public relations generated by the interaction with the media would more than compensate for such a relatively small investment and I gave it little more thought.

The following day we were rewarded with front page coverage of the whole Southeast Asian evacuation operation that Canada had undertaken to relieve the refugee crisis throughout the region. I visited the ambassador a few days later and he was ecstatic at the coverage and had been congratulated by his colleagues in Ottawa for pulling off such a media coup.

After two weeks in this beautiful city, I was ready to go home. I had accomplished more than I set out to do and felt somewhat spare among my new Wardair friends who were busy making preparations for the last refugee flight back to Canada. I visited the screening camp on the outskirts of Bangkok and spent a day watching Canadian doctors, nurses and immigration officials process the flood of homeless people looking to renew their lives in a strange new land.

I can't say that the flight home was uneventful. This time close to five hundred refugees bound for Long Point barracks in Montreal accompanied me. I spent the whole flight moving about the cabin answering the many questions posed by refugees of all ages. What Canada was like, was there snow, how far was Mount Forest from Montreal? Many of the questions were difficult to answer since individual refugees, families and some groups were assigned to sponsoring organisations in many communities of which we had very little knowledge. My touring during the flight was an enjoyable experience for me. It was also a relief for the cabin crew who could get on with their duties without having to respond to the endless questions that continued throughout the flight.

We arrived at Edmonton International airport late in the day, our last refuelling stop between Bangkok and Montreal. We were briefed that the refuelling stop would be of short duration and that we were to remain on board. However, the cabin doors had to be opened to replenish the galley and the sudden rush of cold air was immediately noticeable.

It was Halloween and snowing lightly. The curiosity of the refugees soon got the best of them as they rushed to the doors to see and feel snow. Most were dressed for the tropical climate of Southeast Asia and found their first experience with sub-zero temperatures exhilarating. Fortunately, external-heating units had been connected to the aircraft allowing those who had over-exposed themselves to retreat for relief in a warmer part of the cabin.

We were only thirty minutes on the ground at Edmonton and all of the four hundred and eighty or so passengers had experienced their first snow. Coincidentally, our arrival in Montreal was also accompanied by the first snowfall of the year. A welcome that many refugees now settled into the Canadian culture are not likely to forget.

This flight marked the end of the South East Asian refugee operations undertaken by Canada in the spring of 1980 and it was the beginning of the end of my career in the air force.

CHAPTER TWENTY-THREE
G-7 SUMMIT OTTAWA 1981

Following the termination of the Wardair refugee contract in the fall of 1980, I disposed of my Wardair shares and had a small nest egg with which to enjoy an uninterrupted Christmas.

The two refugee processing centres in Bangkok and Kuala Lumpur were closed and both reception bases at Namao and Long Point returned to normal. Another successful operation had come to a close.

However, the staff had not been idle during my visit to Bangkok. The routine of the office had not significantly changed and in my absence Major Fred Volks looked after the store. He had been monitoring the progress of the government planning for hosting the 1981 G-7 Summit to be held in Ottawa the following year. A special committee under External Affairs had been established for the purpose of developing preliminary plans that were based on fairly sketchy information. Fred had attended most of the initial meetings but the requirement for DND resources had not yet been identified in detail.

Fred briefed me on my return and I was amazed at the magnitude of the support that would be necessary involving many government departments and agencies in order to host this event. This was one of the earlier meetings of the G-7 and the government naturally wanted to impress the Heads of State and the Heads of Government who would be in attendance.

Fred and I attended the final pre-holiday G-7 planning meeting together in early December. It was more of an update and no new information came out of it. The planning committee had adjourned promising to meet in early January. On the way back to the office, Fred and I discussed a variety of military resources that might be needed, the necessity for detailed military logistic planning and the potential security requirements.

As Christmas 1980 neared, planning for the G-7 was placed on the back burner and we all assumed a more relaxed business posture for the season. I was intent on enjoying Christmas this time around as my Yuletide experience the year before had been badly disrupted by the events in Turkey and Iran.

The military had little responsibility for the personal security of the delegations as that function had been assigned to the RCMP. Like ourselves the Mounties had only preliminary information and we both awaited final details of the function to be provided by the bureaucrats before we could proceed to tailor our planning to the grand strategy. However, it didn't take much imagination to understand that an intense level of security would be necessary for the high profile international leaders who would be attending.

The USA, Great Britain, France, Germany, Italy, Japan and Canada made up the original group of seven with the European Economic Community attending as an observer. Later Russia would become a full member of what is now known as the G-8. Each of the member countries of the G-7 sent their leaders and a small support staff. For this reason a high priority was placed on the planning for the event. There was little doubt that security would present us with many problems and it would be necessary for us to work hand in hand with the RCMP for the occasion.

The discussion that Fred and I continued following the meeting came to a close as we arrived at the Army mess on Somerset

Street. Drinks in hand, we proceeded to take our discussion to another level. In a few days it would be Christmas and after all, there were more important things to do, for the time being at least.

Fred had been working for me for about three years by this time. He was the son of retired Major General Chris Volks who had distinguished himself during the war years. Like father like son, Fred had a strong personality and didn't countenance mediocrity. He spoke his mind openly and was a soldier's soldier.

Three years earlier I had a call from Bentley MacLeod to tell me that Fred had approached him looking for a change from a position he held elsewhere in the headquarters. He felt that he did not have much responsibility and was looking for new challenges.

In keeping with his character, Bentley felt responsible for the well being of a fellow infantryman. He knew I had a vacancy for a major in DMOC and wondered if I would be interested in considering Fred for the position. I felt confident in Bentley's high regard for Fred and on review of his file, I found him to be an officer with fine qualities both as a leader in the field and as an outstanding staff officer. I interviewed Fred who informed me right off the bat that he didn't much like air force officers but he found the job intriguing. I advised him that he was welcome to give it a try but if he didn't like it or if things didn't work out between us, then I would be forced to fire his ass off to wherever the career managers wished to send him. We shook hands and Fred reported for duty in DMOC the very next week.

I discovered early on that Fred had ample qualities of initiative and decisiveness. He was forceful and when giving direction he was clear and concise leaving no margin for loose interpretation. He expected the same from his superiors and did not hesitate to insist on clarification of the muddleheaded thinking that often accompanied headquarters edicts.

Our interaction on the job grew very quickly into a friendship that exists today and from the time he jointed our group in early 1978 until his retirement in late1981, Fred had made himself a valuable member of the DMOC tasking team.

We entered 1981 following a quiet Christmas on the tasking front. Nothing unusual had occurred to disrupt the holidays as we returned to the job in the New Year.

The phone began to ring early on the first day back and we immediately went into an intensive detailed planning mode for the summit. The dates had been established for late June and there was barely six months for us to develop our detailed plans.

DND was assigned the task of providing arrival and departure support, ceremonial units, ground transportation, drivers, support to the RCMP for security both for movement of personnel and a quick response force to be on standby if needed during the three day conference. Bureaucratic planners often neglected the requirements of the media in the early planning stages forcing difficult changes to plans as the event loomed. Accordingly, we made some rough estimates of what we thought the media requirements might be.

We set aside two helicopters specifically to move media between venues and issued instructions to our ground support staff to build in ground transportation for up to fifty media. Actual numbers were not yet available but it seemed logical to expect that each of the nations involved would want media coverage of their activities for national coverage back home.

We would need a media centre in Ottawa together with a suitable area for press conferences. In addition a small media facility would be required at the venue where the conference was to be held. There would be numerous ancillary requests for support but at least now we had a good outline of what was expected of DND and we set about identifying resources.

Once again I pulled together a team of DND specialists that would shape the plans into working documents that contained all of the support activities and the military resources assigned to meet them. Medical support, ground transport, air support requirements and a communications network were all identified as supporting functions that DND would provide and we began the laborious process of developing the detailed movement plans and tasking orders that would be necessary for the entire operation.

The number of cars identified to support summit demands was on the order of one hundred not including baggage trucks, buses and other support vehicles. The North American auto industry was approached for assistance in transportation. General Motors agreed to provide the necessary numbers of new cars for a dollar a piece. Pickup trucks and other utility vehicles were added to the list and all that was left for DND was to provide the drivers and the organisation to run the ground transport operation.

Over the remaining winter months, plans were developed, tested and modified. Transport of the senior representatives from the airport into town exposed a variety of security problems and it was decided that each of the visiting delegations would be transported from the airport to the front lawn of Parliament Hill by helicopter. VIP kits were fabricated for the twin Hueys assigned to the task and a simple air movement plan was worked out and tested. According to the US constitution, the President may only fly in US aircraft operated by US personnel. Provision was made to allow helicopter Marine One into the mix.

In consultation with other participating nations, an arrival window of two hours was established on the morning of the first day. This provided the visiting delegations a smaller target within which to establish their individual arrivals at Ottawa. As the summit date neared the arrival times were refined even further until a minute by minute schedule was developed for the sequential arrival of each of the delegations.

A combined operations centre was set up in the basement of the Centre Block of Parliament Hill and would open a week or two before the conference was to start. This would provide us with easy access to the Privy Council Office, the PMO and all of the other offices on the Hill that might be required to assist.

A fifty man Guard of Honour was established for the purpose of honouring the visiting dignitaries on arrival. They would provide a general salute and then be inspected by the leader of each delegation in the sequence dictated by their predetermined arrival times. The leaders were then transported by helicopter to Parliament Hill along with their close personal staff. Other members of the delegation proceeded into town by motorcade. Naturally, arrangements had to be made for the media to witness the arrival from suitable locations close to the arrival activities and in some cases, media arriving on the delegation aircraft had to be provided for in the media locations and in the transportation plan.

According to the schedule, the duration of the stay on Parliament Hill was to be brief and would be followed by a short motorcade to Government House where the leaders of the delegations would pay their respects to the Governor General in accordance with state protocol.

Once these formalities had been completed the delegations were each to move once again by helicopter from the grounds at Government House to the historic Hotel Montebello in the village of Montebello, Quebec.

For 40 years after its completion in 1930, this log structure was the private retreat of the Seigniory Club, whose elite membership included politicians such as former Canadian Prime Minister Lester B. Pearson and foreign dignitaries including Prince Rainier and Princess Grace of Monaco. The resort has a number of historic meetings under its belt and would now include the 1981 International Economic Summit attended by political leaders from Great Britain, France, Germany, Italy, Japan, the US and the host country, Canada.

Apart from its charm, dignity and international reputation, it had been chosen because of the relative ease in securing the area between the Ottawa River to the South and a major through highway just to the north. It enabled the police to rigidly control land access from any direction with relative ease. Police patrols on the Ottawa River were intensified with increased concentrations in the vicinity of Montebello.

With a bit of clearing we were able to establish a heliport just to the west of the hotel but far enough away so that aircraft movements would have a minimal effect on the conference proceedings. We built a golf-cart track and procured on loan a dozen high-end golf carts from one of the local golf clubs in Ottawa.

Once again the media requirements provided us with another unique twist. We expected to accredit fifty or so media who would travel with the delegations. Since we were limited by space and timings we gave the media a preference of covering the departure from Ottawa to Montebello or the arrival at Montebello, but not both. To our relief the media requests split down the middle. Half were happy to cover the departure and the other half saw a need to be at Montebello for the arrivals. We were then able to issue tasking instructions for a Voyageur helicopter, previously earmarked for this eventuality, to ferry accredited media ahead of the delegations so that they would be in place for the arrivals at Montebello. The helicopter would transport them all back to Ottawa following the arrival event.

Since there were far too many media to move efficiently by golf cart, we had to find another solution for their movement about the Montebello grounds. We were able to combine this requirement with our ground movement plans to provide delegation staffs with transport between the heliport and the hotel. Our ingenious ground transportation officer, Flight Lieutenant Ted Latham, located two, twelve-passenger golf-cart like vehicles that he procured on loan from a theme park in southern Ontario and another logistics problem was solved.

A nagging dilemma of serious concern to the RCMP was the helicopter corridor that had been established between Ottawa and Montebello, particularly on the Ontario side of the Ottawa River. The issue centred on the need for a helicopter to go immediately to ground in the event of an in-flight mechanical emergency.

Such an event was not uncommon in helicopter operations and the RCMP were troubled about their capability to reach and secure a downed delegation should an emergency landing along the route be necessary.

To resolve the dilemma we designed a grid that was superimposed over the primary and alternate flight paths. The flight paths within the corridor would be used at random but selected just prior to flight departure. The RCMP on the ground were made aware of the route and adjusted their ground coverage to the agreed predetermined watch points in the grid along the route. There were several police cars located at intervals throughout the grid and a car could be at an emergency-landing site within a few minutes of notification.

On the declaration of an emergency landing, the pilot needed only to broadcast the co-ordinates of the grid point at which he would land. The police officer first on the scene would keep others elsewhere in the grid advised on the police radio net and would make an initial assessment of the need for security back up. Meanwhile a standby helicopter would be dispatched from either Ottawa or Montebello to collect the downed party and resume the safe delivery to their destination. Fortunately, this contingency plan was never needed.

While NORAD resources could be counted upon to defend the area from highflying intruders, the possibility of an attack on the venue by a bomb carrying light aircraft provided another element of concern.

To ensure protection in this area a small detachment of CF-5s from Bagotville and Cold Lake were deployed. Two aircraft on armed standby in the alert hangars at CFB Uplands were maintained throughout the visit. They could be called upon, with five minutes notice, to scramble and investigate suspicious air movements or to deal with any incursions that might develop.

Such was the nature of "Summit" planning as the spring of 1981 approached. While we still had many concerns, a plan had come together and a budget could be prepared that would provide detailed costs of DND participation. In addition we were able to identify specific manpower and resources to be assigned to summit activities. I felt that our planning had entered the final phase and we began to turn our attention to implementation. As the planning pressures eased I began to think a bit about my own future.

I was forty-eight years old and had served in DMOC for nearly five years. There were assurances from some quarters that a promotion to full colonel was in the offing. However the prospects of being posted into a good job as a colonel were rather limited. It became apparent to me that I would likely wind up in some senior position in the headquarters training younger officers as they streamed through to the general officer ranks. This indicated to me that the challenges that I had welcomed so enthusiastically throughout my service career were coming to a close.

The new breed of headquarters officer that I had begun to notice several years earlier had become more common as they manoeuvred their way into senior positions throughout the three services. Many of them were incapable of independent thinking and relied on the consensus they developed through their individual networks. They were indecisive in military matters and yet quick to extol the virtues of the new bilingual policies, women's rights, gay rights and a host of other abominations that have become the Achilles heel of the forces today.

My tolerance level for many of these younger officers was being stretched and the fact that they were now being promoted into positions of authority concerned me. Most of them had filled the squares in each of the operational jobs they had held in the field achieving only the minimum of time on the job and a bare minimum standard for career progression. They knew the numbers but were unabashedly lacking the experience in their application the field. They were remarkably short in the understanding of the military essentials of leadership and the loyalties necessary both up and down the chain of command in any military organisation.

They used their subordinates to fortify their own career goals and on more than one occasion I witnessed the expectations of good high quality officers and men being sacrificed in the interests of some obscure idea inspired by fuzzy thinking that had little to do with sound military principles.

I had to re-examine my own motivation as I contemplated the way ahead. Was the source of my dissatisfaction the fact that these young, well-educated officers were surpassing my own career aspirations? Was I being resentful of the new military that was becoming a political instrument of social change?

The woolly-minded policies emanating from NDHQ were not only being imposed on the headquarters staffs but on the Canadian Forces in general. The political leadership was using the military as a model that they were holding up as an example of what they expected other government departments, agencies and the Canadian society to emulate. I was beginning to question the way ahead for Canada's military.

During one of our many philosophical discussions on the state of the forces back in 1975, Ron Button had said to me that he felt the military should represent the most conservative element of the society it was tasked to protect. It should react to social change no more quickly than the most conservative elements of the society and then only after every aspect of such change was carefully considered. Here we were, the defenders of the country being used as instruments of political will and the furtherance of Liberal government policies inspired by an elitism that had become entrenched in the bureaucracy.

It was also during this period in my career that I became more aware than ever before of the politics and the politicians in whom we placed the trust to govern us. It was not a pretty sight. Our elected representatives were naïve and susceptible to the manipulations of the senior civil servants.

Many of the bureaucrats with whom I worked took advantage of every situation as though it was their God-given right. Everything from travelling on the weekend so that they could collect overtime, to insisting on first class treatment regardless of the length of the trip or duration of stay. Many of them manipulated the system to suit their own convenience.

In planning for major events, the bureaucrat invariably took the easy way out for himself even if it could be done by alternate means with equal effectiveness at less cost.

It was of little comfort to me to notice that this same behaviour was beginning to appear in the habits of the new career officers who were moving up the chain of command in ever increasing numbers. The good of the service had become secondary to the good of the individual. I became acutely aware that I was also a taxpayer and tried with little success to correct the wrongs as I encountered them.

Driving to work one early spring morning, I realised that it was my thirtieth anniversary in the air force. April 14th and all of those thirty years since I had deserted the beginnings of a banking career had gone by so quickly I had hardly noticed.

It was a beautiful day as I drove along the Ottawa River from Rockcliffe. The air was cool and crisp and the sky was an azure blue. The morning promised a pleasant day ahead, a preview of spring and the summer to come. It was in an up-beat mood during my drive to work on this the day I had confronted the decision lurking in the back of my mind for over a year.

I arrived at my office at about seven AM and dashed off a quick scrawl to my secretary for her attention when she arrived a bit later. It was dated April 14th and addressed to the Director of Personnel Senior Appointments and said simply:

"I wish to register my intention to retire in the fall of this year.
May the appropriate administrative action proceed".

I had revealed my intention to leave the service that I had joined thirty years previously. A service that I had grown to love and respect and a service that seemed to be losing it's way.

The idiocy of integration no longer mattered. All three services had been emasculated by even measure. The military ethic once so proudly upheld by all Canadians serving in the forces was slowly disappearing.

My secretary peeked around the corner shortly after she arrived at her desk. "You can't be serious" she said, "what on earth are you going to do?" The question took me somewhat by surprise. It never occurred to me that I would have to "do" anything. It was a question I would have to answer many times for the rest of that day and for the days to come until "the fall of this year" as I had so carefully worded in my memo proposing the timing of my departure.

I had always thought that correspondence on personnel matters was confidential but several friends of mine around Ottawa called the first day to check my sanity. To the question, "what are you going to do", "I don't know and I don't give a damn" became my stock reply to whoever was interested enough to ask. "Why are you leaving" was another prominent question asked of me. It seemed that there had to be something that really pissed Thompson off for leaving the service so early.

A day or two went by and I became more deeply involved in the preparations for the summit. The prospect of early retirement hardly entered my mind and when it did, it was usually with the sense of relief one gets when a sticky decision is finally made and you know that it was the right one. For several days following my momentous decision, I received calls from all over Canada and North America and some from Europe. What's happened, why are you leaving early – what are you going to do? And then I would go into my spiel; "It's time - I don't know and I don't give a damn".

The questions kept coming at me right up until the day I left the service for good. It seemed many of my friends and associates were looking for a reason that they could hang on to. It was difficult to explain that there was no one particular reason for my decision. I would have had to make a speech.

How could I tell those close to me in the culture in which I had spent my entire life that I felt betrayed by the very service I once cherished? I had given unquestioningly, every bit of my energy for the good of the service that now seemed more interested in pursuing the political imperatives of social change.

The final blow was the blatant sacrifice of the merit principle as the primary prerequisite for promotion. The prime principle in all career management considerations was the merit principle and it was being held hostage in order to further the careers of those who supported government imposed philosophies - philosophies that had little to do with the defence and security of Canada and Canadians.

Meanwhile, as we neared the final preparations for the G-7 Summit, I put these considerations aside. We were bringing in military communicators, logisticians, drivers and technicians from across the country. GM had commenced the delivery of the automobiles and we began to store them in the underground parking area at the National Arts Centre that had been designated as our vehicle compound. We took each vehicle on strength as we would any other DND conveyance. Inspections were conducted and any anomalies were recorded and were signed off by the GM liaison officer.

Helicopter training operations interrupted sleepy downtown Ottawa with their "wup-wup" sounds as they conducted pilot familiarisation flights onto the lawn at Parliament Hill. Rockliffe Park was assailed by the same airborne displays of the military at work as the grounds at Government House were utilised for summit helicopter operations.

It was the first time in history that military aircraft had landed on the Hill or at the

Governor General's residence and the whole operation was the cause of some hand wringing among the growing number of vocal pacifists lobbying the federal government. There was still enough sanity in Ottawa in 1981 to ignore the frenetic ramblings of those who saw the end of the world around every corner.

The old Beacon Arms Hotel extensively renovated following it's near destruction by fire in the sixties was reserved exclusively for the military personnel supporting summit operations. The management and staff at the "Beacon" embraced their novel guests and came close to developing a military esprit de corps as they hosted colonels, privates and all ranks between.

Morning briefings were conducted in the banquet rooms of the hotel complete with complimentary breakfasts. Hotel service was everywhere and the troops; many of whom had been previously involved in field operations in the Middle East and elsewhere, had never had it so good. Cleaning staff to clean the rooms daily, clean sheets, good food at all hours of the day or night – what more could a soldier ask for. I was told later that there was a large volunteer list for participation in the next major event calling for similar support.

Some of my civilian and a few military colleagues felt that we were treating our soldiers too well and that we should have put them up in tents. But I didn't agree. It was my belief that our troops, who admittedly were accustomed to roughing it, should not be treated any differently from the civil servant whose union would demand first class accommodations under similar circumstances.

The Canadian soldier is willing to go anywhere he is ordered and adapts to working under any conditions of personal hardship and deprivation. Many of those assigned to us had completed more than one peacekeeping tour abroad and knew what squalor could be. If there was an opportunity to treat our soldiers well, then why not? They didn't travel first class, they were not entitled to overtime pay, they didn't get their airfare paid to go home on weekends when on extended periods of temporary duty. They were doing a mundane job in an urban atmosphere and I could see no reason why they shouldn't be treated well and said so in as many words to anyone who objected.

The G-7 summit day came and the whole support system our federal planning committee had put in place worked like a charm. But there were two or three incidents that challenged the programme we had worked so hard to prepare.

The first was near panic at the air-traffic control centres in Ottawa and Montreal as a small blip appeared on their radar screens. Close observation revealed that it was a low-speed, low-flyer and likely a privately owned aircraft. It was heading directly for Montebello. The area in a ten-mile radius around the hotel had been designated as a prohibited flying area and the airspace was protected up to ten thousand feet.

There was no reason for this aircraft to be there and two CF-5 aircraft were immediately scrambled from their alert status at Uplands.

Within minutes they had intercepted the intruder and after making several threatening gestures as they eased by their target they became convinced that the pilot was a poorly informed farmer out of northern Quebec. The aircraft was identified as a Cessna 150, a light two place aircraft. It had a cruise speed of about 110 knots and the minimum speed of the CF-5 was around 120 depending on fuel load.

The interceptors took turns sliding by on either side and set up a race track pattern ensuring that there was always one of them in the immediate vicinity of the Cessna. In this manner they managed to herd the small aircraft to a landing at the Ottawa airport. Needless to say this part-time pilot and his passenger were terrified at the welcome they had received, not only as they unwittingly entered the restricted airspace around Montebello, but the armed guard that met them after landing gave them additional pause for concern.

As it turned out our intrepid pilot from northern Quebec hadn't read his Notice to Airmen pamphlets that were published monthly or whenever there was need to advise pilots of impending changes to air regulations. He just jumped into his aircraft and headed out for Ottawa, the sort of thing light aircraft owners at one time used to be able to do out of the back forty. His only stroke of luck was that he had chosen to mount his trip in daylight. Had it been in the darkness of night he may never have finished his journey.

Another couple of incidents that gave the military support and security staffs cause for concern but happily ended as humorous anecdotes occurred during the PM's immediate post conference duties.

The Prime Minister was to host the delegates at a formal dinner at the Hotel Montebello following the summit proceedings on the last evening. There was a full agenda in the afternoon and according to plan, the Prime Minister was to fly by helicopter to Ottawa to hold a mass press briefing for the international media. He was to provide an outline of the progress made at the summit and a summary of the major decisions that had been taken by the delegates.

We had the helicopter for the PM standing by at the heliport and I was beginning to pace a bit as there was a weather system moving in from the Northwest. The weather at Montebello was good and forecast to remain so until around seven in the evening. However, the situation required close monitoring.

Finally, at around four-thirty I contacted the PM's staff on the walkie-talkie and asked for his progress. I was told that the meeting had finished at four o'clock and that he had gone to his room to change his shirt. Fine, I thought, the time spent on changing his damn shirt might prevent him from returning in time to carry out his hosting duties.

A few minutes later Mr. Trudeau appeared looking jaunty and waving his umbrella much like the conductor of a philharmonic orchestra. He seemed totally unconcerned as he strolled toward the helicopter that by this time had the engines running and rotor turning in preparation for takeoff.

At first I maintained a discrete distance watching cautiously. However, as he approached the outer diameter of the whirling blades I sensed that he intended to keep swinging his umbrella all the way in to the door of the aircraft.

There is a protocol of behaviour around helicopters and the PM was well aware of it. I knew he had been briefed many times and I myself had briefed him at least once on other occasions. Loose articles like hats, purses and umbrellas can get sucked up into the rotors of the helicopter and can do serious damage to the aircraft. Such items are not allowed under turning rotors and military personnel are subject to serious disciplinary action should they be the cause of an incident of this nature.

I began my advance on the PM at a slow walk at first causing a bit of a stir among the bodyguards. I quickened my step and finally lunged at the PM throwing my arms around him just before he entered into the danger area under the rotors. With my arms still around him and his umbrella, I marched the Prime Minister of Canada right up to the entrance of the aircraft and more or less shoved him inside. A second or two later the door slammed, the engines revved up and the helicopter rose majestically from the helipad. Surrounded by security, I was given a royal wave from an amused Pierre Elliotte Trudeau as the aircraft turned above my head and departed at great speed for Ottawa.

How far Trudeau might have gone with his orchestral conducting artistry one can only speculate. At the time I had visions of an aborted trip in order to repair a damaged helicopter. In later years I began to realise that a great number of the Trudeau escapades were tests to see how far he might be allowed to go in any given situation. Yet in this particular instance, I still wonder how much further he might have gone without my clutching embrace.

The other incident loomed a short while later that evening as the PM's pilot reported deteriorating weather as he approached Ottawa. The PM was delivered on time to the Ottawa Conference Centre, the venue for the international press conference. The conference droned on for the allotted time and as it came to a close it became apparent that the PM's return trip to Montebello would not be made by helicopter.

We had been working on a contingency plan from the time of the PM's departure and we watched with dismay as the weather at Montebello deteriorated to below the weather limits for safe flying operations. The weather in Ottawa was still just above limits with similar ceiling and visibility conditions at a small civil airport in Gatineau just across the river.

With only an hour to spare before the dinner was to commence, we made the decision to move the PM by helicopter to Gatineau where he would be met by a car dispatched from Montebello. In order to save time, the PM's staff prepared a small suitcase containing his formal attire for the evening. He would change in the car as he made his way through the rain from Gatineau to Montebello.

Once again an unexpected weather occurrence had caused a last minute change in plans. Despite the anxiety among the airmen and the ground transportation folks, the PM arrived at the front door of the hotel at five minutes to seven. In full formal dress, he made his way up the stairs and into the reception area with mere seconds to spare. A perfect host and none of the other heads of delegation were any the wiser.

The departure operation commenced early the next day. The airspace between Montebello and the Ottawa International airport was alive with helicopters as each delegation departed in turn. The departures from Ottawa were informal to allow the delegations to begin their homeward journeys without undue delay.

Later that day there was a huge "Wheels Up" party. Wheels Up was the RCMP code-word for, "senior personage or personages are no longer our responsibility". They hosted the party at their mess on Cooper Street and the organisers from all of the participating government departments were invited.

Unfortunately, I had a responsibility of a slightly more lasting nature. I didn't feel comfortable until the last VIP aircraft had passed the "point of no return" to Canada. Had any of the departing delegations had to divert to a Canadian airport along their route, I had to be available to deal with the Ministry of Transport, External Affairs and other responsible government departments to make whatever arrangements may have been required at the diversion airfield.

Fortunately, all of the flights made it past the their critical points a few hours later and I repaired to the RCMP mess to join the party now reaching a crescendo. We toasted one another, the PM, the Queen, members of the G-7 and anyone else that anyone could think of and in the wee small hours I was ceremoniously escorted to an unmarked police car and driven home.

The next day as I sheepishly recovered my vehicle from the RCMP secure parking area, I found that I was not the only one who had been given the VIP treatment and chauffeured to their place of residence. The RCMP had pre-planned this small service for their guests and no one was allowed to get into trouble.

Yet another successful operation had been completed and I was proud of the support that all of the Canadian Forces personnel had provided. Officers, men and women had performed their assigned tasks extraordinarily well in a very high profile activity. In my estimation they had achieved the highest accolade - they were a credit to their service.

An important factor in the success of the 1981 Ottawa G-7 summit was the quality of the team that came together under the federal organising committee chairman. Derek Burney, formerly Canada's Ambassador to Japan, had been given the task of planning for the Ottawa Summit. He not only had the requisite management skills but most importantly, he exhibited the fine qualities of leadership found wanting among many senior civil servants.

He was well liked by all of the personnel representing the participating government departments and agencies and effectively developed a smoothly working team from the beginning. Under his leadership or perhaps because of it, the success of the G-7 Summit '81 inspired the praise and admiration of all of the senior participants.

It is worthy of note that Derek Burney left the civil service shortly after the summit. He worked successfully in the private sector for a number of years before being pressed back into the service of his country as Canada's Ambassador to Washington. Having contributed in no small way to the improvement in Canada/US relations, he returned to the private sector on completion of his ambassadorial tour. Derek Burney served at the pleasure of the Queen but he didn't hitch his wagon to the largesse of the federal trough.

As the summit came to a close and the loose ends were tidied up, files were put away for posterity and military personnel returned to their units, I was beginning to wind down for the summer. One of the heaviest tasking functions of the year had been completed successfully and it was time to turn to the mechanics of terminating of my career.

The social season had wound down for the summer but I had a call from my old friend, Bing Peart from Moose Jaw days who was now Base Commander at Uplands. He was having the final base Mess Dinner of the season and would be delighted if I could attend. It was a wonderful gesture from one, like many who had never been in the headquarters, could not understand the detached, aloof treatment of retiring officers and men. I was honoured as my career was outlined during the proceedings following the dinner and I found a forum in which to say my formal farewells. I made only a brief speech thanking my hosts for reminding me that there was still an airforce and that I had indeed enjoyed a full and rewarding career in the service.

I had accumulated enough outstanding leave to give me almost another year of service and decided to take a month of it and relax before making any of the major career ending decisions that would be required of me.

My good friend Peter Fleming offered the loan of the Punkin and with two of my teenage sons, we set off to explore the Rideau waterway. We took enough stores to last us a month and relied on the many small convenience stores along the way to provide for our daily fresh fruit, vegetable and dairy product needs.

On reaching Big Rideau Lake at the halfway point between Ottawa and Kingston, we spent days drifting, sun tanning, swimming and fishing. Once bored with this activity, we worked our way down the canal system to the City of Kingston and Lake Ontario. We visited several ports along the lakeshore and many of the islands at the entrance to the St. Laurence River.

We became an adept team at the locking protocol and could fit our small craft into the tightest spots in the lock. We became part of the locking community and manned the barge poles every time a houseboat loomed at the entrance to the lock. Most houseboat captains were tenants on their vessels and were inexperienced in the etiquette of the canal. They were generally clumsy sailors and we had to exercise strict vigilance in order to protect our hulls from the bumps and scratches that could be incurred when locking with amateurs.

The weather was perfect for the whole period of our odyssey with endless days of sunshine and warm evenings cooled by the light breezes off the water. As I began to relax, I once again confronted my decision to retire early from the air force. I became even more convinced than ever that I had made the right choice and determined that my first order of priority on my return would be to begin the retirement process.

The several weeks of living on the water had been good for all of us and as we reluctantly made our way back through the canal system to Ottawa we began looking for excuses to slow our journey. Westport, Smith Falls and Merickville, all historic settlements along the Rideau Canal, were explored in detail. The last few miles into Dows Lake and the Marina in Ottawa were navigated at a snail's place and we reluctantly tied up the Punkin after nearly a month on the water. To us it was an epic voyage and one we often talk about whenever we are together.

My final days in uniform were busy. I had handed over the reins of my office to my predecessor and was called upon for advice less and less frequently. DMOC seemed to be in good hands as I concentrated on my terminal procedures. Terminal medical, terminal dental, terminal administrative procedures. Everything was terminal as the service cut me loose from its ties and readied me for the final terminal procedure – the door. On the twenty-eighth day of September 1981 I walked out of the office for the last time wearing the uniform I would never wear again.

It was a green uniform and not a source of any sentimental value for me. I had long since discarded my air force blue. I'd had the wing that I had so painstakingly earned replaced by a cheap imitation and I had not retired as a Wing Commander but as a Colonel.

All of my junior years in the service, I had aspired to be a good air force officer. I had been trained well by officers of high ethical and moral standards. I had been expected to carry on the traditions that I had been taught so early in my career and in some small way I felt that I had failed those who so many years before had placed their trust in me.

I had no feeling of emotion for the institution that I was leaving. In fact I began to feel a sense of relief. Relief that I no longer had to challenge the ridiculous orders and directives issued by incompetent officers striving only for recognition. I was free. I could set the course of my own destiny without too much concern for the well being of others. I was beginning to resent this new organisation that was starting to exaggerate its military capabilities.

It was a good feeling to be free but not without some questioning of my own competence to make a go of life outside. I was eighteen when I had joined the RCAF. The RCAF trained me. They told me when to go to the dentist, the doctor, to church or when to report for pay parade. I had only to read the Daily Routine Orders to know what was required of me administratively. I took the courses as they came my way, I accepted the postings unequivocally and I knew that the air force would look after me.

I suddenly realised that I didn't know how to make a doctor's appointment, find a dentist or negotiate a job contract. I knew little or nothing about the world outside the military.

I had joined from the cradle and was still a long distance away from the grave.

The motto of the squadron on which I had served in the RAF was "Quid Se Coelum Ruat". The literal translation "What if the Sky Should Fall", had particular significance during the battle of Britain

Supported by our squadron crest portraying a Phoenix rising from the fire, we were referred to somewhat irreverently as the "Chicken Lickin' Squadron" and frequently suffered the good-natured derision of other fighter squadrons. It is a motto that I am proud to have served under.

For the RCAF the sky had indeed fallen. This new integrated service was no longer one with which I could identify. As the forces fuelling the cold war began to sputter, the military imperative was lost and in my last few years I began to notice how the operation of the headquarters now resembled any of the other government departments.

The uniqueness of the military had been carefully blended into the fabric of the Ottawa bureaucracy. The colourful characteristics of former fine leaders had given way to the grey prominence of the new breed of civil servant. Essentially a civil servant in uniform who, once assigned his own little piece of turf would defend it to the death in the mistaken belief he was fulfilling his role in the military chain of command.

To be fair, there are some officers in all three services who still hold the service of their country foremost in their priorities. They recognise that loyalty works both ways in the chain of command and their subordinates will follow them faithfully when the necessary respect is earned. Unfortunately, it is unlikely that they will ever become the leaders that are needed in Canada's military of the future. They will not bow to the political imperative. They are outspoken with the truth, their states of readiness, their lack of resources, their training standards and the welfare of their subordinates. They will call spade a spade and do not accept the edicts of the muddled thinking emanating from those unqualified individuals who dominate the bureaucracy.

Unfortunately, until some future government recognises that the Canadian military institution cannot be tampered with to suit political whim, the Canadian forces will never regain its once magnificent level of excellence in the defence of Canada. Nor will the Canadian military exercise a positive influence on Canada's stature abroad.

It is sad to observe the political posturing that is now occurring at the highest levels of government. It is troubling in these trying times since September 11, 2001 to see the Liberal government move quickly to use any major event as an opportunity to further their own agenda.

The proof is now plain for all to see. The Canadian forces, apart from sending a few ill-equipped undermanned ships into an area of the world devoid of conflict cannot mount and sustain a credible operation abroad without extensive help from our allies. Pitifully inadequate defence budgets only exacerbate the problems by keeping personnel levels low and equipment replacement programs out of reach.

Retired military officers and military scientists who have spent their entire careers studying geopolitics and warfare are no match for the political incompetence of the Liberal government. Too bad the politicians who find themselves in positions of power decide that they are invincible. They make decisions based on their own meagre understanding of the military sciences and the specialised disciplines that are studied by military leaders throughout their entire careers.

The morale of the servicemen and women is at record low levels and has little to do with compensation. The government and senior military officers defend this sorry state by questioning the wisdom of their critics that include distinguished retired military officers who have devoted their lives to the country they love and have served.

The politicians tell us that these honourable gentlemen who have given their lives to their country are fighting the last war or that they don't understand the modern aspects of warfare. The Prime Minister, the Minister of National Defence and senior members of cabinet extol the virtues of Canada's military. They exhort the generals and admirals to support the Liberal party line in the definition of military preparedness.

It is an indisputable indication of a somnambulant government and a bureaucratic military hierarchy lulling themselves into a false state of security unwilling to admit that indeed, the sky is falling.

CHAPTER TWENTY-FOUR
WHAT OF THE FUTURE

The year 2001 closed with its horrific images of the savage attack on the World Trade Centre seared into our memories. The event has been symptomatic of the beginning of the new age of raw terrorism. Wild, fanatical interpretations of the word of God have laid bare an unyielding division in human understanding.

Extremist misrepresentation of western intentions and an avowed objective to destroy all peoples whose religion is not based on Islamic radicalism has mounted the world stage. It is revealed as a new, despicable level of man's inhumanity to man.

In looking back on our recent history, diabolical Nazism intent on domination of the free world was confronted and defeated. The hesitant peace following World War II was quickly replaced by the communist threat of world domination and the cold war that followed. The uneasy peace that ensued during the 1990's served only to lull western nations into a false sense of security.

Despite the warnings of military scientists and historians the Canadian government defence policies remain stagnant. A succession of governments since the early 1960s seduced by the lure of political power at home, have relegated the armed forces to an unrealistically low priority. The defence and security of Canada has taken a back seat to other politically motivated programs vying for budget and resources.

The bureaucracy has become a caricature of the party in power and eagerly adopts the crippling social policies that have inhibited the economic development of the country.

The expectations of Canadians have been elevated to unrealistic levels by politicians who promise living standards, growth and economic equality that is unsustainable.

The Canadian Forces are a willing, short-handed, under-equipped and poorly led institution that is losing its once proud identity. Canadian men and women who have devoted their lives and careers to defending the nation have seen successive governments devolve their defence policies to the extent that we now have a defence structure of little consequence. Benevolent government programs promoting unrealistic ideals of a utopian society have proven to be the anchor to our economic progression.

The men and women who serve their country in uniform do so with pride and dedication. That is all that remains of a once distinguished military structure. The training standards are still there and the will to learn and to accept the challenges of often-impossible odds is still the mark of the individual junior officer and soldier in the field.

The success of Canada's modern military has been carried on the backs of young officers, men and women who are dedicated to accomplishing their duties without regard for the lack of resources, their living conditions or their remuneration. They are proud Canadians who are without exception, Canada's best ambassador's abroad in a world searching for peace and security.

While our soldiers toil amid the dirt and the grime and often the blood of the people in far off countries, our politicians continue to praise their achievements at every photo opportunity while denying them the resources that would ease their tasks and contribute to their safety and well-being.

In the fight against terrorism, it has been startling to hear some of the generals parroting the Prime Minister, the defence minister and other members of cabinet as they explain to Canadians that all is well with Canada's military. They enthusiastically claim without reliable evidence that we are contributing more than our fair share to the war on terrorism.

It was startling to hear the announcement in late 2001 that Canada had placed a battalion of light infantry on forty-eight hours notice to move to Afghanistan. A rag tag battalion that had to rely on other units across Canada to bring it up to fighting strength with a questionable combat ready capability. Sending such units into danger courts disaster and signals a government that will risk the lives of others to save face.

The Princess Patricia's Canadian Light Infantry performed their task with honour once they reached the theatre of operations. Indicative of the muddleheaded strategic thinking by the Liberal government and an incompetent bureaucracy, the Canadian contingent was delivered a theatre of war courtesy of USAF transport. Insufficient Canadian military transport was available to perform the task.

Their combat equipment was provided in adequate quantities only because military units across the country had been scavenged to fill the battalion's shortfall. Even their combat uniforms were configured in jungle camouflage and rendered our troops highly visible and therefore vulnerable in the desert landscape. The Canadian battalion gallantly attempted to make do by painting over their jungle-coloured suits to allow them to more readily blend into the blandness of the desert.

The officers and men in the field today are no different than those of their predecessors. They are no different from those I encountered during the early years of my own career. Their patriotism, ambitions and expectations are the same.

During their basic training they have embraced the principles of loyalty and service. They have developed a deep love for their country. They have boundless pride and are eager to demonstrate their skills and the capabilities of their equipment. The Canadian military man or woman has not changed.

What has changed is the new willingness of the politicians to manipulate them to fulfil senseless political objectives designed to make the government in power look good. The soldier knows that through the government he serves the people. He responds to the government executive authority. He is willing and often does lay down his life in the service of his country.

Yet successive governments over the past three decades have betrayed the Canadian soldier. He has been used as a pawn in the political quest for electoral power. Defence budgets have been systematically slashed to provide money for social or make-work programmes. Programmes representing flights of invention that are no more than a political expedient for a government desperate to retain power.

Sadly, the senior bureaucracy in the Department of National Defence has acquiesced to factors that exceed a reasonable government imperative. Generals and senior civil servants have become interchangeable in their daily routine. Their thinking has become politicised and they accede to impossible government demands. They convince themselves that the massively over-stressed resources at their disposal are more than adequate for any task that can be sent their way.

Their charade has yet to be challenged and it is to be hoped that their miscalculations will not ever contribute to the loss of life of Canadians dedicated to the preservation of peace.

Has the deplorable deterioration of Canada's military gone past the point of recovery? Some observers say that it cannot be rapidly mobilised to meet any contingency that may arise. This is probably true, but it's not to say that there is not a sound basis that has been preserved over the years. It rests at the junior officer-senior NCO level in the field. They represent the operational cadre of what is left of the military.

They know and understand the principles of war. They are comfortable in their leadership role and have the respect of those in the forces for whom they are responsible. To them, the aim is clear, as is the road to its fulfilment. Given the resources, they will accomplish the task. If the resources fall short they will improvise because they won't accept failure.

This is the level from which our future military leaders must come. They are untainted by the politics of a bureaucracy that has become ineffective. Given the opportunity to restore military principles and ethics at the most senior levels, they will ensure that Canada will be the better in any future conflict that tests international freedom and democracy.

A lack of focus permeates the defence headquarters. Responsibility for the execution of orders and directives is clear to the field commanders. The responsibility for the formulation of those orders in Ottawa is often fraught with indecisiveness or compromise resulting in confusion and often misrepresentation.

The fiasco of the Somali affair was an outstanding example of how bureaucratic bungling escalated into a public relations nightmare.

One or two individual soldiers of questionable character precipitated the senseless murder of a Somali youth. As the inquiry unfolded, it became apparent that mismanagement at the headquarters level contributed significantly.

The unit selected for the operation was not sufficiently prepared. The battalion that was dispatched had not met established combat ready standards and their commander recommended against their deployment. The pressure to meet the political need trumped what ordinarily would have been a decision based solely on military standards and capabilities.

A Royal Commission was established to investigate all of the dynamics that led to this incredibly bad reflection on the country. As the commission began to uncover the revelations of wide spread incompetence within National Defence Headquarters, the spin-doctors could no longer manipulate the findings in favour of the government.

The investigation ended abruptly when the government declared that the Royal Commission had completed its task before the Commissioner had time to conclude his findings. He was not even permitted to write a comprehensive final report based on a complete inventory of discovery.

The incompetence of the government and its bureaucracy is close to being revealed to an electorate already suspicious of government cover-up. A government that is under siege in other areas of the political spectrum and is morally and politically corrupt. The continuing revelations of government incompetence show no immediate signs of improvement as the nation continues to wallow on the edge of international ridicule.

There can be no doubt that patriotic Canadians who represent a mixture of political party affiliations staff the bureaucracy. Civil servants at all levels are also voters and as such have their biases for and against the parties in the political spectrum. For the most part they remain publicly apolitical. However, in practice, their political preferences are often difficult to hide. Naturally, those senior bureaucrats who are exposed to the political level and demonstrate open support for government philosophies are favoured. They censure the proposals put forward by those in opposition and are given preference with respect to their own career advancement.

Planned force structure priorities are under constant change and subjected to re-rigging to suit the latest government whim. Military planners are constantly being thrown off guard by a government confused in the raison d'être of the military, thrusts its own construct of a military solution upon them.

In the high-tech society of today, solutions to Canada's military problems are not simple but they can be made simpler by leaving things military to the military. Tinkering with military structures, traditions, budgets and social behaviours have produced an institutional organisation that is incapable of effectively defending the country. The capability of the military to provide aid to the civil power since the October crisis of 1970 has been eroded by those who see the military as a threat to the very society the Canadian Forces have been tasked to protect.

Assistance with fire, flood and other disasters rank high on the average Canadian perception of the country's military capabilities. Prior to 9/11 there had developed in the mind of the general public, a feeling of repugnance toward violence of any kind even if it meant turning the other cheek.

The events at the World Trade Centre in New York have changed that mind-set and the government is slow to catch up to the changing reality of public opinion. Public conviction has since pushed critics of our national defence policies to take a more aggressive and realistic view of Canada's role as a responsible member of the international community.

Civilised societies can never stand aside as tyrannical forces attempt to subjugate the free world to evils against the human spirit. Canada can never afford to single-handedly defend its borders or its people. But we must stand strong beside our allies in the common resolve to bring peace and well being to the world in which we live.

Our armed forces must be strong; armed and equipped to serve as a credible deterrent to those who would challenge freedom and democracy. The tens of thousands of soldiers, sailors and airmen who have died in uniform throughout the past century must rest in peace knowing that indeed the torch has been passed and is in worthy hands.

The first step in restoring Canada's military will be to return the command of the military to the military. Development of a clear defence policy based on a rational and realistic foreign policy is crucial. Part of the problem the government faces is that the Canadian Forces have no well-defined role. Without the clarity that definition brings, priorities cannot be established with any surety. Defence dollars are wasted as government priorities change across a broad spectrum of military tasks.

The military integration experiment didn't work. Moreover, the integration of the civilian bureaucratic element into the military chain of command has destroyed the military hierarchical structure. Corrective action must be undertaken soon or the Canadian defence structure will be relegated to a place of irrelevance on the world stage.

The soldiers, sailors and airmen must be left alone to define the military organisation and the resources needed to meet the policies established by the government.

The civilian element must be placed at arms length from the military command structure and leave the military planners to identify the resources needed to carry out the policies without interference from those not qualified to do so.

The will to defend peace-loving peoples everywhere is critical to our future. Surely, a rational approach to our responsibilities is not too much to ask. Those who ignore violence in the hope that it will go away will eventually be consumed by it.

The World Trade Centre massacre was the wake up call. There is now an urgent need to reinforce our resolve to face the challenges ahead. It is a need that will test all elements of our society.

Canadians will rise to the challenge but they must be reassured that their military is strong and capable of joining the international community in preserving the freedoms we all cherish.

Quid Se Coelum Ruat

Lightning Source UK Ltd.
Milton Keynes UK
UKHW041013210619
344816UK00001B/40/P